CLEANING &
STAIN REMOVAL

Other Publications:

AMERICAN COUNTRY

VOYAGE THROUGH THE UNIVERSE

THE THIRD REICH

THE TIME-LIFE GARDENER'S GUIDE

MYSTERIES OF THE UNKNOWN

TIME FRAME

FIX IT YOURSELF

FITNESS, HEALTH & NUTRITION

SUCCESSFUL PARENTING

HEALTHY HOME COOKING

UNDERSTANDING COMPUTERS

LIBRARY OF NATIONS

THE ENCHANTED WORLD

THE KODAK LIBRARY OF CREATIVE PHOTOGRAPHY

GREAT MEALS IN MINUTES

THE CIVIL WAR

PLANET EARTH

COLLECTOR'S LIBRARY OF THE CIVIL WAR

THE EPIC OF FLIGHT

THE GOOD COOK

WORLD WAR II

HOME REPAIR AND IMPROVEMENT

THE OLD WEST

CLEANING & STAIN REMOVAL

TIME-LIFE BOOKS
ALEXANDRIA, VIRGINIA

Fix It Yourself was produced by
ST. REMY PRESS

MANAGING EDITOR	Kenneth Winchester
MANAGING ART DIRECTOR	Pierre Léveillé

Staff for Cleaning & Stain Removal

Series Editor	Brian Parsons
Series Assistant Editor	Kent J. Farrell
Editor	Raymond John Woolfrey
Series Art Director	Diane Denoncourt
Art Director	Francine Lemieux
Research Editor	Fran Slingerland
Designers	Lousnak Abdalian, Chantal Bilodeau, Julie Léger
Contributing Writers	S. J. Anderson, Annelies Epstein, Nina Gilbert, Randy Lake, Christopher LIttle, Geri-Lynn Kushneryk, Roxane Marin, Heather Marinos, Michael McDevitt, Judith J. Ritter, Mary Lee Wholey
Contributing Illustrators	Gérard Mariscalchi, Jacques Proulx
Cover	Robert Monté
Index	Christine M. Jacobs
Administrator	Denise Rainville
Accounting Manager	Natalie Watanabe
Production Manager	Michelle Turbide
Coordinator	Dominique Gagné
Systems Coordinator	Jean-Luc Roy
Studio Director	Maryo Proulx

Time-Life Books Inc. is a wholly owned subsidiary of
THE TIME INC. BOOK COMPANY

President and Chief Executive Officer	Kelso F. Sutton
President, Time Inc. Books Direct	Christopher T. Linen

TIME-LIFE BOOKS INC.

EDITOR	George Constable
Director of Design	Louis Klein
Director of Editorial Resources	Phyllis K. Wise
Director of Photography and Research	John Conrad Weiser
PRESIDENT	John M. Fahey Jr.
Senior Vice Presidents	Robert M. DeSena, Paul R. Stewart, Curtis G. Viebranz, Joseph J. Ward
Vice Presidents	Stephen L. Bair, Bonita L. Boezeman, Mary P. Donohoe, Stephen L. Goldstein, Juanita T. James, Andrew P. Kaplan, Trevor Lunn, Susan J. Maruyama, Robert H. Smith
New Product Development	Trevor Lunn, Donia Ann Steele
Supervisor of Quality Control	James King
PUBLISHER	Joseph J. Ward

Editorial Operations

Production	Celia Beattie
Library	Louise D. Forstall
Correspondents	Elisabeth Kraemer-Singh (Bonn); Christina Lieberman (New York); Maria Vincenza Aloisi (Paris); Ann Natanson (Rome).

THE CONSULTANTS

Consulting editor **David L. Harrison** served as an editor for several Time-Life Books do-it-yourself series, including *Home Repair and Improvement*, *The Encyclopedia of Gardening* and *The Art of Sewing*.

Richard Day is a founder of the National Association of Home and Workshop Writers and has written about home repair subjects for nearly a quarter of a century.

Mark Browning and partner, Don Aslett, founded Aslett-Browning, Inc., of Pocatello, Idaho, which consults, trains, and publishes in the cleaning/maintenance industry.

Kathleen M. Kiely is a former *Fix-it-Yourself* Series Editor. She has served as a writer and editor for other Time-Life Books series including *Home Repair and Improvement*, *Your Home* and *Planet Earth*.

Library of Congress Cataloging-in-Publication Data
Cleaning & stain removal
    p. cm. – (Fix it yourself)
Includes index.
ISBN 0-8094-7400-X.
ISBN 0-8094-7401-8 (lib. bdg.)
1. Spotting (Cleaning).
I. Time-Life Books. II. Title: Cleaning and stain removal. III. Series.
TX324.C59   1990
648'.1—dc20   90-10915
                       CIP

For information about any Time-Life book, please write:
Reader Information
Time-Life Customer Service
P.O. Box C-32068
Richmond, Virginia
23261-2068

CONTENTS

HOW TO USE THIS BOOK	6
EMERGENCY GUIDE	8
CLEANING YOUR HOME	14
DRIVEWAY, WALKS AND PATIOS	16
EXTERIOR WALLS	22
WINDOWS AND DOORS	28
WALLS AND CEILINGS	36
FLOORS	44
CARPETS	56
FURNITURE	66
FIREPLACES AND WOOD STOVES	78
BATHROOMS AND KITCHEN	84
APPLIANCES	92
FIXTURES	110
TOOLS & TECHNIQUES	116
INDEX	126
ACKNOWLEDGMENTS	128

HOW TO USE THIS BOOK

Cleaning & Stain Removal is divided into three sections. The Emergency Guide on pages 8 to 13 provides information that can be indispensable, even lifesaving, in the event of a household emergency. Take the time to study this section *before* you need the important advice it contains.

The Repairs section—the heart of the book—is a comprehensive approach to troubleshooting problems of cleaning and stain removal in the home. Shown below are four sample pages from the chapter on furniture, with captions describing the various features of the book and how they work.

For example, if the wood of a furniture piece is dusty or soiled, the Troubleshooting Guide will send you to page 73 for detailed, step-by-step directions on dusting it, identifying its finish and properly cleaning it. Or, if a glass tabletop or mirror is dusty or smudged, the Troubleshooting Guide will direct you to page 72 for instructions on cleaning it.

Each job is rated by degree of difficulty and by the average time it will take for a do-it-yourselfer to complete; keep in mind that this rating is only a suggestion. Before deciding on a specific job, read all the instructions carefully. Then, be guided by your

Introductory text
Describes common problems in cleaning and stain removal for a specific feature or area of the home.

Troubleshooting Guide
To use this chart, locate the entry that most closely resembles your problem in column 1, then follow the recommended procedures in column 2.

Cleaning Tips
Provide general guidance on strategy and techniques for cleaning and stain removal.

Variations
Differences in approach to cleaning and stain removal are described throughout the book, especially if more than one cleaning agent can be used or may be needed.

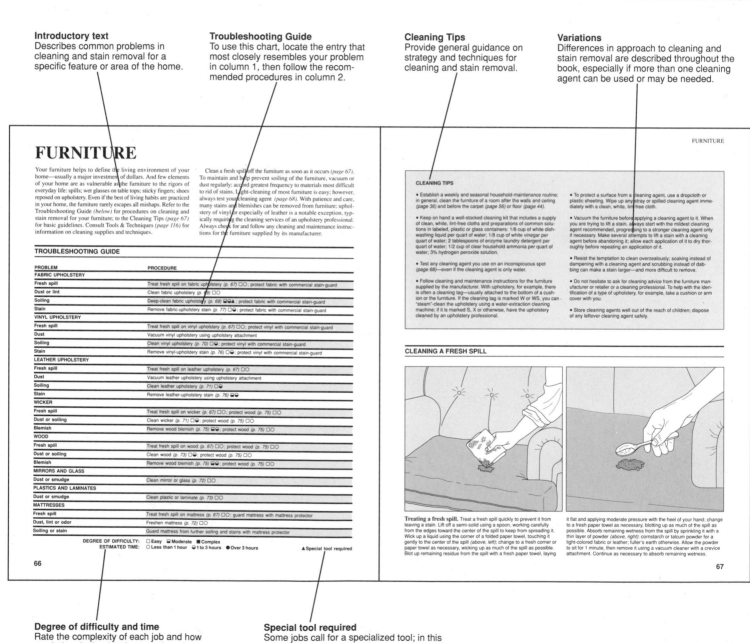

Degree of difficulty and time
Rate the complexity of each job and how much time it should take to perform for a homeowner with average do-it-yourself skills.

Special tool required
Some jobs call for a specialized tool; in this example, a water-extraction cleaning machine is needed to deep-clean fabric upholstery.

own confidence and the time available to you, as well as the supplies and equipment on hand. To lift a stain from leather upholstery, for instance, you may wish to call for professional help; you can still save time by prioritizing your cleaning needs.

Most of the repairs in *Cleaning & Stain Removal* can be made with basic supplies and equipment; occasionally, you may need to buy a special product or rent a specific tool. For information on cleaning supplies and equipment, refer to the chapter entitled Tools & Techniques *(page 116)*; if you are a novice at cleaning and stain removal, read it before starting a job.

Cleaning and stain removal can be simple and worry-free if you work logically and systematically, following all tips and precautions. Wear the safety gear recommended for a job: rubber gloves to protect your hands from caustic or harsh cleaning agents; safety goggles to protect your eyes from splashes.

Exercise caution with cleaning agents. Do not mix different solutions together unless specifically instructed. To prepare a solution of an acid, add it to the water; never pour water into an acid. Follow the manufacturer's instructions with a commercial product. Safely store or dispose of cleaning agents *(page 120)*.

Name of repair
You will be referred by the Troubleshooting Guide to the first page of a specific job.

Lead-ins
Bold lead-ins summarize each step or highlight the key action pictured in the illustration.

Tools and techniques
When a tool or method is required for a job, it is described within the step-by-step repair. General information on tools and supplies, and information about choices of cleaning agents, is included in the Tools & Techniques chapter *(page 116)*.

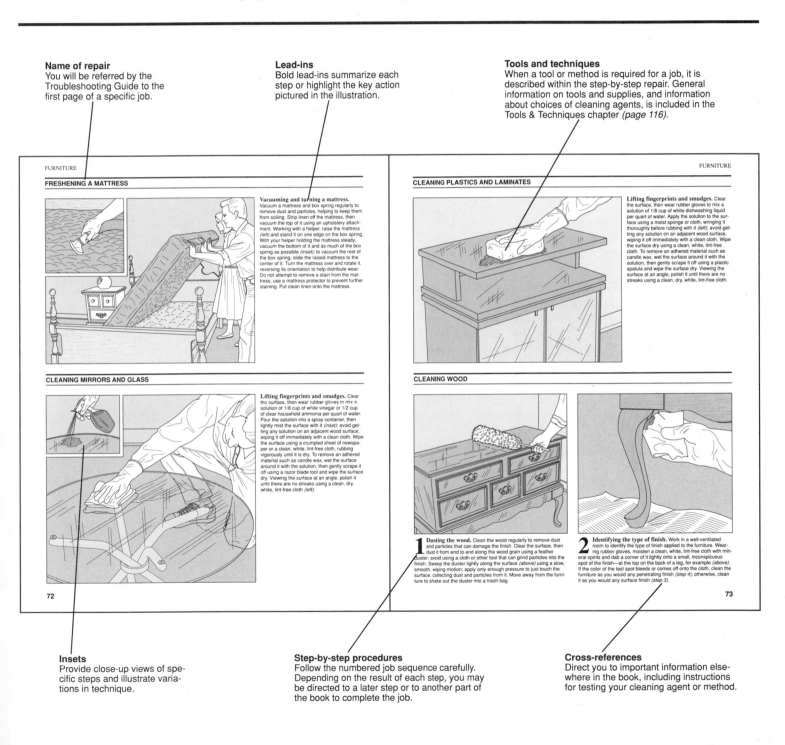

Insets
Provide close-up views of specific steps and illustrate variations in technique.

Step-by-step procedures
Follow the numbered job sequence carefully. Depending on the result of each step, you may be directed to a later step or to another part of the book to complete the job.

Cross-references
Direct you to important information elsewhere in the book, including instructions for testing your cleaning agent or method.

EMERGENCY GUIDE

Preventing problems in home cleaning and stain removal. With common sense and a few precautionary measures, cleaning and stain removal need not be any more dangerous than the most sedentary of activities. Most accidents that can occur during a job of cleaning or stain removal arise from carelessness: improper use of tools and equipment; mishandling of chemical products; and misuse of electricity. The list of safety tips at right covers guidelines for any job of cleaning or stain removal; for more specific advice, consult the particular chapter.

Accidents, however, can befall even the most careful of workers. Prepare yourself to handle an emergency before it occurs by reading the Troubleshooting Guide *(page 9)*, which places emergency procedures at your fingertips; it provides quick-action steps to take and refers you to pages 9 to 13 for detailed information. Also review Tools & Techniques *(page 116)*; it provides guidance on cleaning supplies and techniques, use of ladders and scaffolds, and disposal of chemical products.

Take the time to set up properly for any job of cleaning or stain removal. Protect surfaces from inadvertent contact with cleaning agents by covering them with plastic sheeting or drop-cloths. Keep people and pets away from your job site; restrict access by setting up temporary barricades, if necessary. Before starting a job, assemble all the tools, equipment and supplies you require. Have on hand an adequate stock of clean-up supplies for any spill: clean, white, lint-free cloths or paper towels and an absorbent material such as fuller's earth or cat litter.

Many household cleaning products contain chemicals that are poisonous; others are corrosive or caustic and can burn the eyes or skin or emit toxic fumes and can cause dizziness, faintness or even the loss of consciousness. Follow the instructions provided by the manufacturer for any commercial cleaning product you use; for detailed information on the properties and possible harmful effects to you or the environment of any commercial cleaning product, you can request a copy of its safety data sheet from the retailer or manufacturer.

Keep a well-stocked first-aid kit in a convenient location; in the event of an emergency calling for minor first aid *(page 12)*, you will want anyone to be able to find it quickly. Fire can be a life-threatening emergency. Deprive fire of its element of surprise by installing smoke detectors judiciously throughout your home. Have a fire extinguisher rated ABC on hand, ready to snuff out a blaze before it gains the upper hand; know how to use it *(page 9)*. Regularly test the battery of each smoke detector and check the pressure gauge of the fire extinguisher.

When in doubt about your ability to handle an emergency, do not hesitate to call for help. Post the telephone numbers for your local fire department, hospital emergency room, poison control center and physician near the telephone. In most areas, dial 911 in the event of any life-threatening emergency. Also seek technical help when you need it; consult a cleaning professional—or the manufacturer or retailer of the material you are cleaning. For information on the safe disposal of chemicals, call your local department of environmental protection or public health.

SAFETY TIPS

1. Before attempting any job in this book, read the entire procedure. Familiarize yourself with the specific safety information presented in each chapter.

2. Always use the proper cleaning agent and method for the job. Refer to Tools & Techniques *(page 116)* for information on cleaning supplies and equipment.

3. Wear the safety gear recommended for the job when you are working with any cleaning product containing chemicals: safety goggles to protect your eyes; rubber gloves to protect your hands; a respirator to keep from inhaling vapors.

4. Read the label on the container of any cleaning product you use. Follow the manufacturer's instructions, paying special attention to any hazard warnings and storage information.

5. Work outdoors only in good weather conditions, never when it is wet or windy; wear a hat if it is hot and sunny.

6. Concentrate on the job; keep others away. Never work if you are tired, stressed or have been drinking alcohol or taking medication that causes drowsiness.

7. Keep a first-aid kit on hand; stock it with mild antiseptic, sterile gauze dressings and bandages, adhesive tape, scissors, tweezers and a packet of needles.

8. When working with chemical products that are flammable, keep a fire extinguisher rated ABC nearby; be prepared to use it if necessary *(page 9)*. Work only in a well-ventilated area, away from sources of heat and out of direct sunlight.

9. Never work with electricity in damp conditions. To guard against electrical shock, plug an electrical tool only into an outlet protected by a GFCI (ground-fault circuit interrupter).

10. Turn off and unplug an appliance before you clean it; make sure that it is dry before you plug it in and turn it on.

11. Follow basic safety precautions when you are working with ladders or scaffolds *(page 122)*.

12. Do not mix together different cleaning solutions; mixing together ammonia and bleach, for example, produces a lethal gas. When mixing an acid and water, add the acid to the water; never add water to acid.

13. Store chemical products in airtight containers away from sources of heat. Wash cloths soaked with chemicals for reuse or store them for disposal in airtight metal or glass containers—preferably outdoors, out of direct sunlight.

14. Bag chemical waste separately from other household refuse and keep it outdoors until it can be disposed of. Call your local department of environmental protection or public health for recommended disposal procedures.

15. Post the telephone numbers of your local fire department, hospital emergency room, poison control center and physician near the telephone.

TROUBLESHOOTING GUIDE

SYMPTOM	PROCEDURE
Fire	Have someone call fire department immediately; control fire using fire extinguisher rated ABC *(step below)*
Chemical product swallowed	Immediately call poison control center, hospital emergency room or physician; provide information on victim's age and weight, and type and amount of chemical swallowed
	If professional medical treatment necessary, bring chemical container with you; do not give victim anything to eat or drink or induce vomiting unless advised by medical professional
Chemical product fumes inhaled; faintness, dizziness, nausea or blurred vision	Escape chemical vapors *(p. 10)*; if symptoms persist, seek medical help immediately
Chemical product splashed in eye	Flush chemical from eye *(p. 10)*, then seek medical help immediately
Chemical product splashed on skin	Immediately brush off dry chemical; treat chemical burn *(p. 10)*
Chemical product spilled in work area	For spill of more than 1 quart of flammable chemical, evacuate house and call fire department from home of neighbor; otherwise, clean up spilled chemical *(p. 10)*
Electrical tool or fixture sparks or shocks	Immediately shut off electricity to circuit or system *(p. 11)*
Electrical shock	If victim immobilized by live current, knock him free using wooden implement *(p. 12)*
	Have someone call for medical help immediately
	If victim not breathing, administer artificial respiration; if victim has no pulse, administer cardiopulmonary resuscitation (CPR) only if qualified
	If victim breathing and has pulse, and has no back or neck injury, place in recovery position *(p. 12)*
Foreign particle in eye	Do not remove particle if on cornea, embedded or adhered, or cannot be seen; otherwise, remove particle from eye *(p. 12)*
Splinter	Pull out splinter *(p. 13)*
Scratch or minor wound	Treat cut *(p. 13)*; if bleeding persists or wound deep or gaping, seek medical help immediately
Fall from roof, ladder or top of stairs	Have someone call for medical help immediately; treat victim of fall *(p. 13)*

CONTROLLING A FIRE

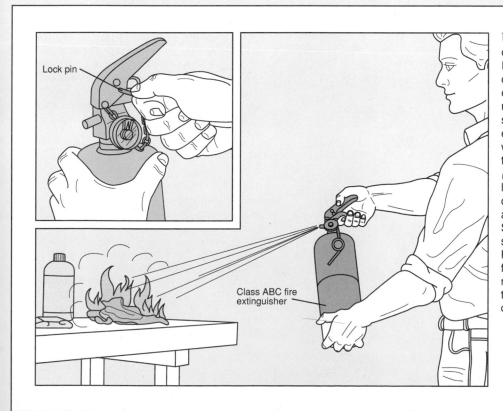

Lock pin

Class ABC fire extinguisher

Using a fire extinguisher. Have someone call the fire department immediately. If flame or smoke comes from the walls or ceilings, or the fire is large or not contained, evacuate the house and call the fire department from a neighbor's home. To control a small, contained fire, use a dry-chemical fire extinguisher rated ABC. **Caution:** Never use water on an electrical or a chemical fire. Pull the lock pin out of the extinguisher handle *(inset)*. Keeping the extinguisher upright, lift it and aim its nozzle or hose at the base of the fire, positioning yourself 6 to 10 feet away with your back to an accessible exit. Squeeze the handle levers together and spray in a quick side-to-side motion *(left)*. Keep spraying until the fire is out. Watch for flashback—rekindling of the fire—and be ready to spray again. If the fire spreads or the extinguisher empties before the fire is out, evacuate the house immediately.

TREATING EXPOSURE TO CHEMICALS

Escaping chemical vapors. Chemical vapors can be toxic, causing faintness, dizziness or nausea; at the first sign of a symptom, go outdoors for fresh air. Loosen your clothing at the neck, chest and waist, then sit with your head lowered between your knees *(above)*. If any symptom persists, seek medical help immediately; otherwise, have someone ventilate the work area and close all chemical containers.

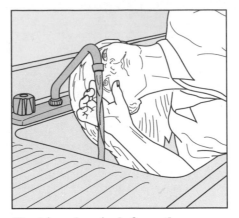

Flushing chemicals from the eye. Holding the eyelids of the injured eye apart with your fingers, position the eye under a gentle flow of cool water, tilting the head to prevent the chemical from washing into the uninjured eye *(above)*. Flush the eye for at least 10 minutes, then cover it with a sterile gauze bandage and seek medical attention immediately.

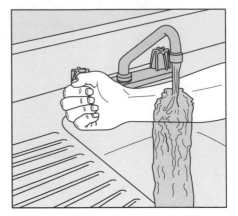

Flushing chemicals from the skin. Gently remove any clothing from the burn; do not remove any clothing adhered to it. If the burn is severe, cover it with a gauze dressing and seek medical help immediately. Otherwise, flush the burn with a gentle flow of cool water from a faucet *(above)* for at least 5 minutes, then bandage it. Do not apply antiseptic spray or ointment, butter or oil, or baking soda or alcohol.

HANDLING A CHEMICAL SPILL

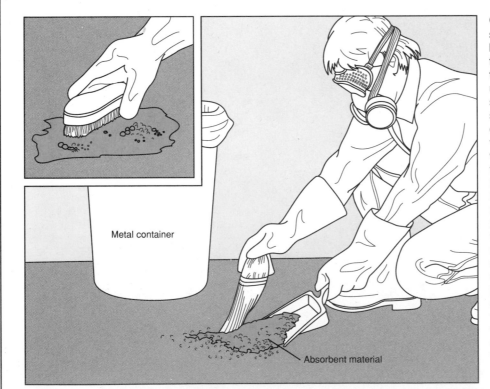

Metal container

Absorbent material

Cleaning up spilled chemicals. For a spill of more than 1 quart of a product labeled EXTREMELY FLAMMABLE, call the fire department; otherwise, ventilate the site, turn off nearby sources of heat and electrical units, and keep others away. Clean up the spill wearing rubber boots, rubber gloves and safety goggles; also a respirator if the spill is of a product labeled with POISON vapor or ventilation warnings. Soak up a small spill with cloths or paper towels, disposing of them in a metal container double-lined with heavy-duty plastic trash bags. Soak up a large spill by covering it with an absorbent material such as fuller's earth or cat litter; if necessary, first neutralize it to help protect the surface *(page 11)*. When the absorbent material soaks up the spill, sweep it up into a dustpan *(left)*, disposing of it the same way. Clean any remaining residue using an appropriate solvent *(page 11)*, rinsing the site thoroughly with water; scrub using a stiff-bristled fiber brush *(inset)* or rub using a cloth. Seal the waste materials and dispose of them safely following the environmental regulations of your community.

HANDLING A CHEMICAL SPILL (continued)

PRODUCT SPILLED	CLEAN-UP PROCEDURE
Acetone	Clean up residue using solution of 1/2 cup of commercial all-purpose cleaner per gallon of water, then rinse thoroughly with water
Ammonia	Neutralize large spill using white vinegar; clean up residue by rinsing thoroughly with water
Ammonium sulfamate	Neutralize large spill using sodium bicarbonate (baking soda); clean up residue using solution of 1/2 cup of commercial all-purpose cleaner per gallon of water, then rinse thoroughly with water
Citrus-based solvent	Clean up residue using solution of 1/2 cup of commercial all-purpose cleaner per gallon of water, then rinse thoroughly with water
Dry-cleaning fluid (1,1,1 trichloroethane)	Clean up residue using solution of 1/2 cup of commercial all-purpose cleaner per gallon of water, then rinse thoroughly with water
Linseed oil	Clean up residue using mineral spirits, then solution of 1/2 cup of commercial all-purpose cleaner per gallon of water and rinse thoroughly with water
Mineral spirits	Clean up residue using solution of 1/2 cup of commercial all-purpose cleaner per gallon of water, then rinse thoroughly with water
Muriatic, oxalic or phosphoric acid	Neutralize large spill using sodium bicarbonate (baking soda); clean up residue using solution of 1/2 cup of commercial all-purpose cleaner per gallon of water, then rinse thoroughly with water
Sodium metasillicate (truck wash)	Neutralize large spill using undiluted white vinegar; clean up residue using solution of 1/2 cup of commercial all-purpose cleaner per gallon of water, then rinse thoroughly with water

Choosing a neutralizing agent and solvent. Refer to the chart at left to clean up a spill of a chemical product. For a large spill of a product such as an acid, quick action to neutralize it can help to minimize any damage to the site—as well as make its waste least harmful to you and the environment. For any residue remaining after a spill, choose an appropriate solvent to clean it. Always check the label of the product spilled to determine if a special solvent is required. In most instances, only a solution of a commercial all-purpose cleaner is necessary. Carefully read and follow the manufacturer's instructions for any commercial product you use, noting if there is a risk of damage to the material of the surface you are cleaning. **Caution:** Do not mix different solvents together; combinations of solvents can be lethal. Be sure to rinse the site thoroughly with water. For information on the safe disposal of waste materials, call your local department of environmental protection or public health.

SHUTTING OFF ELECTRICITY

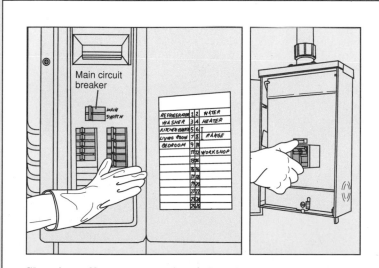

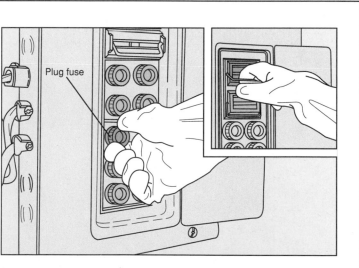

Shutting off power at a circuit breaker panel. If the area around the panel is damp, stand on a dry board or wear dry rubber boots. Wearing heavy rubber gloves, work only with one hand and avoid touching anything metal. Locate the circuit breaker controlling the circuit and flip it to OFF *(above, left)*. If the circuit is not labeled, locate the main circuit breaker (a double breaker usually above the other circuit breakers and labeled MAIN) and flip it to OFF. If there is no main circuit breaker, locate the service disconnect breaker in a separate panel nearby or outdoors by the electricity meter and flip it to OFF *(above, right)*.

Shutting off power at a fuse panel. If the area around the panel is damp, stand on a dry board or wear dry rubber boots. Wearing heavy rubber gloves, work only with one hand and avoid touching anything metal. Locate the plug fuse or the fuse block controlling the circuit. Grasp a plug fuse only by its insulated rim and unscrew it *(above)*; grip a fuse block by its handle and pull it straight out. If the circuit is not labeled, locate the main fuse block or blocks and pull each one straight out *(inset)*. If there is no main fuse block, flip the main circuit breaker or service disconnect breaker to OFF *(step left)* or pull down the main shutoff lever.

RESCUING A VICTIM OF ELECTRICAL SHOCK

 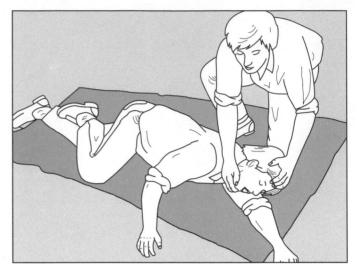

Freeing a victim of electrical shock. A person who contacts live electrical current is usually thrown back from the source; sometimes, however, muscles contract involuntarily around the source. Do not touch the victim or the source. Immediately shut off power at the main circuit breaker, the service disconnect breaker or the main fuse block *(page 11)*. If power cannot be shut off immediately, unplug the source, if possible, or use a wooden broom handle or other implement to knock the victim free *(above)*.

Handling a victim of electric shock. Call for medical help immediately. Check the victim's breathing and pulse; administer artificial respiration if there is no breathing and cardiopulmonary resuscitation (CPR) if there is no pulse and you are qualified. If the victim is breathing and has no back or neck injury, place him in the recovery position *(above)*, tilting the head back with the face to one side and the tongue forward to maintain an open airway. Keep the victim calm until medical help arrives.

PROVIDING MINOR FIRST AID

Removing a foreign particle from the eye. Facing a mirror, use a thumb and finger to hold open the injured eye. Check the eye for the particle; if necessary, slowly rotate the eye to expose it. **Caution:** Do not remove a particle that is on the cornea, is embedded or adhered, or cannot be seen. Otherwise, gently wipe away the particle using the twisted end of a tissue moistened with water

(above, left). Or, fill an eye irrigator with cool water and use it to flush out the particle. Lean forward with your eyes closed and press the rim of the irrigator to the injured eye, then tilt back your head. Open your eyes *(above, right)* and blink several times to flush out the particle. Lean forward again to remove the irrigator. If the particle cannot be removed, seek medical help immediately.

PROVIDING MINOR FIRST AID (continued)

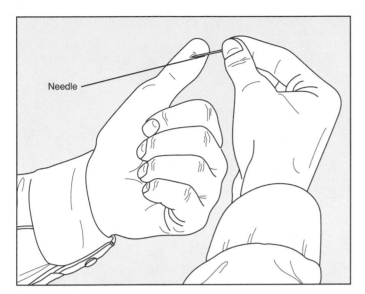

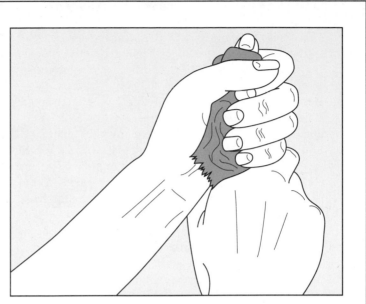

Pulling out a splinter. Wash the skin around the splinter with soap and water. A metal splinter may require treatment for tetanus; seek medical help. Otherwise, sterilize a needle and tweezers with rubbing alcohol or over a flame. Ease out the splinter from the skin using the needle *(above)*, then pull it out with the tweezers. Wash the wound again with soap and water. If the splinter cannot be removed or the wound becomes infected, seek medical help.

Treating a cut. To stop the injury from bleeding, elevate it and apply pressure with a clean cloth or gauze dressing *(above)*. If the cloth or dressing becomes blood-soaked, add another one over it; avoid lifting it to inspect the wound. Continue elevating the injury and applying pressure until the bleeding stops. If the wound is minor, wash it with soap and water, then bandage it. If the bleeding persists or the wound is deep or gaping, seek medical help.

TREATING A VICTIM OF A FALL

Treating a fall victim. Have someone call for medical help immediately. **Caution:** Do not move the victim if a spinal injury is suspected or he is in pain. Loosen the victim's clothing at the neck, chest and waist. Monitor the victim's vital life signs, checking for breathing and taking a pulse until medical help arrives. Keep the victim warm, covering him with a blanket *(left)*; keep others away. Do not apply a hot water bottle or heating pad or give the victim anything to drink.

CLEANING YOUR HOME

One may dispute the axiom that cleanliness is next to godliness, but for the typical do-it-yourselfer there is no arguing that cleaning and stain removal is one of the most fundamental and universal elements of any home fix-it strategy. Regular, proper cleaning not only ensures that your home looks and feels pleasant and comfortable, but helps to guarantee that each item in the house—from the window blinds to the major appliances—stays in top condition and in good working order, providing the greatest return on each investment of money and time you make in modeling your home.

There is not a surface or object in the house that escapes the need for cleaning. Dust and dirt are carried in the air through open windows and doors, and tracked into the house on the muddy feet of children and paws of pets. Indoor sources of grime and grease abound; humidity in the bathrooms, kitchen and basement, cooking fumes, and candle, tobacco and wood smoke all create airborne residues that settle on household surfaces, coating and discoloring them. And any household surface, even with the best of care, is accident-prone; spills of every shape, size and color can mar the vulnerable surfaces of floors, carpets, furniture, and bathroom and kitchen fixtures.

Keeping household surfaces clean is not difficult, but requires careful planning and perseverance. Cleaning a particular household surface properly also requires knowing which one of possibly dozens of different cleaning tools, cleaning agents and cleaning techniques is most appropriate. Even the most self-assured and conscientious homeowner is likely to shrink from a cleaning job that is judged intimidating or tedious, but modern cleaning agents and tools can make cleaning even the toughest dirt from a delicate surface a simple task.

You can keep the upper hand in the endless battle against household dirt, dust and grime by establishing regular cleaning schedules for your home that suit your lifestyle and available time. Every home has its own particular cleaning needs and you should give careful thought to the specific cleaning requirements of yours. For instance, if you have a large family and pets, you will probably have to give greater priority to cleaning floors and carpets than will a young married couple. Or, if you live near a city, your windows and exterior walls may be a greater cleaning priority than if you live in the country.

As a general rule of thumb, however, clean any household surface the moment you feel it needs cleaning, ensuring you prepare properly for the job. Assemble all the necessary tools and cleaning agents. Wear the safety gear recommended and follow label instructions carefully when mixing cleaning agents. Always test your cleaning agent and technique on an inconspicuous spot of the surface before you start to clean it; if necessary, adjust your cleaning agent or technique. Work carefully and patiently while cleaning, prepared to make repeated applications of a cleaning agent to thoroughly clean a surface. After you finish a cleaning job, safely dispose of leftover cleaning agents.

Walls and ceilings (page 36)
Vacuum or dust walls and spot-clean high-traffic areas regularly. Remove stains the moment you notice them. Clean walls and ceilings once each year to prevent dirt from wearing their finishes and coverings.

Driveway, walks and patios (page 16)
Sweep driveways, walks and patios regularly. Hose-wash surfaces at least twice a year. Spray-clean stained surfaces with an appropriate cleaning solution. Protect clean surfaces by sealing them.

Exterior walls (page 22)
Hose-wash exterior wall surfaces at least once a year. Spray-clean stained walls with an appropriate cleaning solution. Pressure-wash extensively-discolored brick or wood siding.

Windows and doors *(page 28)*
Clean windows and doors at least twice a year. Choose the best cleaning strategy for a window, removing it to clean it or cleaning it in place from the outside and the inside or from only the inside.

Bathrooms and kitchen *(page 84)*
Clean the porcelain, enamel, stainless steel, ceramic and plastic-laminate surfaces of the bathrooms and kitchen regularly to prevent permanent damage from grease and grime. Ventilate the bathrooms and kitchen properly to keep humidity and fumes from dirtying surfaces.

Appliances *(page 92)*
Regularly clean and polish the exteriors of major appliances to keep them looking like new. Also clean the accessible working parts of appliances to prevent dirt and grime from hampering their proper operation.

Fixtures *(page 110)*
Draperies and blinds are dust traps; vacuum them regularly to protect their surfaces and minimize household dust.

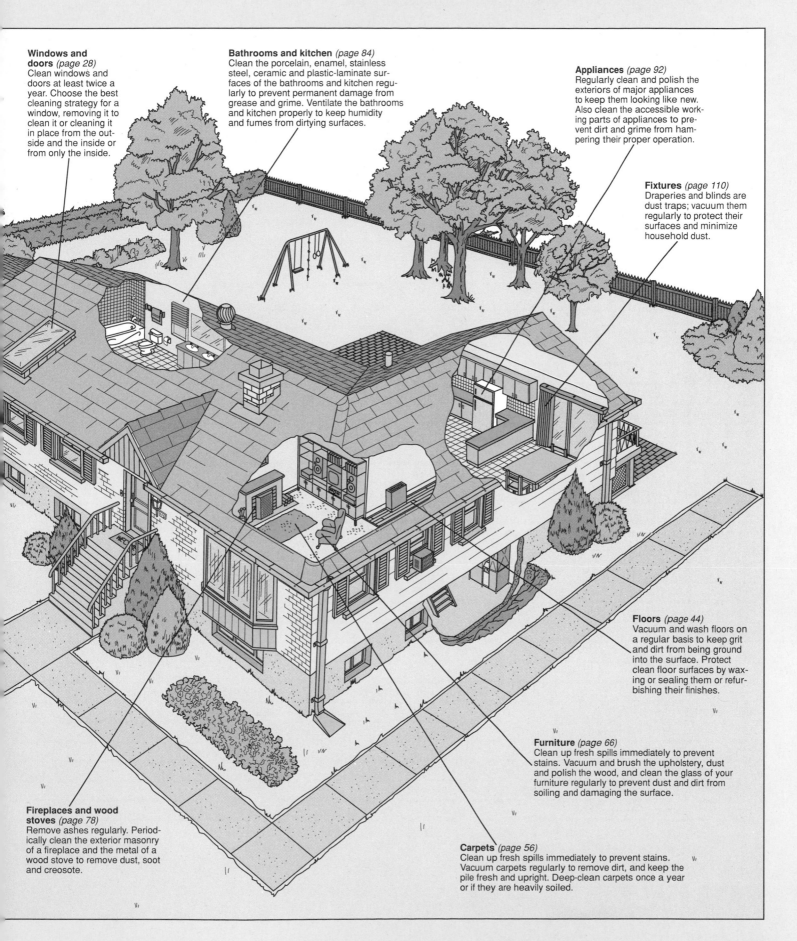

Fireplaces and wood stoves *(page 78)*
Remove ashes regularly. Periodically clean the exterior masonry of a fireplace and the metal of a wood stove to remove dust, soot and creosote.

Floors *(page 44)*
Vacuum and wash floors on a regular basis to keep grit and dirt from being ground into the surface. Protect clean floor surfaces by waxing or sealing them or refurbishing their finishes.

Furniture *(page 66)*
Clean up fresh spills immediately to prevent stains. Vacuum and brush the upholstery, dust and polish the wood, and clean the glass of your furniture regularly to prevent dust and dirt from soiling and damaging the surface.

Carpets *(page 56)*
Clean up fresh spills immediately to prevent stains. Vacuum carpets regularly to remove dirt, and keep the pile fresh and upright. Deep-clean carpets once a year or if they are heavily soiled.

DRIVEWAY, WALKS AND PATIOS

The driveway, walks and patios around the exterior of your home are an integral part of its style and beauty. However, driveway, walk and patio surfaces are exposed to relentless wear, whether from foot, automobile and bicycle traffic or from the rigors of the elements; their location at the entries to your home also makes them vulnerable to spills of all types. Even with the best of care, the porous materials of your driveway, walks and patios—whether simple, traditional materials such as asphalt and cast concrete or increasingly-popular, decorative materials such as concrete paving stones (pavers), exposed aggregate and bricks—make them more likely than any other exterior surface to show the punishing effects of everyday wear and tear.

Refer to the Troubleshooting Guide *(below)* for procedures on cleaning and stain removal for the driveway, walks and patios around the exterior of your home. For basic guidelines and general strategy on cleaning and removing stains from these surfaces, read the Cleaning Tips *(page 17)*. Consult Tools & Techniques *(page 116)* for information on cleaning supplies and techniques.

Clean a fresh spill off your driveway, walk or patio as soon as it occurs *(page 18)*. To remove common dirt and debris from a driveway, walk or patio, sweep the surface, then hose-clean it. You can remove a small stain from your driveway, walk or patio by hand-cleaning it *(page 19)*; if the surface is stained extensively, spray-clean it *(page 20)*. After cleaning your driveway, walk or patio, consider sealing the surface *(page 21)* to give it a fresh, uniform and stain-resistant finish. Knowledge about the material of a driveway, walk or patio simplifies the job of cleaning or removing a stain from it. Never hesitate to ask for cleaning advice from the manufacturer or installer of your driveway, walk or patio material or from a building or cleaning professional.

TROUBLESHOOTING GUIDE

PROBLEM	PROCEDURE
DRIVEWAY	
Fresh spill	Treat fresh spill on driveway *(p. 18)* □○; if desired, seal driveway *(p. 21)* □●
Surface dirty or debris-covered	Clean dirt and debris off driveway using garden hose and stiff-bristled fiber push broom
Surface soiled; dingy, grimy or discolored	Spray-clean driveway *(p. 20)* □◑▲; if desired, seal driveway *(p. 21)* □●
Surface deposit; gummy or encrusted material	Lift off deposit; remove stain *(p. 19)* □○
Surface efflorescence (white, powdery deposits)	Remove efflorescence *(p. 19)* □○ or spray-clean driveway *(p. 20)* □◑▲
Surface stained	Remove stain *(p. 19)* □○ or spray-clean driveway *(p. 20)* □◑▲
Surface stained repeatedly	Seal driveway *(p. 21)* □●
WALK	
Fresh spill	Treat fresh spill on walk *(p. 18)* □○; if desired, seal walk *(p. 21)* □●
Surface dirty or debris-covered	Clean dirt and debris off walk using garden hose and stiff-bristled fiber push broom
Surface soiled; dingy, grimy or discolored	Spray-clean walk *(p. 20)* □◑▲; if desired, seal walk *(p. 21)* □●
Surface deposit; gummy or encrusted material	Lift off deposit; remove stain *(p. 19)* □○
Surface efflorescence (white, powdery deposits)	Remove efflorescence *(p. 19)* □○ or spray-clean walk *(p. 20)* □◑▲
Surface stained	Remove stain *(p. 19)* □○ or spray-clean walk *(p. 20)* □◑▲
Surface stained repeatedly	Seal walk *(p. 21)* □●
PATIO	
Fresh spill	Treat fresh spill on patio *(p. 18)* □○; if desired, seal patio *(p. 21)* □●
Surface dirty or debris-covered	Clean dirt and debris off patio using garden hose and stiff-bristled fiber push broom
Surface soiled; dingy, grimy or discolored	Spray-clean patio *(p. 20)* □◑▲; if desired, seal patio *(p. 21)* □●
Surface deposit; gummy or encrusted material	Lift off deposit; remove stain *(p. 19)* □○
Surface efflorescence (white, powdery deposits)	Remove efflorescence *(p. 19)* □○ or spray-clean patio *(p. 20)* □◑▲
Surface stained	Remove stain *(p. 19)* □○ or spray-clean patio *(p. 20)* □◑▲
Surface stained repeatedly	Seal patio *(p. 21)* □●

DEGREE OF DIFFICULTY: □ Easy ◪ Moderate ■ Complex
ESTIMATED TIME: ○ Less than 1 hour ◑ 1 to 3 hours ● Over 3 hours
▲ Special tool required

CLEANING TIPS

• Establish a seasonal and yearly exterior-maintenance routine; in general, sweep dirt and debris off driveway, walk and patio surfaces once a week and wash the surfaces every spring and fall. Also wash the exterior walls *(page 22)* as well as the windows and doors *(page 28)* of your home.

• Wait for a calm, dry day to clean a driveway, walk or patio surface; avoid working in direct sunlight or in a temperature below 50°F or above 80°F.

• To protect a surface from a cleaning agent, use plastic sheeting. Wipe up any stray or spilled cleaning agent immediately with a clean, white cloth.

• Test any cleaning agent and method you use on an inconspicuous spot of the surface *(page 24)*—even if you are only dabbing or wiping using a cloth dampened with water.

• Follow the cleaning instructions supplied by the manufacturer for any commercial cleaning product you use.

• When you are trying to lift a stain from a driveway, walk or patio, always start with the cleaning agent recommended, progressing to a stronger concentration of it or another cleaning agent only if necessary. Make several attempts to lift a stain with a cleaning agent before abandoning it; allow each application of it to dry before repeating an application of it.

• After cleaning or removing a stain from a driveway, walk or patio, consider applying a sealer to prevent staining of the cleaned surface; to help prevent mildew and organic stains on a surface, trim back adjacent vegetation growing onto it.

• Store cleaning agents well out of the reach of children; dispose of any leftover cleaning agent safely.

PREPARING TO CLEAN A DRIVEWAY, WALK OR PATIO

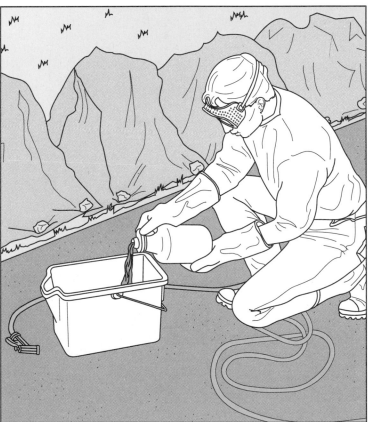

Preparing for the job. To clean, etch or seal a driveway, walk or patio, protect any nearby surface adjacent to it. For a small shrub or plant or the lawn adjacent to a driveway, walk or patio, loosely cover it with plastic sheeting *(above, left)*, then weight the edges of the sheeting with stones to prevent it from blowing away. To keep traffic off a driveway, walk or patio while you clean, etch or seal it, set up a temporary barrier around the edges of it. If you plan to spray-clean a driveway, walk or patio, tape plastic sheeting over any adjacent house surface, and close any windows and doors. When nearby surfaces are protected, assemble all the tools and supplies you need for the job. Wear the safety gear recommended: rubber gloves, safety goggles and rubber boots to mix *(above, right)* or apply a cleaning or etching solution and to apply a sealer; also a respirator to spray-clean with other than a solution of detergent. If you plan to spray-clean, keep people and pets away from the area.

CLEANING A FRESH SPILL

Treating a fresh spill. Treat a spill quickly to prevent it from leaving a stain; to keep from spreading it, do not try to mop it up. For a chemical spill, wear rubber boots, rubber gloves and safety goggles. For a spill of a semi-solid, work carefully from the edges to the center to lift it off the surface: using a putty knife if the spill is small; using a squeegee and a dustpan if the spill is large *(above, left)*. For a small spill of a liquid, use the corner of a clean, folded cloth to wick it up, changing to a fresh corner or cloth as necessary. For a large spill of a liquid, soak it up by covering it with an absorbent material: mechanic's oil absorbent for oil; cat litter *(above, right)* or fuller's earth otherwise. For a large spill of an undiluted acid, first neutralize it by sprinkling sodium bicarbonate (baking soda) on it. Allow the absorbent material to soak up the liquid completely—this may take 24 hours. Then, use a squeegee and a dustpan to lift the absorbent material off the surface. After treating a spill, rinse the surface thoroughly with fresh water from a garden hose.

REMOVING A STAIN

STAIN	CLEANING AGENT
Efflorescence	Dry stiff-bristled fiber brush; water-dampened stiff-bristled fiber brush; solution of 1 part phosphoric acid per 9 parts of water, then neutralize using solution of 1/8 cup of sodium bicarbonate (baking soda) per gallon of water
Embedded dirt or grime	Solution of 1/8 cup of all-purpose cleaner per gallon of water
Grease, oil, tar or rubber mark	For asphalt, a solution of 1/8 cup of all-purpose cleaner per gallon of water
	For other materials, commercial oil and grease remover; undissolved powdered laundry detergent; undiluted citrus-based solvent
Mildew	Solution of 1/4 pound of oxygen bleach powder and 1/8 cup of dishwashing liquid per gallon of water
Organic	Solution of 1 ounce of ammonium sulfamate powder (herbicide) per gallon of water, then neutralize using solution of 1/8 cup of sodium bicarbonate (baking soda) per gallon of water; solution of 1/4 pound of sodium metasilicate powder per gallon of water, then neutralize using solution of 1 quart of white vinegar per gallon of water
Rust	For cast concrete or brick, solution of 1/4 pound of oxalic acid powder per gallon of water, then neutralize using solution of 1/8 cup of sodium bicarbonate (baking soda) per gallon of water
	For other materials, commercial rust remover; solution of 1 part phosphoric acid per 9 parts of water, then neutralize using solution of 1/8 cup of sodium bicarbonate (baking soda) per gallon of water

Choosing a cleaning agent. Remove a stain as soon as you notice it—and be patient; repeated applications of a cleaning agent may be necessary. To help identify a stain, use its color and texture as clues. Consult the chart at left to choose an appropriate cleaning agent; also follow any specific procedures on stain removal recommended by the manufacturer of your driveway, walk or patio material. Always start with the cleaning agent recommended for a stain; if it does not remove the stain, try a slightly stronger concentration of it or another cleaning agent, continuing as necessary. Work outdoors to prepare a cleaning solution; wear rubber gloves and safety goggles. **Caution:** When preparing a solution of an acid, add the acid to the water; never add acid to water.

TESTING A CLEANING AGENT

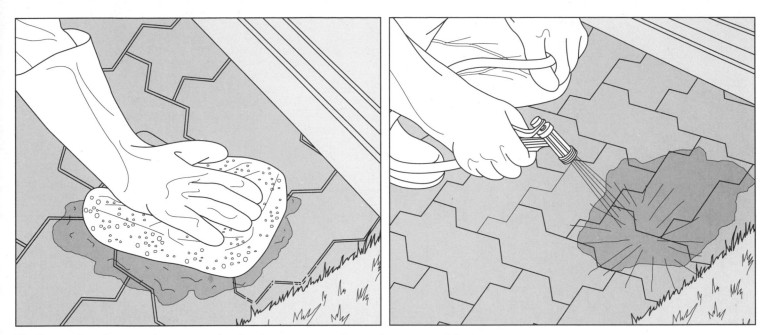

Testing a cleaning agent. Always test a cleaning agent on an inconspicuous spot of the surface. With a cleaning solution, wear safety goggles and rubber gloves to soak a clean sponge with it, then squeeze it onto the test spot *(above, left)*; saturate the test spot completely. Wait at least 30 minutes, then rinse the test spot thoroughly with water from a garden hose *(above, right)*. Allow the test spot to dry thoroughly—this may take up to 48 hours. If the test spot becomes discolored, streaked or otherwise damaged, try a milder form of the cleaning agent or a different cleaning agent, testing it first.

REMOVING STAINS

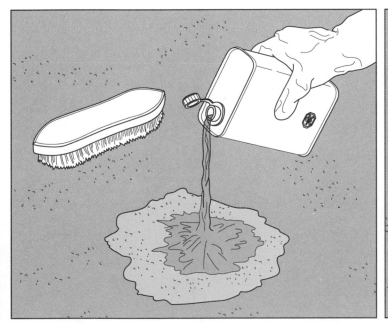
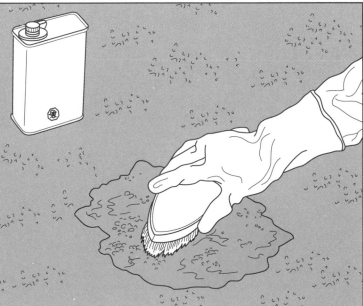

Hand-cleaning the surface. If the surface is stained extensively, spray-clean it *(page 20)*; for a localized stain, hand-clean it. For a stubborn deposit of encrusted particles or gummy material, gently work the edge of a putty knife under it to dislodge it; apply moderate pressure and use a slight scraping motion. To remove a localized stain, choose a cleaning agent *(page 18)* and test it *(step above)*. Soak the stain with water from a garden hose, then wear safety goggles and rubber gloves to apply the cleaning agent. With an undiluted liquid cleaning agent such as a citrus-based solvent, for example, pour it onto the stain *(above, left)*, then scrub the surface using a stiff-bristled fiber brush *(above, right)*; apply moderate pressure. Rinse the surface thoroughly with water from the garden hose, then allow it to dry completely—this may take 48 hours. If necessary, repeat the procedure to remove any remaining traces of the stain.

SPRAY-CLEANING THE SURFACE

Using a pump-up sprayer. To clean everyday dirt and debris off the surface, wear rubber boots and use a garden hose fitted with a spray nozzle to wash one section of it 5 feet wide at a time. Soak the section with water and scrub it with a stiff-bristled fiber push broom, then rinse it. Hand-clean any localized stain *(page 19)*. If the surface is heavily soiled or stained extensively, spray-clean it using a pump-up sprayer. Prepare to clean the surface *(page 17)*, then choose a cleaning agent *(page 18)* and test it *(page 19)*. Rent a pump-up sprayer at a tool rental center and follow the manufacturer's instructions to set it up. Wearing rubber boots, rubber gloves and safety goggles, spray-clean the surface one section 5 feet square at a time; to spray other than a solution of detergent, wear a respirator. Holding the wand with the nozzle about 12 inches from the surface, use a steady side-to-side motion to soak the section; wait several minutes, then scrub using a stiff-bristled fiber push broom. Rinse the section thoroughly with water from a garden hose. Continue the same way *(left)*, pressurizing and refilling the sprayer as necessary. Let the surface dry thoroughly—this may take 48 hours.

Pump-up sprayer

ETCHING CONCRETE

Etching solution

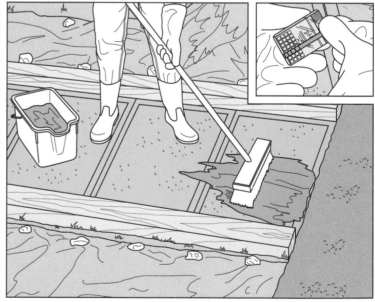

Etching a surface of cast concrete. Before sealing a surface of cast concrete, etch it if it has a patchy, uneven hue; do not etch a surface of concrete pavers or concrete that is colored or textured. For etching, buy muriatic acid at a building supply center; also buy a pH test kit. Prepare to etch the surface *(page 17)*. Wearing safety goggles and rubber gloves, mix an etching solution of 1 1/2 cups of muriatic acid per gallon of water in a plastic bucket. **Caution:** Add the acid to the water; never add water to acid. To apply the etching solution, use a stiff-bristled fiber push broom. Test your etching solution and method on an inconspicuous spot, letting it dry for 48 hours; if necessary, mix a milder solution or use a gentler technique. Use a garden hose to soak the sur-

face with water, then etch it one section at a time. Pour the etching solution onto the section *(above, left)*, then scrub it *(above, right)*. Etching occurs for as long as the etching solution bubbles. To neutralize the etching solution, sprinkle sodium bicarbonate (baking soda) on the section, wait 15 minutes, then flush it thoroughly with water. Check that the etching solution is neutralized using the pH test kit, touching a test strip to the surface and comparing its color with the colors of the test chart *(inset)*. If the test strip matches less than a pH 7 of the test chart, the etching solution is not neutralized; repeat the procedure until it is neutralized. Otherwise, continue section by section the same way until the surface is etched. Wait one week before sealing the surface *(page 21)*.

SEALING THE SURFACE

1 Preparing to apply a sealer. After cleaning a driveway, walk or patio, seal the surface to provide a uniform, stain-resistant finish. Do not apply a sealer if: the surface is less than 6 months old; asphalt was sealed less than 2 years ago; or concrete was sealed less than 3 years ago. If a surface of cast concrete has a patchy, uneven hue, first etch it *(page 20)*. Buy enough of a recommended sealer to coat the surface at a building supply center. For an asphalt surface, ask for a rubberized, coal tar-derived sealer with a 25-35% solids content; if it is sloped steeply, ensure that the sealer also has a filler. For other surfaces, ask for an acrylic resin-based, a solvent-based silane or a silicone sealer. Test the sealer on an inconspicuous spot of the surface. Wearing rubber boots, rubber gloves and safety goggles, follow the manufacturer's instructions to pour a small amount of the sealer onto the test spot *(left)*, then use a squeegee to spread it out evenly. Let the sealer dry—this may take 3 days. If the test spot becomes discolored or damaged, try another sealer, testing it first.

2 Applying the sealer. Work on a calm, dry day between 50°F and 80°F when no rain is expected; if possible, avoid working in direct sunlight. Prepare to seal the surface *(page 17)*. Wear rubber boots, heavy rubber gloves and safety goggles; if recommended by the manufacturer of the sealer, also a respirator. To apply sealer on an asphalt surface, use a long-handled squeegee; on another surface, use a medium-nap roller fitted with an extension pole. Follow the manufacturer's instructions to prepare the sealer and the surface—in some cases, the surface must be dampened with water. Coat the surface with the sealer one section at a time, working across it from one end to the other end of it. Pour the sealer onto the section, then make steady back-and-forth strokes with the roller *(inset)* or the squeegee to spread it evenly. Continue applying the sealer *(above)* without overlapping sections until the entire surface is coated. Keep traffic off the surface until the sealer is dry—this may take 3 days.

EXTERIOR WALLS

The exterior walls of your home are an integral part of its structure, adding style to its appearance as well as shielding its interior from the elements. Whether of a material such as brick, stone, wood or concrete, or of a manufactured siding such as aluminum or vinyl, the exterior walls are designed to stay attractive in the face of changing weather conditions. Even with the best of care, however, any exterior wall is vulnerable to the effects of airborne particles, extremes of heat and cold, water, and sunlight—eventually becoming dirty, soiled or stained.

Routine maintenance can prolong the life of the exterior walls of your home. Clean dirt and debris off the exterior walls at least once each year—helping to postpone the need for an expensive repair such as refinishing or replacing the materials of which they are made. Remove a stain from an exterior wall as soon as you spot it. Cleaning an exterior wall is not difficult, but time, patience and orderliness are needed to do it efficiently. Refer to the Troubleshooting Guide (below) for procedures on cleaning and stain removal for the exterior walls of your home. For basic guidelines and strategy on cleaning and stain removal for an exterior wall, read the Cleaning Tips (page 23). Consult Tools & Techniques (page 116) for general information on cleaning supplies and techniques.

Always take the time to prepare properly for a cleaning job (page 23); set up any ladder or scaffolding necessary to reach high surfaces comfortably—and safely (page 122). To remove common, everyday dirt, hose-wash the surface (page 25) using a garden hose fitted with an automobile brush and extension-pole attachment; for a soiled surface of a material other than aluminum or vinyl siding, you can pressure-wash it (page 25) with a pressure-washer—available at a tool rental center. To remove stains, spray-clean the surface if stains are extensive (page 26); hand-clean the surface if a stain is localized (page 27). Choose a cleaning solution appropriate for the type of stain (page 24), testing it and your cleaning method on an inconspicuous spot of the surface (page 24).

Knowledge about the materials of the exterior walls of your home simplifies the job of cleaning or removing stains—and reduces the risk of inadvertent damage. For siding of a material such as wood, aluminum or vinyl, always save any cleaning and maintenance instructions supplied by its manufacturer. Keep samples of the bricks, stones or siding of other materials used on your exterior walls for testing cleaning solutions and methods. Never hesitate to ask for cleaning advice from the manufacturer or retailer of your exterior-wall material or from a building professional.

TROUBLESHOOTING GUIDE

PROBLEM	PROCEDURE
BRICK OR STONE	
Wall dirty	Hose-wash wall (p. 25) □●
Wall soiled; dingy or discolored	Pressure-wash wall (p. 25) ▱●▲
Wall efflorescence (white, powdery deposits)	Remove efflorescence (p. 26) □◗
Wall stained	Spray-clean (p. 26) □◗▲ or hand-clean (p. 27) □○ wall
Wall deposit; gummy or encrusted material	Remove deposit (p. 27) □○
WOOD	
Wall dirty	Hose-wash wall (p. 25) □●
Wall soiled; dingy or discolored	Pressure-wash wall (p. 25) ▱●▲
Wall stained	Spray-clean (p. 26) □◗▲ or hand-clean (p. 27) □○ wall
Wall deposit; gummy or encrusted material	Remove deposit (p. 27) □○
ALUMINUM OR VINYL	
Wall dirty	Hose-wash wall (p. 25) □●
Wall soiled; dingy or discolored	Hose-wash (p. 25) □●, spray-clean (p. 26) □◗▲ or hand-clean (p. 27) □○ wall
Wall stained	Spray-clean (p. 26) □◗▲ or hand-clean (p. 27) □○ wall
Wall deposit; gummy or encrusted material	Remove deposit (p. 27) □○
CONCRETE OR MASONRY	
Wall dirty	Hose-wash wall (p. 25) □●
Wall soiled; dingy or discolored	Pressure-wash wall (p. 25) ▱●▲
Wall efflorescence (white, powdery deposits)	Remove efflorescence (p. 26) □◗
Wall stained	Spray-clean (p. 26) □◗▲ or hand-clean (p. 27) □○ wall
Wall deposit; gummy or encrusted material	Remove deposit (p. 27) □○

DEGREE OF DIFFICULTY: □ Easy ▱ Moderate ■ Complex
ESTIMATED TIME: ○ Less than 1 hour ◗ 1 to 3 hours ● Over 3 hours   ▲ Special tool required

CLEANING TIPS

• Establish a seasonal and yearly exterior-maintenance routine; in general, wash the exterior walls of your home once each year—before the windows *(page 28)*. Clean the exterior walls from top to bottom: the siding before the foundation. Also clean the driveway, walks and patios *(page 16)*.

• To prevent run-down stains on an exterior wall, repair any rusted or damaged roofing material, gutter or downspout at the top of the wall; to prevent mildew and organic stains on an exterior wall, trim back vegetation adjacent to or growing on the wall.

• Wait for a calm, dry day to clean the exterior walls of your home; avoid working in direct sunlight or hot temperatures.

• Follow the cleaning instructions supplied by the manufacturer for any commercial cleaning product you use.

• Test any cleaning agent and method you use on an inconspicuous spot of the surface *(page 24)*—even if you are only dabbing or wiping using a cloth dampened with water.

• To protect a surface from a cleaning agent, use plastic sheeting. Wipe up any stray or spilled cleaning agent immediately with a clean, white, lint-free cloth.

• When you are trying to lift a stain, always start with the cleaning solution recommended, progressing to a stronger concentration of it or another solution only if necessary. Make several attempts to lift a stain with a cleaning solution before abandoning it; allow each application of it to dry thoroughly before repeating an application of it.

• Store cleaning agents well out of the reach of children; dispose of any leftover cleaning agent safely.

PREPARING TO CLEAN AN EXTERIOR WALL

Plastic sheeting

Preparing for the cleaning job. Protect the area around the surface you are cleaning. For a small shrub or plant or the lawn near a wall, cover it with plastic sheeting *(above, left)*; leave the sheeting loose enough to provide adequate ventilation and weight the edges of it with stones to prevent it from blowing away. To protect a large shrub or small tree adjacent to a wall, tie back any obstructing branch. If you are cleaning an entire wall, tape plastic sheeting over lighting fixtures, outlets and vents, and close windows and doors. When the area around the surface you are cleaning is protected properly, assemble all the tools and supplies you need for the cleaning job. If necessary, set up a ladder *(page 122)*. Always wear the safety gear recommended for the cleaning job: rubber gloves and safety goggles to mix any cleaning solution *(above, right)* or to pressure-wash, spray-clean or hand-clean a wall; also a respirator to spray-clean other than a solution of detergent. If you plan to pressure-wash or spray-clean a wall, also keep people and pets away from the area.

REMOVING A STAIN

STAIN	CLEANING AGENT
Chalking (aluminum siding)	Solution of 1/4 pound of sodium metasilicate powder (truck wash) per gallon of water, then neutralize using solution of 1 quart of white vinegar per gallon of water
Efflorescence (brick, stone or concrete)	Solution of 1 part phosphoric acid per 9 parts of water, then neutralize using solution of 1/8 cup of sodium bicarbonate (baking soda) per gallon of water
Embedded dirt or grime	Solution of 1/8 cup of all-purpose cleaner per gallon of water
Mildew	Solution of 1/4 pound of oxygen bleach powder and 1/8 cup of dishwashing liquid per gallon of water
Oil, tar, caulking compound	Undiluted citrus-based solvent
Organic	Solution of 1 ounce of ammonium sulfamate powder (herbicide) per gallon of water, then neutralize using solution of 1/8 cup of sodium bicarbonate (baking soda) per gallon of water; solution of 1/4 pound of sodium metasilicate powder (truck wash) per gallon of water, then neutralize using solution of 1 quart of white vinegar per gallon of water
Rust	Solution of 1/4 pound of oxalic acid powder per gallon of water, then neutralize using solution of 1/8 cup of sodium bicarbonate (baking soda) per gallon of water

Choosing a cleaning agent. Remove a stain as soon as you notice it—and be patient; repeated applications of a cleaning solution may be necessary. To help identify a stain, use its color and texture as clues. Consult the chart at left to choose an appropriate cleaning agent; also follow any specific procedures on stain removal recommended by the siding manufacturer. Always start with the cleaning solution suggested for a stain; if it does not remove the stain, try a slightly stronger concentration of it, continuing as necessary. Work outdoors to prepare a cleaning solution; wear rubber gloves and safety goggles. **Caution:** When preparing a solution of an acid, add the acid to the water; never add water to acid.

TESTING A CLEANING AGENT AND METHOD

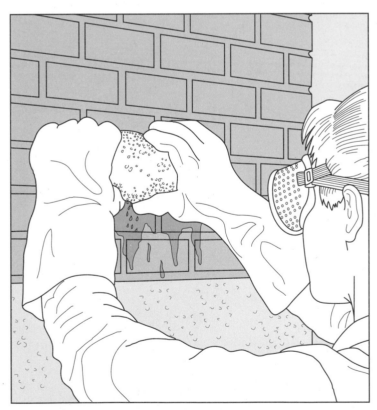

Testing the cleaning solution. Always test a cleaning agent on an inconspicuous spot of the surface. Wearing rubber gloves and safety goggles, soak a clean sponge with the cleaning agent and squeeze it onto the test spot *(above)*. Saturate the test spot with the cleaning agent, then wait several minutes and rinse it with water from a garden hose. Allow the test spot to dry thoroughly. If the test spot becomes discolored or otherwise damaged, try a milder form of the cleaning agent or a different cleaning agent, testing it first.

Testing the cleaning method. Always test your cleaning method on an inconspicuous spot of the surface. With a scrub brush, for example, wear rubber gloves and safety goggles to load it with the cleaning agent, then scrub the test spot lightly *(above)*, gradually increasing your pressure. If the test spot is damaged, try scrubbing more gently or change to a cleaning tool or method that is less abrasive. With a cloth, for example, try rubbing lightly, gradually increasing your pressure. If the test spot is damaged, try wiping gently.

HOSE-WASHING AN EXTERIOR WALL

Cleaning with a garden hose. If an exterior wall of a material other than aluminum or vinyl siding is heavily soiled, pressure-wash it *(step below)*. Otherwise, prepare to clean the wall *(page 23)* using a garden hose fitted with an automobile brush and an extension-pole attachment. Wearing rubber gloves and rubber boots, fit the extension pole onto the hose and the brush onto it *(inset)*, then connect the hose to a water supply. Turn on the water and wash the wall from the top to the bottom of it in successive sections about 5 feet wide. Start at one end of the wall and apply moderate pressure to scrub the surface with the brush; work carefully to avoid splashing windows or doors. Continue to the other end of the wall the same way *(left)*, overlapping sections slightly. Turn off the water and let the wall dry.

PRESSURE-WASHING AN EXTERIOR WALL

Pressure washer

Cleaning with a pressure washer. If an exterior wall of a material other than aluminum or vinyl siding is heavily soiled, rent a gas-powered pressure washer rated 1000 to 1500 pounds per square inch (psi) at a tool rental center; ensure that it is equipped with a sufficient length of hose for the job. Prepare to clean the wall *(page 23)*, then follow the manufacturer's instructions to set up the pressure washer, fitting it with the hose, wand and proper nozzle attachment. Wearing rubber gloves, rubber boots and safety goggles, start the pressure washer and wash the wall from the top to the bottom of it in successive sections about 5 feet wide. Starting at one end of the wall, grip the wand firmly with both hands and brace it against you to steady it; do not aim it at windows or doors. Keeping the wand almost perpendicular to the wall with the nozzle 12 to 18 inches from the surface, squeeze the trigger to start the water flow; release the trigger to stop it. Work to the other end of the wall *(left)*, overlapping sections slightly. Turn off the pressure washer, then let the wall dry.

REMOVING EFFLORESCENCE

Cleaning off efflorescence. Prepare to clean the wall *(page 23)*. Wearing work gloves and safety goggles, work from top to bottom along the wall to scrub off efflorescence using a stiff fiber brush; apply moderate pressure, making short, brisk strokes. If necessary, dip the brush in water and shake it thoroughly, then scrub with it. For stubborn or recurring efflorescence, wear rubber gloves to mix a solution of 1 part phosphoric acid per 9 parts of water in a plastic bucket. **Caution:** Add the acid to the water; never add water to acid. Carefully wash off the efflorescence by applying the cleaning solution with the brush, first testing your cleaning solution and method *(page 24)*. Soak the brush in the cleaning solution, then shake it thoroughly and scrub with it *(left)*. After washing off the efflorescence, neutralize the cleaning solution using a solution of 1/8 cup of sodium bicarbonate (baking soda) per gallon of water, mixing it in a plastic bucket and applying it with the brush the same way. Rinse off the neutralizing solution using water from a garden hose and let the wall dry.

REMOVING STAINS

Pump-up sprayer

Spray-cleaning the surface. For a localized stain, hand-clean the surface *(page 27)*. Otherwise, rent a pump-up sprayer at a tool rental center; ensure that it is equipped with a fan-type spray nozzle *(inset)*. Prepare to clean the surface *(page 23)*, then choose a cleaning solution *(page 24)*. Wearing rubber gloves, rubber boots and safety goggles, mix enough cleaning solution to fill the sprayer; for other than a solution of detergent, wear a respirator. Set up and fill the sprayer following the manufacturer's instructions, pumping the pressure-pump handle to pressurize it. Test your cleaning solution *(page 24)*. To clean the surface, work from the top to the bottom of it in successive sections about 5 feet wide. Starting at one end of the surface, hold the wand at a slight angle to the surface with the nozzle about 12 inches from it; do not aim the wand at windows or doors. Squeeze the trigger to start the spray; release the trigger to stop it. Work to the other end of the surface *(left)*, repressurizing and refilling the sprayer as necessary. Rinse the surface thoroughly using a garden hose fitted with a spray nozzle and let it dry.

REMOVING STAINS (continued)

 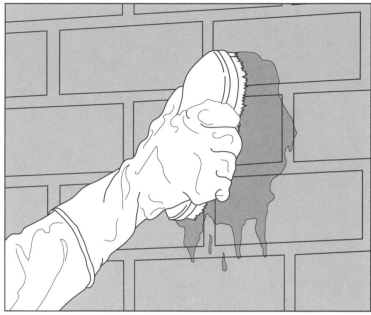

Hand-cleaning the surface. If the surface is stained extensively, spray-clean it *(page 26)*. For a localized stain, prepare to clean the surface *(page 23)*, then choose a cleaning solution *(page 24)*. Wearing rubber gloves and safety goggles, mix enough cleaning solution for the job in a plastic bucket. To apply the cleaning solution, use a scrub brush: a soft-bristled fiber type for aluminum or vinyl siding; a stiff-bristled fiber type otherwise. Test your cleaning solution and method *(page 24)*. Soak the stain with water using a sponge *(above, left)*. Dip the brush in the cleaning solution and shake it thoroughly, then apply moderate pressure to scrub the surface with it *(above, right)*. Continue until the surface is clean, reloading the brush as necessary. Rinse the surface thoroughly using a garden hose fitted with a spray nozzle and let it dry.

REMOVING DEPOSITS

Cleaning off gummy or encrusted deposits. To remove a stubborn deposit of encrusted particles or gummy material from aluminum, vinyl or wood siding, use a plastic spatula; otherwise, use a putty knife. Wearing work gloves and safety goggles, gently work the edge of the tool under the deposit *(above, left)*; apply moderate pressure and use a slight scraping motion to dislodge it. To soften the deposit or clean remaining residue off the surface, wear rubber gloves to apply a chemical solvent such as a citrus-based type. Test the cleaning solvent and method *(page 24)*. Dampen a clean, white, lint-free cloth with the solvent *(above, right)*, then gently dab the surface using a corner of it; if necessary, use a gentle rubbing or wiping motion. Continue the same way, refolding or changing cloths as they become stained. Rinse the surface using a clean cloth dampened with water, then blot it dry with another cloth.

WINDOWS AND DOORS

Your home's windows and doors are subjected to more use and abuse than most other surfaces in your home. The exterior sides of windows and doors are exposed to airborne dust and pollutant-carrying rain, the interior sides to condensation and to the soot, smoke and grease of appliances, fireplaces, candles and tobacco. As well, the never-ending opening and closing of a window or door makes it vulnerable to unsightly smudges and fingerprints. The windows and doors, however, are among the most satisfying surfaces of the house to clean, often producing a startling improvement to its overall appearance. A clean window not only sparkles; the extra light that it lets into a room makes every surface in the interior seem brighter and cleaner. A clean door can speak volumes to guests about the kind of home you keep.

Refer to the Troubleshooting Guide (below) for procedures on cleaning your windows and doors. For basic guidelines and general strategy on cleaning your windows and doors, refer to the Cleaning Tips (page 29). Consult Tools & Techniques (page 116) for information on cleaning supplies and techniques. Prepare for the job properly (page 29), setting up any ladder or scaffold needed to reach a high surface comfortably—and safely (page 122).

While cleaning a single window or door is rarely a difficult task, cleaning all the windows or doors of an average house can be a formidable task requiring careful planning. If you cannot clean both sides of all the windows of your home in a single day, divide the job into more manageable segments. In general, clean the windows of an upper story before the windows of a lower story; or, you may wish to clean all the interior sides of the windows in one day and leave the exterior sides for another day.

As well, you will need to evaluate the best cleaning strategy for each window. For a window with removable sashes (page 30), you can remove the sashes one by one and clean them at a convenient cleaning site. For a window with non-removable sashes (page 31), you will need to determine if it is easier to clean the interior side of the window from the inside and the exterior side of the window from the outside, or if you will need to clean both sides of the window from the inside. You will also need to choose the best tool and technique for cleaning each pane of a window (page 33); and you may need to use a special cleaning method to remove a deposit or stain (page 34). As well, you will need to clean the screen (page 32) and frame of any window or door you are cleaning.

TROUBLESHOOTING GUIDE

PROBLEM	PROCEDURE
DOUBLE-HUNG WINDOW	
Window dirty	Clean double-hung window: removable sashes (p. 30) □○; non-removable sashes (p. 31) □○
Screen dirty	Clean screen (p. 32) □○
Stubborn dirt on pane	Remove stubborn dirt (p. 34) □○
Stubborn film on pane	Remove stubborn film (p. 34) □○
Hardened deposit on pane	Remove deposit (p. 35) □○
Mildew on frame	Remove mildew (p. 35) □○
SLIDING WINDOW OR DOOR	
Window or door dirty	Clean sliding window or door: removable sashes (p. 30) □○; non-removable sashes (p. 31) □○
Screen dirty	Clean screen (p. 32) □○
Stubborn dirt on pane	Remove stubborn dirt (p. 34) □○
Stubborn film on pane	Remove stubborn film (p. 34) □○
Hardened deposit on pane	Remove deposit (p. 35) □○
Mildew on frame	Remove mildew (p. 35) □○
SWINGING OR FIXED WINDOW	
Window dirty	Clean swinging or fixed window (p. 31) □○
Screen dirty	Clean screen (p. 32) □○
Stubborn dirt on pane	Remove stubborn dirt (p. 34) □○
Stubborn film on pane	Remove stubborn film (p. 34) □○
Hardened deposit on pane	Remove deposit (p. 35) □○
Mildew on frame	Remove mildew (p. 35) □○
DOOR	
Door dirty	Clean door (p. 35) □○

DEGREE OF DIFFICULTY: □ Easy ▪ Moderate ■ Complex
ESTIMATED TIME: ○ Less than 1 hour ◖ 1 to 3 hours ● Over 3 hours

CLEANING TIPS

• Establish a seasonal cleaning schedule for your windows and doors corresponding to your interior and exterior household-maintenance routines; in general, clean windows and doors every 4 months, cleaning the interior sides after cleaning the walls and ceilings *(page 36)*, the exterior sides after cleaning the exterior walls *(page 22)*.

• Plan an effective cleaning strategy for windows and doors; for example, if you cannot finish cleaning all the windows in one day, divide the work to clean the windows of one story or one side of the house at a time. In general, finish cleaning all the surfaces of one window before starting to clean the next one.

• If you cannot comfortably and safely reach the exterior side of a window from the inside using a safety harness or from the outside using a ladder or extension pole, have a professional window cleaner clean the exterior side of the window.

• Clean windows on a calm, dry day; avoid working in direct sunlight or wind that can cause any cleaning solution you apply to the pane to evaporate too quickly and leave streaks.

• To prevent a cleaning solution from icing on the exterior side of a window in freezing weather, follow the manufacturer's directions on the label of a commercial automobile windshield anti-freeze product to mix it with the cleaning solution.

• To speed the cleaning of the exterior side of a window, shut it tightly before cleaning it and use a garden hose fitted with a spray nozzle to thoroughly wet the pane, softening and rinsing off dirt.

• To protect a surface from a cleaning solution, use a dropcloth or plastic sheeting. Wipe up any stray or spilled cleaning solution immediately with a clean, white, lint-free cloth.

• When you are cleaning a pane, always start with the cleaning solution recommended, progressing to a stronger cleaning agent only if necessary. Make several attempts to wash the pane with a cleaning solution before abandoning it; dry each application of it thoroughly before repeating an application of it.

• Store cleaning agents well out of the reach of children; dispose of any leftover cleaning agent safely.

PREPARING TO CLEAN WINDOWS AND DOORS

Preparing for a cleaning job. Inside the house, move furniture away from the window or door to be cleaned; for a window, open or take down any curtain or other covering. To protect a surface such as the floor, cover it with plastic sheeting or a dropcloth. Outside the house, protect vegetation near the window or door. Cover a small shrub or plant or the lawn with plastic sheeting and weight down the edges with stones. To protect a large shrub or small tree, tie branches of it back from the window or door. Assemble all the tools and supplies necessary for the job, then wear rubber gloves to mix any cleaning solution needed in a plastic bucket. For window panes, use a solution of 1 tablespoon of dishwashing liquid per gallon of water; or, if they are of glass, a solution of 1/8 cup of white vinegar or 1/8 cup of clear household ammonia *(left)* per gallon of water. For window frames, tracks and screens and for doors, use a solution of 1/8 cup of all-purpose cleaner per gallon of water; ensure that it is recommended for the material of the surface. Set up any ladder or scaffold necessary *(page 122)*.

1 Removing the sashes. Choose a cleaning site, then prepare to clean the window *(page 29)*. Remove any screen from the window, if possible, and clean it *(page 32)*; otherwise, remove and clean the sashes, then clean the screen in place before reinstalling the sashes. Starting with the inner sash, remove the sashes one at a time from the window following the manufacturer's instructions; note the position of each sash in the frame for later reinstallation. For a sliding window like the one shown, slide open the sash a few inches, then

grasp it firmly by the sides and lift it as far as possible, pulling the bottom of it toward you to angle it out of the frame *(above, left)*. For a double-hung window like the one shown, lift the sash as far as possible, then pull the bottom of it toward you to angle it out of the frame *(above, right)*. Carefully carry the sash to your cleaning site and stand it on its edge on a dropcloth, leaning it against a vertical surface to steady it. Clean any non-removable sash in place *(page 31)*, then clean any sash you removed *(step 2)*.

2 Cleaning the sashes. Wearing rubber gloves, clean the sashes one at a time. To protect the surface behind a sash, cover it with a dropcloth or plastic sheeting or shield it with plywood. Using a suitable cleaning technique *(page 33)*, clean one side of the pane, then turn the sash around to clean the other side of the pane. For a large pane of plain glass like the one shown, use a strip washer soaked in your cleaning solution to wash it *(above)*, then use a squeegee to dry it. Remove any deposit from the pane *(page 34)*. When the sashes are clean, clean the window frame *(step 3)*.

3 Cleaning the frame. Clean the frame before reinstalling the sashes. Working from top to bottom, vacuum the frame with a soft brush attachment; vacuum any window track with a crevice attachment *(above)*. Then, use a clean, white, lint-free cloth dampened with your cleaning solution to wipe the frame and any track. To remove compacted dirt from the corner of the frame or the inside of a track, scrub gently using an old toothbrush soaked with your cleaning solution *(inset)*. Wipe the frame and any track dry with another cloth. Then, reinstall the sashes in the window.

CLEANING WINDOWS: NON-REMOVABLE SASHES

Cleaning a window from the inside and outside. If you cannot reach the exterior of the window from the outside, clean both sides of it from the inside *(steps below)*; otherwise, clean its interior from the inside and its exterior from the outside. Prepare to clean the window *(page 29)*. Remove any screen from the window, if possible, and clean it *(page 32)*. Work from top to bottom to clean the frame, vacuuming it with a soft brush attachment. Wipe the frame clean using a clean, white, lint-free cloth dampened with your cleaning solution, then wipe it dry with another cloth. Using a suitable cleaning technique *(page 33)*, wear rubber gloves to clean each side of the window in turn one pane at a time. For a high, large pane of plain glass like the one shown, soak a strip washer fitted with an extension pole in your cleaning solution and wash with it. Dry the pane using a squeegee fitted with an extension pole *(above, left)*. For a large pane of plain glass on the exterior of a skylight, wash *(above, right)* and dry it the same way without using an extension pole. When the exterior and interior of each pane is clean, reinstall any screen you removed.

Cleaning a double-hung window from the inside. Prepare to clean the window *(page 29)*. Remove any screen from the window and clean it *(page 32)*. Work from top to bottom to clean the frame, vacuuming it with a soft brush attachment. Wipe the frame clean using a clean, white, lint-free cloth dampened with your cleaning solution, then wipe it dry with another cloth. Using a suitable cleaning technique *(page 33)*, wear rubber gloves to clean first the exterior, then the interior of the window one pane at a time. To clean the exterior of the inner sash, raise the inner sash until the opening at the top of it is just large enough to reach through and lower the outer sash. For the large pane of plain glass shown, wash it using a strip washer soaked in your cleaning solution, then dry it using a squeegee *(above, left)*. To clean the remaining exterior of the sashes, raise both sashes. Wearing a safety harness tied with bowline knots to a brace of boards *(inset)*, work with a helper to sit on the window sill and lower the inner sash to your lap, then clean each pane of the outer sash and the remaining portion of each pane of the inner sash *(above, right)*. To clean the interior of the sashes, close the sashes and work from top to bottom one pane at a time. When the exterior and interior of each pane is clean, reinstall any screen you removed.

Graphite

Cleaning a swinging window from the inside. Prepare to clean the window *(page 29)*. Remove any screen from the window and clean it *(page 32)*. Work from top to bottom to clean the frame, vacuuming it with a soft brush attachment. Wipe the frame clean using a clean, white, lint-free cloth dampened with your cleaning solution, then wipe it dry with another cloth. Using a suitable cleaning technique *(page 33)*, wear rubber gloves to clean first the exterior, then the interior of the window one pane at a time. To clean the exterior of the window, open the sash enough to reach it. For the large pane of plain glass shown, wash it using a strip washer soaked in your cleaning solution *(left)*, then dry it using a squeegee. To clean the interior of the window, close the sash, then work from top to bottom to wash and dry one pane at a time the same way. When the exterior and interior of each pane is clean, reinstall any screen you removed. If any moving part of the window sticks, follow the manufacturer's instructions to apply a recommended lubricant *(inset)*.

CLEANING SCREENS

Vacuuming and washing screens. If the screen is removable, remove it and take it to your cleaning site; otherwise, clean it in place, working from the side of it most easily reached. To clean dust off the screen, work from top to bottom across it using a vacuum with a soft brush attachment *(above, left)*; apply only light pressure. To clean dirt off the screen, wear rubber gloves and safety goggles to work from top to bottom of it, scrubbing it using a soft-bristled fiber brush soaked with water *(above, right)*; apply gentle pressure and use a circular motion. Rinse the screen using a sponge soaked with water. To clean stubborn dirt or grime off the screen, wash it the same way with a solution of 1/8 cup of all-purpose cleaner per gallon of water.

CLEANING WINDOW PANES

Using a cloth and newspaper. For a large pane of plain glass, use a strip washer and squeegee *(step below)*. For a small pane of plain glass or any pane of textured glass, glass block or acrylic, wear rubber gloves and use one cloth to wash it, another cloth to dry it; or, to dry a pane of other than acrylic, use newspaper. To wash the pane, soak a clean, white, lint-free cloth in your cleaning solution, then wring it until it does not drip. Working from top to bottom across the pane, rub lightly with the cloth using a circular motion *(above, left)*. To dry the pane, fold a clean, white, lint-free cloth into a pad slightly larger than your hand; or, crumple a sheet of newspaper into a loose ball. Working from top to bottom across the pane, use a vigorous circular motion to wipe it dry *(above, right)*, rubbing until it is shiny and streak-free. Refold the cloth or change the newspaper as it becomes saturated.

Using a strip washer and a squeegee. For a small pane of plain glass or any pane of textured glass, glass block or acrylic, use a cloth *(step above)*. For a large pane of plain glass, wear rubber gloves and use a strip washer to wash it, a squeegee to dry it; if necessary, extend the reach of the strip washer and squeegee with an extension pole. To wash the pane, soak the strip washer in your cleaning solution, then squeeze it until it does not drip. Starting at a top corner of the pane and working across it, wipe the washer down and up it in slightly overlapping passes *(above, left)*. To dry the pane, use the squeegee: making a continuous, side-to-side pass if the width of the pane is equal to or more than double the width of the squeegee blade *(page 34)*; making straight, overlapping passes otherwise. Position the squeegee with its blade against the top edge of the pane at one corner. Apply firm pressure to pull the squeegee down the pane to the bottom, then lift it off the pane and use a clean, white, lint-free cloth to wipe its blade dry. Reposition the squeegee at the top edge of the pane in the opposite corner and repeat the procedure, drying a strip that slightly overlaps the first strip *(above, right)*. Use a clean, white, lint-free cloth to wipe the edges of the pane dry and to blot up any cleaning solution on the window sill.

Using a squeegee on a large pane of glass. If the width of a pane of glass is equal to or more than double the width of a squeegee blade, dry it with a squeegee in a continuous side-to-side pass. Position the squeegee with its blade against the side of the pane at a top corner. Apply firm pressure to pull the squeegee across the pane toward the opposite side, then pivot it without lifting the blade off the pane, reversing direction to pull it back across the pane toward the starting side in a slightly overlapping strip. Continue the same way, pivoting the squeegee to pull it one way across the pane and back again in continuous overlapping strips *(left)*, moving down the pane until you reach the bottom of it. Then, lift the squeegee off the pane and use a clean, white, lint-free cloth to wipe the blade dry *(inset)*. Use a clean, white, lint-free cloth to wipe the edges of the pane dry and to blot up any cleaning solution on the window sill.

REMOVING WINDOW DEPOSITS AND STAINS

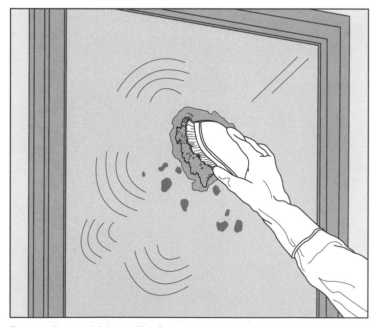

Removing stubborn dirt from a pane. For a pane of plain glass, wear rubber gloves and safety goggles to mix and apply a solution of 1 1/2 teaspoons of clear household ammonia per quart of water. Apply the solution to the pane using a clean, white, lint-free cloth, then scrub gently in a circular motion with a soft-bristled fiber brush *(above)*, softening and dislodging the dirt. Wipe the pane dry using a folded cloth, rubbing vigorously in a circular motion until it is shiny and streak-free. For a pane of acrylic, wet it with water using a clean, white, lint-free cloth, then scrub it gently with a white scrubbing pad.

Removing stubborn film from a pane. For a pane of plain glass, wear rubber gloves and safety goggles to apply a spray oven cleaner following the manufacturer's instructions. Mist the pane with the cleaner and let it sit for the time specified, then use a clean, white, lint-free cloth dampened with water to wipe it off *(above)*. Then, apply a solution of 1/8 cup of white vinegar per quart of water to the pane using a clean cloth. Wipe the pane dry using another cloth, rubbing vigorously in a circular motion until it is shiny and streak-free. For a pane of acrylic, apply a commercial acrylic cleaner following the manufacturer's instructions.

REMOVING WINDOW DEPOSITS AND STAINS (continued)

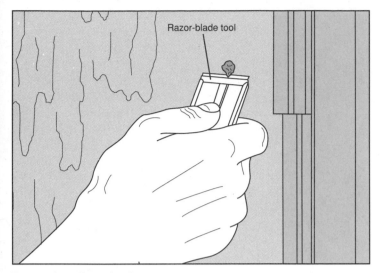

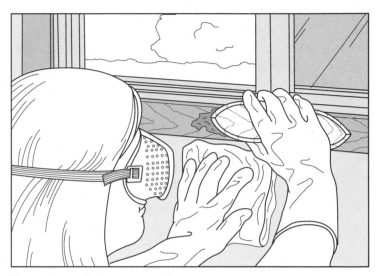

Removing deposits from a pane. For a pane of plain glass, use a clean, white, lint free cloth dampened with water to wet the pane, then work the blade of a razor-blade tool under the deposit *(above)*; apply moderate pressure and use a slight scraping motion to dislodge it. To clean remaining residue off the pane, apply a solution of 1/8 cup of white vinegar per quart of water using a clean cloth. Wipe the pane dry using another cloth or a crumpled sheet of newspaper, rubbing vigorously in a circular motion until it is shiny and streak-free. For a pane of acrylic, clean a deposit off it by rubbing gently using a clean, white, lint-free cloth dampened with mineral spirits.

Removing mildew from a frame. To remove mildew from a frame, use a bleach solution. Wear rubber gloves and safety goggles to mix a solution of 1/4 cup of household laundry bleach per quart of water in a bucket. Apply the solution using a soft-bristled fiber brush. Test your cleaning solution and method on an inconspicuous spot of the frame; if necessary, mix a milder solution or use a gentler technique. Soak the brush in the solution, then shake it thoroughly and lightly scrub the surface with it, using a clean, white, lint-free cloth to catch drips *(above)*. Rinse the surface using a cloth dampened with water. Wipe the surface dry with a dry cloth.

CLEANING DOORS

Cleaning a door. Prepare to clean the door *(page 29)*. For a door of a material other than wood with a penetrating finish, wipe it using a clean, white, lint-free cloth dampened with water. Wearing rubber gloves, use a sponge to wash the door with your cleaning solution, working from top to bottom across it. Rinse the door thoroughly using a sponge dampened with water, then dry it with a clean cloth *(left)*. For a door of wood with a penetrating finish, dust it with a clean, white, lint-free cloth, then apply boiled linseed oil to it with another cloth. Work in a well-ventilated area and wear rubber gloves to rub the oil onto the surface, working on a small section at a time in the direction of the grain; continue until the oil no longer soaks into the wood. Fold another cloth into a pad slightly larger than your hand and rub the section vigorously until it is dry. Continue, changing to clean cloths as necessary. After cleaning the door, clean any pane in it *(page 33)*. To clean a metal fitting on the door, apply a commercial product recommended for the metal following the manufacturer's instructions, rubbing vigorously with a clean, white, lint-free cloth *(inset)*.

WALLS AND CEILINGS

The walls and ceiling of the living room, dining room and bedrooms in your home are not as prone to the traffic- and function-induced cleaning demands of your kitchen, bathrooms and appliances. But even if you enjoy a tranquil, childfree lifestyle, follow disciplined living habits and practice vigilant housekeeping, the walls and ceiling of any room eventually show the signs of a gradual accumulation of dust and dirt. Airborne particles are carried into the house through open windows and doors. Telltale evidence of furniture arrangements and picture groupings, along with the passage of children and pets, appear on the walls. As well, the ceiling and walls are vulnerable to discoloration from the soot, smoke and grease of appliances, fireplaces, candles and tobacco.

Vacuum the ceiling and walls of each room in your home regularly to remove the dust and dirt that settle on them; also take steps to eliminate sources of airborne particles, soot, smoke and grease that can mark them. Once each year, clean the ceiling and walls of the room thoroughly to help prevent them from soiling and discoloring—postponing the expense and hassle of redecorating. While cleaning the ceiling and walls of a room is not a difficult job, time, patience and orderliness are necessary to do it well.

Refer to the Troubleshooting Guide *(below)* for procedures on cleaning and stain removal for the walls and ceilings in your home; to the Troubleshooting Guide in the chapter entitled Bathrooms And Kitchen for procedures on cleaning and stain removal for surfaces of special material such as ceramic tiles, laminates and acrylics. For basic guidelines and general strategy on cleaning and stain removal for the walls and ceiling of a room, read the Cleaning Tips *(page 37)*. Consult Tools & Techniques *(page 116)* for information on cleaning supplies and techniques. If you plan to clean the ceiling and walls of an entire room, prepare for the job properly *(page 37)*; set up any ladder or scaffold necessary to reach high surfaces comfortably—and safely *(page 122)*.

Knowledge about the material of a ceiling or wall simplifies the job of cleaning or removing stains—and reduces the risk of damage. Always save the maintenance instructions supplied by the manufacturer for the paint, wallcovering or other material applied to a ceiling or wall. Keep samples of the wallcoverings, wood paneling or bricks in your home for testing cleaning agents and methods. Never hesitate to ask for cleaning advice from the material manufacturer or retailer or a cleaning professional.

TROUBLESHOOTING GUIDE

PROBLEM	PROCEDURE
ROOM	
Ceiling and walls dirty	Clean ceiling of drywall or plaster *(p. 38)* ☐◖, accoustic tiles *(p. 39)* ☐◖ or stucco *(p. 39)* ☐◖; then, clean wall of drywall or plaster *(p. 40)* ☐◖, stucco *(p. 39)* ☐◖, wallcovering *(p. 40)* ☐◖, wood paneling *(p. 41)* ☐◖ or bricks *(p. 41)* ☐◖
Ceiling or wall stained	Remove stain from ceiling or wall with liquid cleaner *(p. 42)* ☐○; "dry" cleaner *(p. 43)* ☐○
CEILING	
Drywall or plaster dirty	Clean ceiling of drywall or plaster *(p. 38)* ☐◖
Drywall or plaster stained	Remove stain from ceiling of drywall or plaster with liquid cleaner *(p. 42)* ☐○; "dry" cleaner *(p. 43)* ☐○
Accoustic tiles dirty	Clean ceiling of accoustic tiles *(p. 39)* ☐◖
Accoustic tiles stained	Remove stain from ceiling of accoustic tiles with liquid cleaner *(p. 42)* ☐○; "dry" cleaner *(p. 43)* ☐○
Stucco dirty	Clean ceiling of stucco *(p. 39)* ☐◖
Stucco stained	Remove stain from ceiling of stucco with liquid cleaner *(p. 42)* ☐○; "dry" cleaner *(p. 43)* ☐○
WALL	
Drywall or plaster dirty	Clean wall of drywall or plaster *(p. 40)* ☐◖
Drywall or plaster stained	Remove stain from wall of drywall or plaster with liquid cleaner *(p. 42)* ☐○; "dry" cleaner *(p. 43)* ☐○
Stucco dirty	Clean wall of stucco *(p. 39)* ☐◖
Stucco stained	Remove stain from wall of stucco with liquid cleaner *(p. 42)* ☐○; "dry" cleaner *(p. 43)* ☐○
Wallcovering dirty	Clean wall of wallcovering *(p. 40)* ☐◖
Wallcovering stained	Remove stain from wall of wallcovering with liquid cleaner *(p. 42)* ☐○; "dry" cleaner *(p. 43)* ☐○
Wood paneling dirty	Clean wall of wood paneling *(p. 41)* ☐◖
Wood paneling stained	Remove stain from wall of wood paneling with liquid cleaner *(p. 42)* ☐○; "dry" cleaner *(p. 43)* ☐○
Bricks dirty	Clean wall of bricks *(p. 41)* ☐◖
Bricks stained	Remove stain from wall of bricks with liquid cleaner *(p. 42)* ☐○; "dry" cleaner *(p. 43)* ☐○

DEGREE OF DIFFICULTY: ☐ Easy ◖ Moderate ■ Complex
ESTIMATED TIME: ○ Less than 1 hour ◖ 1 to 3 hours ● Over 3 hours

CLEANING TIPS

• Establish a weekly and seasonal household-maintenance routine; in general, vacuum the ceiling and walls of a room every week and clean the ceiling and walls of a room once each year—before the furniture *(page 66)* and the carpet *(page 56)* or floor *(page 44)*. Vacuum or clean the ceiling before the walls of a room.

• Keep on hand a well-stocked spot-cleaning kit that includes a supply of clean, white, lint-free cloths and preparations of common solutions in labeled, plastic or glass containers: 1/8 cup of white dishwashing liquid per quart of water; 1/2 cup of household laundry bleach per quart of water; commercial all-purpose cleaner.

• Test any cleaning agent and method you use on an inconspicuous spot *(page 38)*—even if you are only dabbing or wiping using a cloth dampened with water.

• Follow the cleaning instructions supplied by the manufacturer for any commercial cleaning product you use.

• Clean a fresh spill, splash or mark off a ceiling or wall as soon as it occurs. To minimize dirt buildup and soiling, spot-clean frequently around high-traffic surfaces of a room such as at doors, windows, switches, outlets and thermostats.

• To protect a surface from a cleaning agent, use a dropcloth or plastic sheeting. Wipe up any stray or spilled cleaning agent immediately with a clean, white, lint-free cloth.

• Vacuum the ceiling or wall before applying a cleaning agent to it. When you are trying to lift a stain, always start with the mildest cleaning agent recommended, progressing to a stronger cleaning agent only if necessary. Make several attempts to lift a stain with a cleaning agent before abandoning it; allow each application of it to dry thoroughly before repeating an application of it.

• Store cleaning agents well out of the reach of children; dispose of any leftover cleaning agent safely.

PREPARING THE ROOM

Preparing for the cleaning job. Move small items, breakables and freestanding furniture away from a surface to be cleaned—preferably to another room. Take down any mounted furnishings: wall hangings, bookshelves or window coverings, for example. If necessary, also remove hardware such as brackets or hangers. To protect surfaces from a cleaning agent, use dropcloths or plastic sheeting, covering the carpet or floor as well as furniture left in the room and immovables such as balustrades; to prevent slips, do not use plastic sheeting to cover the treads and risers of a staircase. To prevent trips, use masking tape to tape the edges of dropcloths or plastic sheeting. Clean dust off trim and fixtures using a vacuum cleaner and a soft brush attachment, then protect them the same way, if necessary. When the room is prepared *(left)*, set up any ladder or scaffold necessary for the job *(page 122)*.

TESTING A CLEANING AGENT AND METHOD

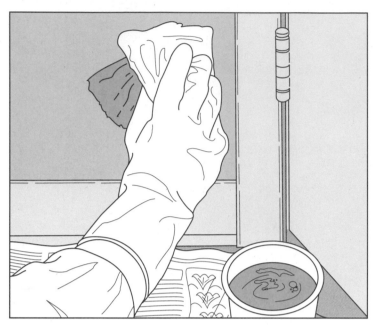

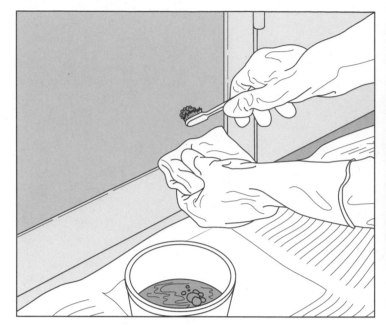

Testing the cleaning agent. Always test a cleaning agent on an inconspicuous spot. Wearing rubber gloves, moisten a clean, white, lint-free cloth with the cleaning agent and dab it lightly onto the test spot *(above)*; ensure that each color of a wallcovering is included. Allow the test spot to dry thoroughly. If the test spot bleeds, discolors or otherwise is damaged, try a milder form of the cleaning agent or a different cleaning agent, testing first; if the test spot of a wallcovering absorbs the cleaning agent, use only a "dry"-cleaning method to clean *(page 40)* or remove a stain *(page 43)*.

Testing the cleaning method. Always test your cleaning method on an inconspicuous spot. With a toothbrush, for example, wear rubber gloves and safety goggles to load it with the cleaning agent. Holding a clean, white, lint-free cloth below the test spot to catch drips, try scrubbing lightly *(above)*, gradually increasing your pressure. If the test spot is damaged, try scrubbing more gently or change to a cleaning tool or method that is less abrasive. With a cloth, for example, try rubbing lightly, gradually increasing your pressure. If the test spot is damaged, try wiping gently or use a dabbing motion.

CLEANING THE CEILING: DRYWALL OR PLASTER

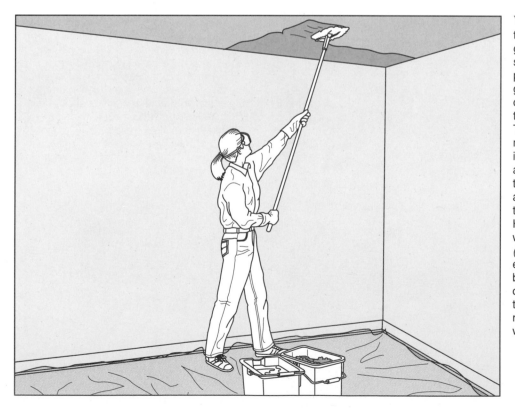

Washing and rinsing the ceiling. Prepare to clean the ceiling *(page 37)*. Wear rubber gloves and safety goggles to mix a cleaning solution in a plastic bucket: for a surface with flat paint, 1/2 cup of white dishwashing liquid per gallon of warm water; otherwise, an all-purpose cleaner following the manufacturer's instructions. For rinsing, fill another bucket with water. To clean the ceiling, use a swivel-headed flat mop with detachable wool pads: one for washing; one for rinsing. Test your cleaning solution and method *(steps above)*. Wash a section of the ceiling at a time, working from end to end along it. Fit a pad onto the mop and soak it in the cleaning solution, then wring it thoroughly. Holding the pad at an angle away from you, wipe back and forth along the section with it *(left)*; apply uniform pressure and overlap passes slightly. Rinse the section the same way before it dries using the other pad. Change the cleaning solution and rinse water as soon as they become dirty. On spots that are hard to reach, wash and rinse by hand with clean, white, lint-free cloths.

CLEANING THE CEILING: ACCOUSTIC TILES

Washing and rinsing the ceiling. Wear rubber gloves to mix a cleaning solution of 1/8 cup of white dishwashing liquid per quart of warm water in a spray container; or, use a commercial spray cleaner for tiles following the manufacturer's instructions. For rinsing, fill another spray container with water. To clean the ceiling, use sponges or clean, white, lint-free cloths: one for washing; one for rinsing. Test your cleaning solution and method *(page 38)*. If the tiles are grid-mounted, remove one at a time for cleaning. Dust your hands with cornstarch or talcum powder to avoid marking the tile, then push it up and carefully tilt it to slide it out *(above, left)*. Stand the tile on end and wash from the top to the bottom of it. Mist the tile with the cleaning solution, then wipe it gently in one direction using a sponge *(above, center)* or cloth, overlapping passes slightly. Rinse the tile the same way before it dries using the other sponge or cloth. Before reinstalling the tile, wipe the grid clean using a cloth dampened with the cleaning solution. If the tiles are not grid-mounted, prepare to clean the ceiling *(page 37)*, then clean the tiles in place one at a time, washing and rinsing the same way *(above, right)*.

CLEANING THE CEILING OR WALLS: STUCCO

Washing and rinsing the ceiling or wall. Prepare the room for cleaning *(page 37)*. Wear rubber gloves and safety goggles to mix a cleaning solution in a plastic bucket: for a surface with flat paint, 1/2 cup of white dishwashing liquid per gallon of warm water; otherwise, an all-purpose cleaner following the manufacturer's instructions. For rinsing, fill another bucket with water. To clean, use a soft-bristled fiber brush; for the ceiling, a pole-mounted type. Test your cleaning solution and method *(page 38)*. Wash a section of the ceiling at a time, working from end to end along it. Fit the brush onto the pole and soak it in the cleaning solution, then shake it thoroughly. Holding the brush at an angle away from you, scrub gently back and forth along the section with it *(far left)*; apply uniform pressure and overlap passes slightly. Rinse the section the same way before it dries. Wash and rinse a section of a wall at a time using the same procedure, working from bottom to top across it and using a clean, white, lint-free cloth to wipe off drips *(near left)*. Change the cleaning solution and rinse water as soon as they become dirty.

CLEANING THE WALLS: DRYWALL OR PLASTER

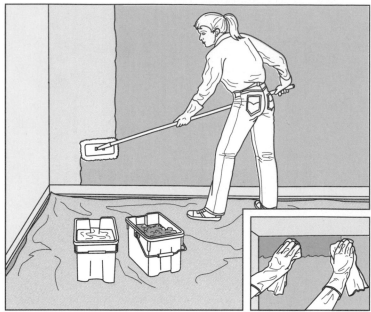

Washing and rinsing the wall. Prepare to clean the wall *(page 37)*. Wear rubber gloves to mix a cleaning solution in a plastic bucket: for a surface with flat paint, 1/2 cup of white dishwashing liquid per gallon of warm water; otherwise, an all-purpose cleaner following the manufacturer's instructions. To wash the wall, use a swivel-headed flat mop with a detachable wool pad. For rinsing, fill another bucket with water and use a clean, white, lint-free cloth. Test your cleaning solution and method *(page 38)*. Wash a section of the wall at a time, working from bottom to top across it. Fit the pad onto the mop and soak it in the cleaning solution, then wring it thoroughly. Holding the pad at an angle away from you, wipe up and stop short of the ceiling, then wipe down *(above, left)*; apply uniform pressure and overlap passes slightly. Wash the top of the section using a cloth dampened with the cleaning solution *(inset)*, wiping carefully to avoid touching the ceiling. Rinse the section from top to bottom before it dries using another cloth dampened with water, wiping in a slight circular motion *(above, right)*. Change the cleaning solution and rinse water as soon as they become dirty.

CLEANING THE WALLS: WALLCOVERINGS

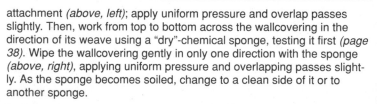

Dry-chemical sponge

"Dry"-cleaning the wallcovering. To test a wallcovering for washability, use a clean, white, lint-free cloth dampened with water to gently dab an inconspicuous spot. If the test spot does not absorb the water, clean the wallcovering as you would a wall of drywall or plaster *(step above)*. Otherwise, prepare the room for cleaning *(page 37)*, then "dry"-clean the wallcovering. Working from top to bottom across the wallcovering in the direction of its weave, vacuum it using a soft brush attachment *(above, left)*; apply uniform pressure and overlap passes slightly. Then, work from top to bottom across the wallcovering in the direction of its weave using a "dry"-chemical sponge, testing it first *(page 38)*. Wipe the wallcovering gently in only one direction with the sponge *(above, right)*, applying uniform pressure and overlapping passes slightly. As the sponge becomes soiled, change to a clean side of it or to another sponge.

CLEANING THE WALLS: WOOD PANELING

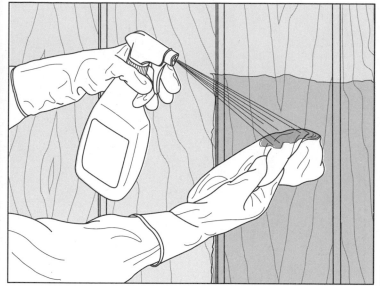 

Cleaning the wood. Prepare to clean the wall *(page 37)*. To remove scuff marks or other blemishes, use mineral spirits. Wearing rubber gloves, moisten a clean, white, lint-free cloth with the mineral spirits, then gently rub the surface with it. For light-cleaning, apply a commercial liquid polish for wood following the manufacturer's instructions. Pour the polish into a spray container, then dampen a clean, white, lint-free cloth with it *(above, left)*. Wipe the surface with the cloth, working on a section of it at a time in the direction of the wood grain. As the cloth dries, rub the section of the surface vigorously, buffing it until it shines. Continue the same way, changing to a clean cloth as necessary. For deep-cleaning, mix a solution of 1 tablespoon of white dishwashing liquid per quart of warm water, then whip it using an eggbeater to create as much foam as possible. Soak a clean, white, lint-free cloth with the solution *(above, right)* and scrub the surface vigorously, working on a section of it a time in the direction of the wood grain. Wipe the surface dry using a clean cloth. After deep-cleaning, wait 1 to 2 days, then protect the finish by applying a commercial liquid polish for wood.

CLEANING THE WALLS: BRICK

Cleaning the bricks. Prepare to clean the wall *(page 37)*. Wearing safety goggles, work from top to bottom across the wall to vacuum the bricks using a floor brush attachment *(left)*; apply uniform pressure and overlap passes slightly. To clean efflorescence (white, powdery mineral deposits) off the bricks, scrub using a stiff fiber brush; apply moderate pressure, making short, brisk strokes. If necessary, dip the brush in water and shake it thoroughly, then scrub with it. To clean stubborn or recurring efflorescence off the bricks, wear rubber gloves to mix a solution of 1 part phosphoric acid per 9 parts of water in a plastic bucket. **Caution:** Add the acid to the water; never add water to acid. Carefully apply the solution to the bricks using the brush, first testing your cleaning solution and method *(page 38)*. Then, rinse the bricks and neutralize the cleaning solution using a solution of 1/8 cup of sodium bicarbonate (baking soda) per gallon of water, mixing it in a plastic bucket and applying it with the brush the same way.

REMOVING A STAIN WITH A LIQUID CLEANER

1 **Applying an all-purpose cleaner.** For a washable surface, first try an all-purpose cleaner. Test your cleaner and method *(page 38)*. Wearing rubber gloves, dampen a clean, white, lint-free cloth with the cleaner, then gently dab or wipe the surface with it. Or, lightly mist the surface with the cleaner *(above)* and wait several minutes, using the cloth to catch drips and gently rub the surface. If the stain persists, wear safety goggles and lightly scrub the surface with the cleaner using a toothbrush or a soft-bristled fiber brush. For mildew or a water mark, try a bleach solution *(step 2)*; otherwise, next try an abrasive cleaner *(step 3)*.

2 **Applying a bleach solution.** For mildew or a water mark, try a bleach solution. Wear rubber gloves and safety goggles to mix a solution of 1/2 cup of household laundry bleach per quart of water in a plastic bucket. Apply the cleaning solution to the surface using a soft-bristled fiber brush. Test your cleaning solution and method *(page 38)*. Soak the brush in the cleaning solution, then shake it thoroughly and lightly scrub the surface with it, using a clean, white, lint-free cloth to catch drips *(above)*. Rinse the surface using a cloth dampened with water, wiping gently with it. Wipe the surface dry with a dry cloth.

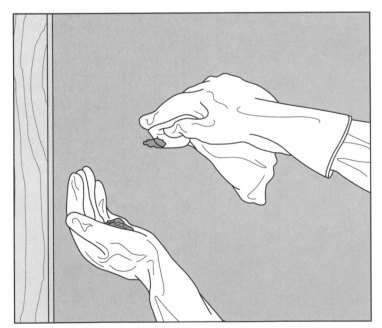

3 **Applying an abrasive cleaner.** Wear rubber gloves to mix an abrasive cleaner of household scouring powder and water. Pour a tablespoon of the powder in your hand and add water a few drops at a time, mixing the cleaner into a thick paste. Apply the cleaner to the surface using a clean, white, lint-free cloth. Test your cleaner and method *(page 38)*. Dampen the cloth with water, then dip a corner of it in the cleaner and gently rub the surface with it *(above)*. Use a cloth dampened with water to wipe off residue, then wipe the surface dry with a dry cloth.

4 **Applying a chemical solvent.** Work in a well-ventilated room and wear rubber gloves to apply a chemical solvent to the surface using a clean, white, lint-free cloth; start with rubbing alcohol or mineral spirits, if necessary progressing to dry-cleaning fluid. Test your cleaning agent and method *(page 38)*. Dampen a corner of the cloth with the solvent and gently blot the surface with it *(above)*; avoid using a rubbing or wiping motion. Use a cloth dampened with water to wipe off residue, then wipe the surface dry with a dry cloth. If the stain persists, next try a poultice *(page 43)*.

REMOVING A STAIN WITH A "DRY" CLEANER

1 **Using a "dry"-cleaning pad.** For a non-washable surface such as a wallcovering, first try a draftsman's "dry"-cleaning pad—a powder-filled, eraser-type pad for artwork, available at a stationery or art supply store. Test your cleaning method *(page 38)*. Gently rub the pad back and forth on the surface, holding a dustpan below it to catch particles *(above)*. Remove traces of the pad from the surface using a soft-bristled brush or a vacuum and a soft brush attachment. If the stain persists, try a commercial spotter *(step 2)*.

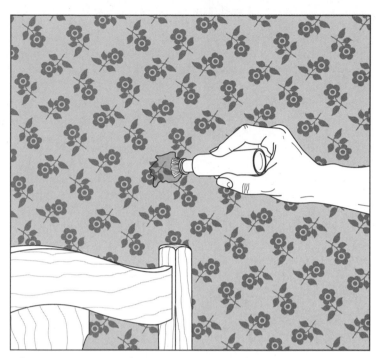

2 **Using a commercial spotter.** Apply a fast-drying commercial spotter recommended for use on the surface following the manufacturer's instructions. Test your cleaning method *(page 38)*. Gently brush *(above)*, dab or mist the spotter onto the surface and allow it to set for the time specified by the manufacturer. Remove traces of the spotter from the surface using a soft-bristled brush or a vacuum and a soft brush attachment. If the stain persists, try a poultice *(step 3)*.

3 **Using a poultice.** Wearing rubber gloves, prepare a poultice of mineral spirits and a dry ingredient: cornstarch or talcum powder for a light-colored surface; fuller's earth otherwise. Mix the poultice in a clean container into a thick, uniform paste that is the consistency of putty, adding a small amount of the dry ingredient and pouring in the mineral spirits a little at a time. Test your cleaning agent and

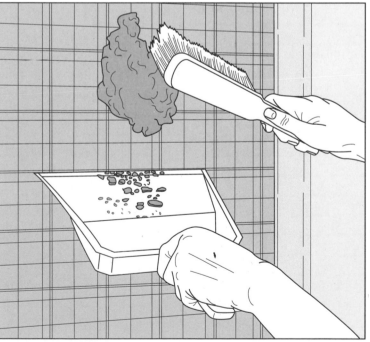

method *(page 38)*. Apply a thick, even coat of the poultice onto the surface *(above, left)* and allow it to dry—this may take hours. When the poultice is dry, gently sweep it off the surface into a dustpan using a soft-bristled fiber brush *(above, right)*. Remove traces of the poultice from the surface by wiping it using a clean, white, lint-free cloth dampened with water. Wipe the surface dry with a dry cloth:

FLOORS

Virtually all of today's floor materials and finishes are designed for toughness and easy maintenance—handy features, considering that your floors are exposed to more daily wear and tear than most of the other surfaces in your home. A typical floor may be crisscrossed daily by everything from dirty boots and bare feet to pet paws and the tricycle tires of tots. Indeed, the floor is the final resting ground for most dropped objects and spilled liquids, as well as virtually all of the dust and dirt in the house.

Whether of functional resilient tile or sheeting, colorful ceramic tile, elegant marble or lustrous wood, no floor escapes the need for regular cleaning—making floor cleaning the most frequently-performed housekeeping task of most homes. Refer to the Troubleshooting Guide (below) for procedures on cleaning and stain removal for your floors; to the Cleaning Tips (page 45) for basic guidelines and general strategy. Consult Tools & Techniques (page 116) for information on cleaning supplies and techniques.

Clean a fresh spill off the floor the moment it occurs (page 45). To prevent dirt and grit from being ground into the floor and damaging it, dust and vacuum it regularly (page 46). For other than a waxed wood floor, you can wash the floor as soon as it begins to look dirty and dingy (page 46). With patience and care, along with the right choice of cleaning agent and technique, most stains and deposits can be removed from the floor (page 54).

You can take steps to protect some types of floors: waxing a resilient floor (page 47); sealing a ceramic-tile floor (page 49). Refurbishing a wood floor is easier if it has a penetrating finish (page 50) than if it has a surface finish (page 53). Always prepare properly for a floor cleaning job. To dust and vacuum, clear the floor of small objects; to wash or wax, clear the floor entirely. Assemble all the cleaning tools and supplies needed for the job before starting it. For any cleaner, stripper, sealer or finish you use, always test it first on an inconspicuous spot of the surface.

TROUBLESHOOTING GUIDE

PROBLEM	PROCEDURE
RESILIENT	
Fresh spill	Treat fresh spill on resilient floor (p. 45) □○
Dust or grit	Dust and vacuum resilient floor (p. 46) □○
Dirt, grime or soiling	Wash resilient floor (p. 46) □○
Finish dullness	Polish resilient floor (p. 47) □◗
Stain or deposit	Remove stain or deposit from resilient floor (p. 54) □○
CERAMIC TILE	
Fresh spill	Treat fresh spill on ceramic-tile floor (p. 45) □○
Dust or grit	Dust and vacuum ceramic-tile floor (p. 46) □○
Dirt, grime or soiling	Wash ceramic-tile floor (p. 46) □○, clean grout (p. 49) □○; seal ceramic-tile floor (p. 49) □○, seal grout (p. 49) □○
Stain or deposit	Remove stain or deposit from ceramic-tile floor (p. 54) □○, clean grout (p. 49) □○
MARBLE	
Fresh spill	Treat fresh spill on marble floor (p. 45) □○
Dust or grit	Dust and vacuum marble floor (p. 46) □○
Dirt, grime or soiling	Wash marble floor (p. 48) □○
Finish dullness	Polish marble floor (p. 48) □◗
Stain or deposit	Remove stain or deposit from marble floor (p. 54) □○
WOOD	
Fresh spill	Treat fresh spill on wood floor (p. 45) □○
Dust or grit	Dust and vacuum wood floor (p. 46) □○
Dirt, grime or soiling	Refurbish wood floor with penetrating finish (p. 50) □◗; wash wood floor with surface finish using commercial all-purpose cleaner
Finish dullness	Refurbish wood floor with penetrating finish (p. 50) □◗; refurbish wood floor with surface finish (p. 53) ◪●▲
Stain or deposit	Remove stain or deposit from wood floor (p. 54) □○

DEGREE OF DIFFICULTY: □ Easy ◪ Moderate ■ Complex

ESTIMATED TIME: ○ Less than 1 hour ◗ 1 to 3 hours ● Over 3 hours   ▲ Special tool required

CLEANING TIPS

• Establish a weekly and seasonal household-maintenance routine; in general, dust and vacuum a floor once a week—more often for a high-traffic floor. Wash a floor whenever it appears dirty—after cleaning of the walls and ceilings *(page 36)* and furniture *(page 66)* and before cleaning of the carpets *(page 56)*.

• To minimize dirt and grit on floors, use a boot mat at each house entrance and keep trays under pet food dishes.

• Before vacuuming a floor, set up the vacuum cleaner properly. Empty or change the dust bag if it is more than half full. Ensure that all attachments are clean and unclogged. Pick or sweep up small objects and large debris to avoid sucking them into and damaging the vacuum cleaner.

• After dusting and vacuuming other than a waxed wood floor, damp-mop it using a sponge mop or string mop with a solution of 1 squirt of dishwashing liquid per gallon of water.

• After dusting and vacuuming a waxed wood floor, use a household floor polisher fitted with felt pads to buff the wax until it has a uniform luster.

• Test any cleaning agent and method you use on an inconspicuous spot of the surface—even if you are only dabbing or wiping using a cloth dampened with water.

• Follow the cleaning instructions supplied by the manufacturer for any commercial cleaning product you use.

• To protect a surface from a cleaning agent, use a dropcloth or plastic sheeting. Wipe up any stray cleaning agent immediately with a clean, white, lint-free cloth.

• When you are trying to lift a stain, always start with the mildest cleaning agent recommended, progressing to a stronger cleaning agent only if necessary. Make several attempts to lift a stain with a cleaning agent before abandoning it; allow each application of it to dry thoroughly before repeating an application of it.

• Do not hesitate to ask for cleaning advice from the manufacturer, retailer or installer of your floor or a cleaning professional.

• Store cleaning agents well out of the reach of children; dispose of any leftover cleaning agent safely.

CLEANING A FRESH SPILL

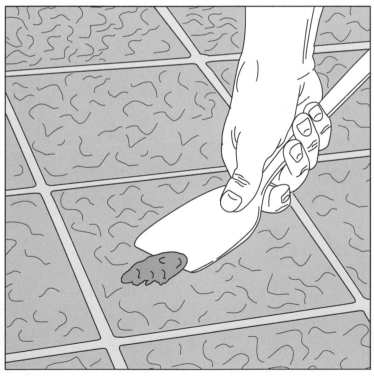 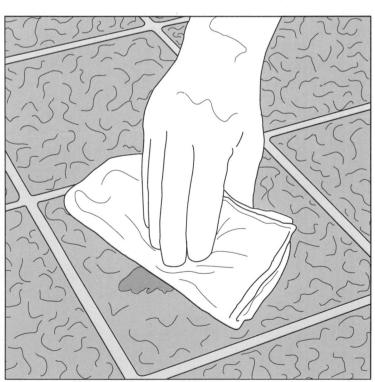

Treating a fresh spill. Treat a fresh spill quickly to prevent it from leaving a stain. For a dry-solid spill, sweep it into a dustpan or vacuum it. For a semi-liquid spill, use a plastic spatula to scoop up as much of it as possible *(above, left)* without spreading it, then blot up any residue with a clean, white, lint-free cloth *(above, right)* or paper towels; for an oily residue, first moisten the cloth or towel with a few drops of dish-washing liquid. For a liquid spill, blot it up by laying a clean, white, lint-free cloth or paper towels on it and pressing down firmly, soaking up as much of it as possible; repeat with more dry cloths or paper towels until all the liquid is absorbed. Use a clean cloth dampened with water to wipe the surface, then rub it dry with another cloth.

CLEANING THE FLOOR

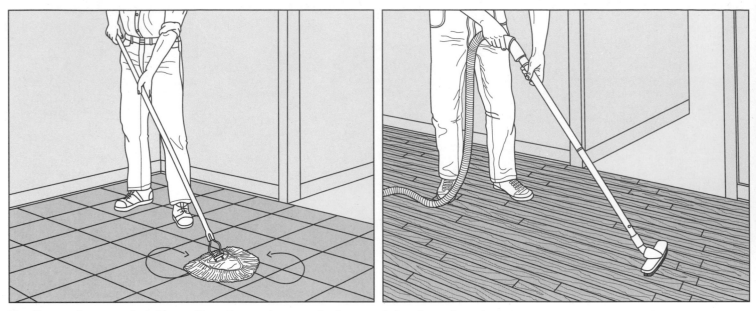

Dusting and vacuuming the surface. Dust and vacuum the floor regularly to keep dirt and grit from being ground into it. Starting in a corner of the room and working back to the door, dust the floor a section at a time using a dust mop *(above, left)*. Keep the head of the dust mop flat and sweep it from side to side in a figure-eight pattern. Work the same way to vacuum the floor using a vacuum cleaner fitted with a floor-brush attachment. Move the floor-brush attachment slowly back and forth across the floor in overlapping passes, making several passes over a high-traffic section; on a strip wood floor, work along the grain *(above, right)*. Or, sweep the floor using a soft-bristled nylon broom and a dustpan; wipe up any bits you cannot sweep into the dustpan using a clean, white, lint-free cloth dampened with water.

WASHING THE FLOOR: RESILIENT OR CERAMIC TILE

Mop-washing the surface. Clear the floor, then dust and vacuum it *(step above)*. Wearing rubber gloves, mix a solution of an all-purpose cleaner recommended for the surface following the manufacturer's instructions. Wearing clean, white, soft-soled shoes, use a string mop to apply the solution. Starting in a corner of the room and working back to the door, wet the floor a section at a time with the solution *(left)*. Load the mop with solution and partially wring it, then sweep it across the floor from side to side in a figure-eight pattern; reload it as necessary. Mix a fresh solution and work the same way to scrub the floor. Load the mop with solution and thoroughly wring it, then scrub the floor vigorously with it; as it absorbs the solution used to wet the floor, wring it into a waste bucket. Continue the same way, mixing a fresh solution and emptying the waste bucket as necessary. For stubborn dirt and encrusted particles, scrub using a white scrubbing pad *(inset)*. Use the same procedure to rinse the floor with water.

POLISHING THE FLOOR: RESILIENT

1 **Applying a floor-polish stripper.** Clear the floor, then dust and vacuum it *(page 46)*. Work in a well-ventilated room and wear rubber gloves to mix a solution of a water-based "rinseless" (one-rinse) stripper following the manufacturer's instructions; avoid using an ammonia-based stripper. Wearing clean, white, soft-soled shoes, start in a corner of the room and work back to the door, stripping polish off the floor one section 3 feet square at a time. Load a sponge mop with solution and partially wring it, then mop back and forth across the floor in slightly overlapping passes *(left)*. Allow the solution to sit for the time specified—usually 5 to 15 minutes. Scrub the floor using a swivel-headed flat mop fitted with a black or brown scrubbing pad *(inset)*, loosening the polish. Remove the loosened polish from the floor immediately *(step 2)*.

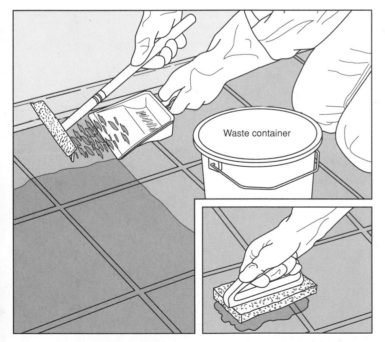

2 **Removing the loosened polish.** Remove the loosened polish from the section of the floor using a squeegee and a dustpan. Position the squeegee at one edge of the section and draw its blade firmly across the floor, scraping the loosened polish and stripping solution into the dustpan *(above)*; empty the dustpan into a waste container. Continue until all the loosened polish and stripping solution is removed from the section. Scrub adhered bits of polish off the floor using a black or brown scrubbing pad soaked with stripping solution *(inset)*. Rinse the stripped section of the floor immediately *(step 3)*.

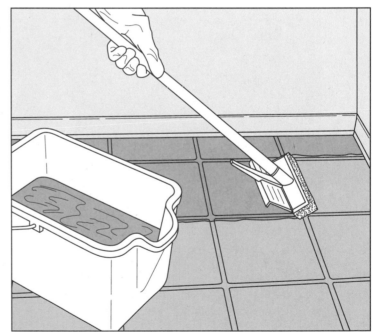

3 **Rinsing the surface.** To rinse the stripped section of the floor, fill a bucket with water and use a clean sponge mop. Load the mop with water and partially wring it, then mop back and forth across the floor in slightly overlapping passes *(above)*. Thoroughly wring the mop into a waste container, then mop back and forth across the floor again, continuing until all the water is removed from the section. Repeat the procedure for the other sections of the floor, applying stripper *(step 1)* and removing the loosened polish *(step 2)*, then rinsing. Let the floor dry before applying a fresh coat of polish *(step 4)*.

POLISHING THE FLOOR: RESILIENT (continued)

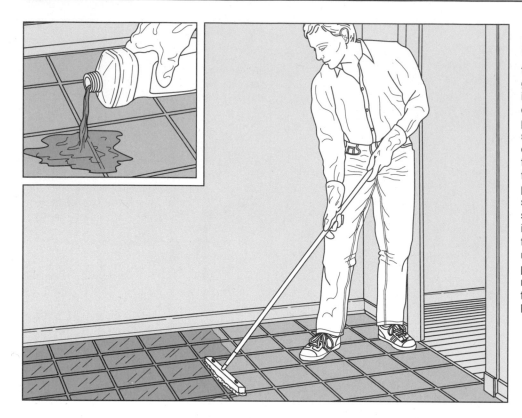

4 Applying a floor polish. Vacuum the floor, then apply an acrylic floor polish recommended for the surface following the manufacturer's instructions. Wearing rubber gloves and clean, white, soft-soled shoes, start in a corner of the room and work back to the door, using a wax applicator with a lamb's wool pad to apply polish to the floor one section 3 feet square at a time. Pour a small pool of polish onto the floor *(inset)* and spread it evenly with the applicator, moving back and forth across the floor in slightly overlapping passes. When the polish begins to spread spottily, pour another small pool of it onto the floor and spread it the same way *(left)*, smoothing out any unevenness immediately. Continue until the floor is coated, then let the polish dry for the time specified—usually 30 to 45 minutes. Apply another coat of polish on heavy-traffic sections of the floor. If recommended by the polish manufacturer, buff the floor for a high-gloss finish using a household floor polisher fitted with felt buffing pads.

WASHING AND POLISHING THE FLOOR: MARBLE

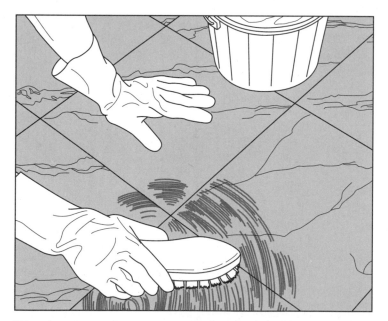

Washing the surface. Clear the floor, then dust and vacuum it *(page 46)*. Wearing rubber gloves and clean, white, soft-soled shoes, work from a corner of the room back to the door to wash the floor a section at a time. Wet the floor with water using a string mop. Mix a solution of a marble cleaner or liquid stone soap following the manufacturer's instructions and apply it to the floor using a soft-bristled nylon brush. Soak the brush in the solution and shake it out, then gently scrub with it *(above)*. Rinse the floor using a sponge soaked with water, then dry it with a clean, white, lint-free cloth. Change the solution and rinse water when they become dirty.

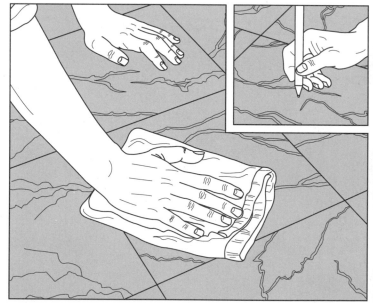

Polishing the surface. Wash the floor *(step left)*, then polish it a section at a time using a marble-floor polish. Wearing rubber gloves and clean, white, soft-soled shoes, work from a corner of the room to the door to apply a thin, uniform coat of polish with a clean, white, lint-free cloth. Moisten the cloth with polish, then wipe the floor with it. Let the polish dry, then buff it by hand with a clean cloth *(above)* or using a household floor polisher fitted with felt pads. For any small, white etch mark, rub the tip of a marble-polishing stick over it to level it with the surrounding surface *(inset)*, then rub it using a piece of burlap dampened with water.

CLEANING AND SEALING GROUT: CERAMIC TILE

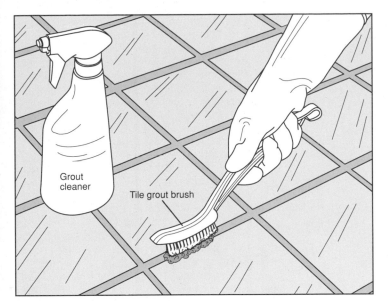

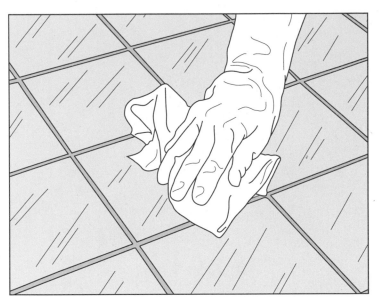

1 **Cleaning the grout.** Wash the floor *(page 46)*, then clean the grout with a grout or ceramic-tile cleaner following the manufacturer's instructions. Wearing rubber gloves, moisten a tile grout brush or an old toothbrush with cleaner and shake it, then gently scrub with it *(above)*. Wipe the grout dry using a clean, white, lint-free cloth. For mildew, work the same way using a solution of 1 cup of household laundry bleach per quart of water or a commercial mildew remover following the manufacturer's instructions. Let the grout dry; to protect it, consider sealing it *(step 2)* or the floor *(step below)*.

2 **Sealing the grout.** For ceramic tiles that can be sealed, consider sealing the entire floor *(step below)*. For glazed or other tiles that do not require a sealer, seal only the grout with a silicone-based grout sealer following the manufacturer's instructions. Wearing rubber gloves, start at a corner of the room and work back to the door to seal the grout one joint at a time. Moisten a clean, white, lint-free cloth with sealer, then wipe the grout with it *(above)*. Work carefully to avoid applying sealer to the tiles, immediately wiping off any stray sealer with another cloth. Let the sealer dry thoroughly.

SEALING THE FLOOR: CERAMIC TILE

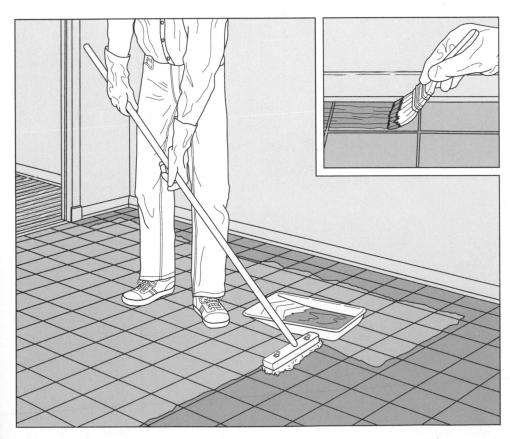

Sealing the surface. Wash the floor *(page 46)*, then seal it with a water-based sealer recommended for the tile following the manufacturer's instructions; for glazed or other tiles that do not require a sealer, seal only the grout *(step 2, above)*. Wearing rubber gloves and clean, white, soft-soled shoes, prepare the sealer and apply it; if recommended by the manufacturer, also ventilate the room and wear a respirator. Pour a small amount of sealer into a roller tray, then use a paintbrush to apply a band of it 3 to 4 inches wide to the perimeter of the floor *(inset)*. Starting at a corner of the room and working to the door, apply sealer to the rest of the floor a section at a time using a wax applicator with a lamb's wool pad. Load the applicator with sealer, then move it back and forth across the floor in slightly overlapping passes, spreading the sealer evenly *(left)*. Immediately wipe off any white residue left by evaporating sealer using a clean, white, lint-free cloth dampened with sealer. Let the sealer dry thoroughly.

IDENTIFYING THE FINISH: WOOD

Identifying the type of finish. To determine if there is wax on the floor, scrape a low-traffic spot with a fingernail; if you can scrape off material, it is wax. If there is no wax on the floor, determine if the finish on it is a surface type or a penetrating type by scraping it with the edge of a coin *(left)*. If the coin makes no mark, the finish is a penetrating type; if it makes a powdery, white mark, the finish is a surface type. To determine if a surface finish is polyurethane or varnish, choose one for a compatibility test. Wearing work gloves, roughen an inconspicuous spot of the floor using super-fine (grade 4/0) steel wool, then wipe off particles using a tack cloth. Apply a thin coat of the test finish to the spot and let it dry. Then, scrape the test finish with the edge of a coin. If the test finish flakes off, it is incompatible with the surface finish on the floor; otherwise, it is compatible with the surface finish on the floor and can be applied.

REFURBISHING A PENETRATING FINISH: WOOD

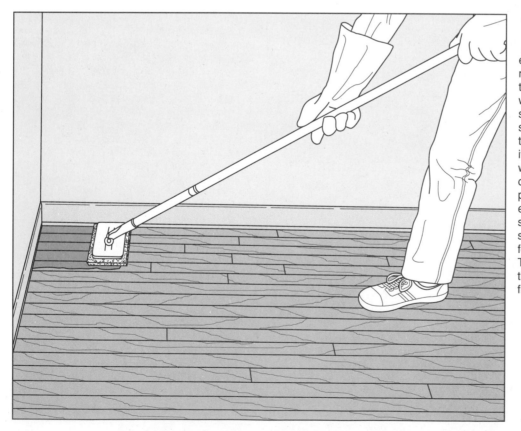

1 **Applying a wax stripper.** Clear the floor, dust and vacuum it *(page 46)*, then identify its finish *(step above)*. If the penetrating finish of the floor is not waxed, spot-refinish it *(step 3)*. If the penetrating finish of the floor is waxed, strip it with a wood-floor wax stripper following the manufacturer's instructions. Working in a well-ventilated room, start at a corner and work to the door to strip the floor one section 3 feet square at a time; if recommended by the stripper manufacturer, wear a respirator. Wearing rubber gloves and clean, white, soft-soled shoes, pour a small pool of stripper onto the floor, then spread it evenly in the direction of the grain using a swivel-headed flat mop fitted with a green scrubbing pad *(left)*. Allow the stripper to sit for the time specified—usually 5 to 15 minutes. Then, scrub the floor with the mop to loosen the wax. Remove the loosened wax from the floor immediately *(step 2)*.

REFURBISHING A PENETRATING FINISH: WOOD (continued)

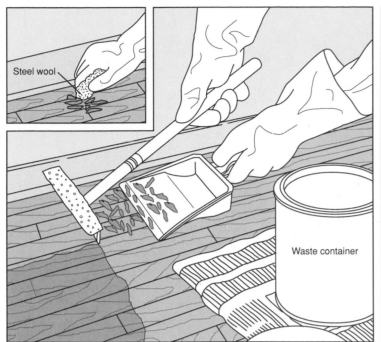

2 **Removing the loosened wax.** Remove the loosened wax from the section of the floor using a squeegee and a dustpan. Position the squeegee at one edge of the section and draw its blade firmly across the floor, scraping the loosened wax and stripper into the dustpan *(above, left)*; empty the dustpan into a waste container. Continue until all the loosened wax and stripper is removed from the section. Scrub adhered bits of wax off the floor using super-fine (grade 4/0) steel wool or a green scrubbing pad soaked with stripper *(inset)*. Wipe the stripped section of the floor dry immediately using a clean, white, lint-free cloth *(above, right)*. Repeat the procedure for the other sections of the floor, applying stripper *(step 1)*, then removing the loosened wax. Let the floor dry thoroughly. If the penetrating finish of the floor is not damaged, apply a fresh coat of paste wax *(step 4)* or liquid buffing wax *(step 5)*.

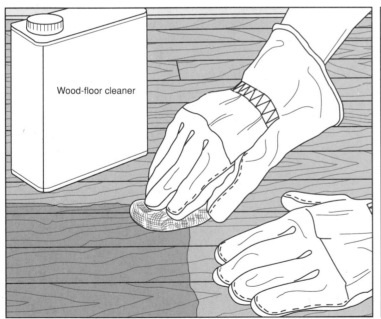

3 **Spot-refinishing the floor.** Work in a well-ventilated room and wear a respirator to spot-refinish each section of the floor with damaged finish. Wearing work gloves, clean and smooth the section using super-fine (grade 4/0) steel wool moistened with a solvent-based wood-floor cleaner, rubbing gently in the direction of the grain *(above, left)*; feather the edges slightly to help disguise them. Wipe the section clean using a tack cloth. Wear rubber gloves to apply a matching penetrating finish to the section using a paintbrush; if necessary, first test for color compatibility at an inconspicuous spot. Apply a uniform coat of penetrating finish to the section, brushing in the direction of the grain *(above, right)*; lap back at the end of each stroke to feather the edges. Continue the same way until the section is coated, overlapping parallel strokes only slightly and smoothing any unevenness immediately. Allow the penetrating finish to sit for the time specified by the manufacturer, then wipe off excess using a clean, white, lint-free cloth. Let the penetrating finish dry. If necessary, apply another coat of penetrating finish. If desired, apply a fresh coat of paste wax *(step 4)* or liquid buffing wax *(step 5)*.

REFURBISHING A PENETRATING FINISH: WOOD (continued)

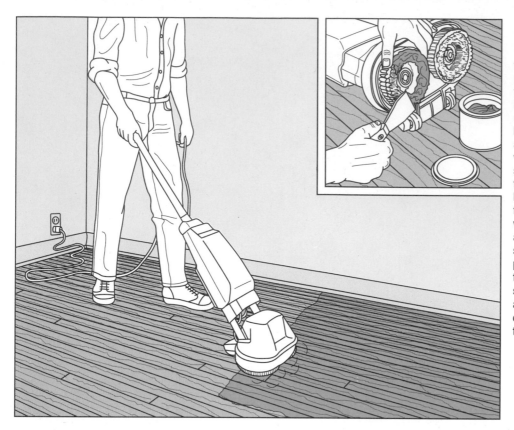

4 **Applying a paste wax.** Vacuum the floor, then apply a liquid buffing wax *(step 5)* or a paste wax recommended for the floor and its color. Work from a corner of the room back to the door, applying the wax on the floor one section 3 feet square at a time. Wearing clean, white, soft-soled shoes, apply the wax using a household floor polisher fitted with stiff-bristled, natural-fiber waxing brushes or disposable waxing pads. Load the brushes or pads with paste wax using a putty knife *(inset)*, then stand the floor polisher upright. Gripping the floor polisher firmly by its handle, turn it on at low speed and immediately move it back and forth in the direction of the grain, spreading the wax evenly; overlap passes slightly and smooth any unevenness immediately. When the wax spreads spottily, turn off and unplug the floor polisher to reload the brushes or pads. Continue the same way *(left)* until the floor is coated; on spots hard to reach, wear rubber gloves and apply the wax using a clean, white, lint-free cloth. Let the wax dry for the time specified, then polish and buff the floor *(step 6)*.

5 **Applying liquid buffing wax.** Vacuum the floor, then apply a paste wax *(step 4)* or a liquid buffing wax recommended for the floor and its color. Work from a corner of the room back to the door, applying the wax on the floor one section 3 feet square at a time. Wearing clean, white, soft-soled shoes, apply the wax using a wax applicator fitted with a lamb's wool pad. Wearing rubber gloves and clean, white, soft-soled shoes, pour a small pool of wax onto the floor, then spread it evenly in the direction of the grain; overlap passes slightly and smooth any unevenness immediately. When the wax spreads spottily, reload the pad. Continue the same way *(left)* until the floor is coated; on spots hard to reach, wear rubber gloves and apply the wax using a clean, white, lint-free cloth. Let the wax dry for the time specified, then polish and buff the floor *(step 6)*.

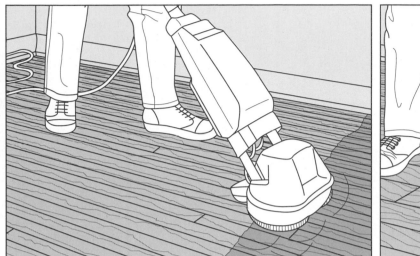

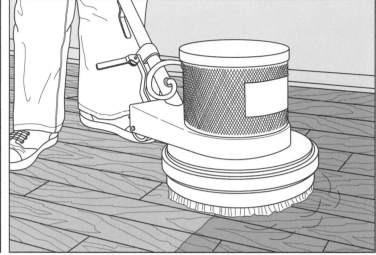

6 **Polishing and buffing the floor.** Polish, then buff the floor as soon as the wax is dry, starting at a corner of the room and working back to the door. Wearing clean, white, soft-soled shoes, polish the floor a section at a time using a household floor polisher fitted with soft-bristled, natural-fiber polishing brushes. Gripping the polisher firmly by its handle, turn it on and immediately move it back and forth in the direction of the grain, overlapping passes slightly. Continue the same way *(above, left)* until the floor is polished and the wax has a

smooth, uniform luster. Buff the floor the same way until the wax shines using the polisher fitted with felt buffing pads; on spots hard to reach, buff by hand using a clean, white, lint-free cloth. Or, use the same procedure to polish and buff the floor with a commercial floor polisher—available at a tool rental center. Use the polisher fitted with a soft-bristled, natural-fiber polishing brush for polishing the floor *(above, right)*; fitted with a felt buffing pad for buffing the floor.

REFURBISHING A SURFACE FINISH: WOOD

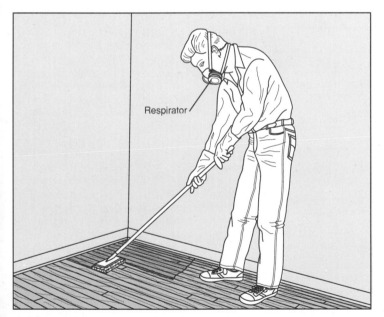

Respirator

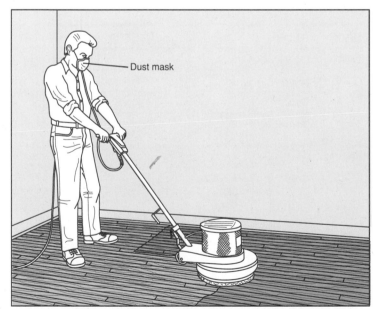

Dust mask

1 **Cleaning the floor.** Clear the floor, dust and vacuum it *(page 46)*, then identify its finish *(page 50)*. If the surface finish of the floor is damaged, refurbish it. Working in a well-ventilated room, start at a corner of the room and work to the door to clean the floor one section 3 feet square at a time with a wood-floor cleaner; if recommended by the manufacturer, wear a respirator. Wearing rubber gloves and clean, white, soft-soled shoes, pour a small pool of cleaner onto the floor and spread it evenly in the direction of the grain using a swivel-headed flat mop fitted with a green scrubbing pad *(above)*. Then, scrub the floor with the mop until it is clean. Wipe the floor dry using a clean, white, lint-free cloth.

2 **Abrading the surface.** Prepare the floor for a finish by abrading it using a commercial floor polisher—available at a tool rental center. Wearing a dust mask, start at a corner of the room and work to the door to abrade the floor one section 3 feet square at a time. Fit the polisher with a black or brown scrubbing pad or a medium sanding screen, then stand it upright. Gripping the polisher firmly by its handle, turn it on and immediately move it back and forth in the direction of the grain, overlapping parallel passes slightly; keep it moving to avoid gouging. Continue the same way *(above)* until the floor is uniformly abraded; on spots hard to reach, wear work gloves and abrade by hand using a black or brown scrubbing pad.

REFURBISHING A SURFACE FINISH: WOOD (continued)

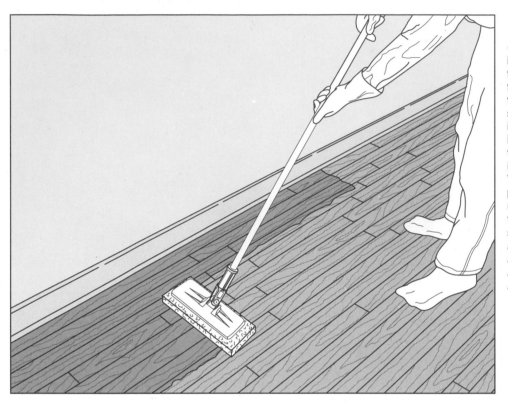

3 **Applying new finish.** Vacuum the floor and wipe it using a tack cloth. Wearing a respirator and rubber gloves, work in stockinged feet to apply a matching surface finish to the floor using a swivel-headed flat mop fitted with a lamb's wool pad; if necessary, first test for color compatibility at an inconspicuous spot. Starting at a corner of the room and working back to the door, apply a uniform coat of finish to the floor one section 3 feet square at a time. Load the pad with finish, then draw it lightly in one direction across the floor along the grain. When the finish starts to spread spottily, lift the pad gently to avoid creating air bubbles and reload it. Continue the same way *(left)* until the floor is coated, overlapping parallel strokes only slightly and smoothing any unevenness immediately; on spots hard to reach, apply finish using a paintbrush. Let the finish dry. If necessary, abrade the surface again *(step 2)* and apply another coat of finish.

REMOVING STAINS AND DEPOSITS

FLOOR	STAIN	CLEANING AGENT
Resilient	Candle wax, tar or chewing gum	Undiluted dishwashing liquid; mineral spirits
	Mildew	Solution of 1 cup of laundry bleach per quart of water
	Oil or grease	Undiluted dishwashing liquid
	Unknown origin	Solution of 1/8 cup of dishwashing liquid per quart of water; undiluted dishwashing liquid; mineral spirits; rubbing alcohol
Ceramic	Candle wax, tar or chewing gum	Undissolved scouring powder
	Mildew	Solution of 1 cup of laundry bleach per quart of water
	Oil or grease	Undiluted dishwashing liquid
	Unknown origin	Undiluted dishwashing liquid; undissolved scouring powder; commercial water-based ceramic-tile stripper
Marble	Candle wax, tar or chewing gum	Undiluted dishwashing liquid
	Mildew	Undiluted dishwashing liquid; solution of 2 tablespoons of laundry bleach per quart of water
	Oil or grease	Undiluted dishwashing liquid
	Unknown origin	Undiluted dishwashing liquid; commercial solvent-based marble-floor polish stripper; poultice of laundry bleach and dry ingredient: cornstarch or talcum powder for light-colored surface, fuller's earth otherwise
Wood	Candle wax, tar or chewing gum	Mineral spirits
	Mildew	Solution of 1 cup of laundry bleach per quart of water
	Oil or grease	Undiluted dishwashing liquid; white vinegar
	Unknown origin	Undiluted dishwashing liquid; white vinegar; mineral spirits

Choosing a cleaning agent. Remove a stain or deposit as soon as you notice it—and be patient; repeated applications of a cleaning agent may be necessary. To help identify a stain or deposit, use its color, texture and odor as clues. Following any specific cleaning procedures recommended by the manufacturer of your floor material, consult the chart at left to choose an appropriate cleaning agent. Always start with the mildest cleaning agent suggested for a stain, listed first in the chart; if it does not remove the stain, try the next cleaning agent suggested, continuing as necessary. When using any cleaning agent, wear rubber gloves; when using a solvent-based cleaning agent, work in a well-ventilated room and wear a respirator if recommended by the manufacturer.

REMOVING STAINS AND DEPOSITS (continued)

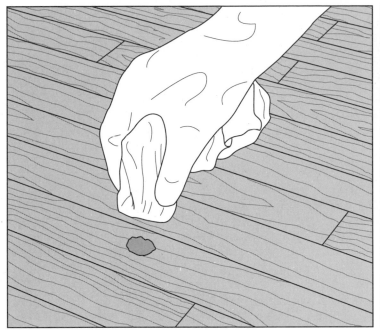

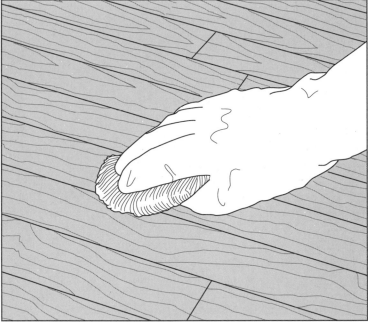

Removing a stain. Choose an appropriate cleaning agent *(page 54)* and test it on an inconspicuous spot of the surface. Wearing rubber gloves, moisten a clean, white, lint-free cloth with the cleaning agent and gently wipe the test spot with it. Let the cleaning agent dry. If the test spot is discolored or otherwise damaged by the cleaning agent, try a milder form of it or another cleaning agent. Otherwise, repeat the procedure to remove the stain, dabbing the surface gently *(above, left)* and working from the edges to the center of the stain to keep from spreading it. Rinse the surface using a clean cloth dampened with water, then blot it dry with another cloth. Continue the same way, refolding or changing cloths as they become stained. If necessary, apply the cleaning agent using a pad of super-fine (grade 4/0) steel wool, rubbing the surface gently with it; on a wood floor, in the direction of the grain *(above, right)*.

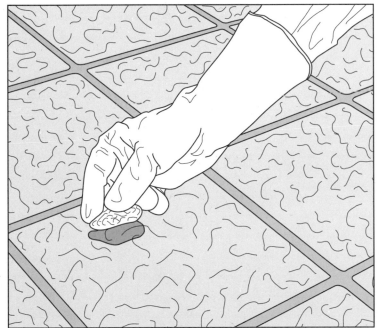

Removing a deposit. For a deposit of gummy material, hold an ice cube wrapped in plastic or an ice pack against it until it hardens *(above, left)*. Remove a deposit of encrusted particles with a plastic spatula. Gently work the edge of the spatula under the deposit, applying moderate pressure and using a slight scraping motion to dislodge it. To clean any remaining residue off the surface, choose an appropriate cleaning agent *(page 54)* and test it on an inconspicuous spot. Wearing rubber gloves, moisten a clean, white, lint-free cloth with the cleaning agent *(above, right)* and gently wipe the test spot with it. Let the cleaning agent dry. If the test spot is discolored or otherwise damaged by the cleaning agent, try a milder form of it or another cleaning agent. Otherwise, repeat the procedure to clean off the residue, dabbing the surface gently and working from the edges to the center of the residue to keep from spreading it. Rinse the surface using a clean cloth dampened with water, then blot it dry with another cloth. Continue the same way, refolding or changing cloths as they become stained. If necessary, apply the cleaning agent using a pad of super-fine (grade 4/0) steel wool, rubbing the surface gently with it; on a wood floor, in the direction of the grain.

CARPETS

Stylish and practical, a carpet can grace the path through any room of the modern home—thanks to today's choice of fabrics, textures and colors. A wall-to-wall carpet or an area rug in the living room, the dining room or a bedroom can add a touch of warmth and comfort to the room, visually highlighting or muting its structural features and other furnishings. And by gracing the path through a room of the home, a carpet is vulnerable to the mishaps that inevitably occur along any route. Few other types of surfaces indoors are as prone to and revealing of the rigors of everyday life as a carpet. The dust, dirt and stains that usually can be quickly wiped off another surface often can be scarring to a carpet.

Refer to the Troubleshooting Guide *(below)* for procedures on cleaning and stain removal for the carpets in your home. For basic guidelines and strategy on cleaning and stain removal for carpets, read the Cleaning Tips *(page 57)*. Consult Tools & Techniques *(page 116)* for general information on cleaning supplies and techniques. Routine maintenance can prolong the life of a carpet. Vacuum a carpet regularly *(page 58)* to prevent the dust, lint and dirt that settles on it from being ground into the pile and the backing—saving yourself from the premature expense of a new carpet.

Clean a fresh spill off a carpet the moment it occurs *(page 57)*. With patience and careful technique, a stain can usually be removed from a carpet; however, always test your cleaning solution before trying to lift a stain with it *(page 59)*. If a carpet is soiled, cleaning it is rarely difficult, but the job takes time, patience and orderliness to do well. You can hand-clean a small area rug *(page 64)*. However, to deep-clean a heavily-soiled wall-to-wall carpet or large area rug *(page 62)*, you will need to obtain special equipment at a tool rental center: a floor polisher equipped with a carpet bonnet and a water-extraction cleaning machine. Ask for a demonstration of the equipment, if possible, before you take it home.

Knowledge about the materials of the carpets in your home simplifies the job of cleaning or removing stains—and reduces the risk of inadvertent damage. Follow any cleaning and maintenance instructions for a carpet supplied by its manufacturer. Keep remnants of the carpets in your home for testing cleaning agents and methods. For any carpet of a fabric you cannot identify or have doubts about cleaning, consult the manufacturer or retailer; for an area rug of a fabric that is fragile or antique—delicate, oriental silk, for example—you may wish to entrust cleaning to a professional.

TROUBLESHOOTING GUIDE

PROBLEM	PROCEDURE
WALL-TO-WALL CARPET	
Fresh spill	Treat fresh spill on wall-to-wall carpet *(p. 57)* □○; protect carpet with commercial stain-guard
Dust, lint or dirt	Vacuum wall-to-wall carpet *(p. 58)* □○
Soiling	Deep-clean wall-to-wall carpet *(p. 62)* □◖▲
Stain	Remove stain from wall-to-wall carpet *(p. 59)* □○
Burn mark	Remove burn mark from wall-to-wall carpet *(p. 60)* □○
Chewing gum	Remove chewing gum from wall-to-wall carpet *(p. 61)* □○
AREA RUG	
Fresh spill	Treat fresh spill on area rug *(p. 57)* □○; protect rug with commercial stain-guard
Dust, lint or dirt	Vacuum area rug *(p. 58)* □○
Soiling	Deep-clean large area rug *(p. 62)* □◖▲; hand-clean small area rug *(p. 64)* □◖
Stain	Remove stain from area rug *(p. 59)* □○
Burn mark	Remove burn mark from area rug *(p. 60)* □○
Chewing gum	Remove chewing gum from area rug *(p. 61)* □○
STAIR RUNNER	
Fresh spill	Treat fresh spill on stair runner *(p. 57)* □○; protect runner with commercial stain-guard
Dust, lint or dirt	Vacuum stair runner *(p. 58)* □○
Soiling	Deep-clean stair runner *(p. 62)* □◖▲
Stain	Remove stain from stair runner *(p. 59)* □○
Burn mark	Remove burn mark from stair runner *(p. 60)* □○
Chewing gum	Remove chewing gum from stair runner *(p. 61)* □○

DEGREE OF DIFFICULTY: □ Easy ◖ Moderate ■ Complex
ESTIMATED TIME: ○ Less than 1 hour ◖ 1 to 3 hours ● Over 3 hours   ▲ Special tool required

CLEANING TIPS

- Establish a weekly and seasonal household-maintenance routine; in general, vacuum the carpeting of a room every week and clean the carpeting of the room once each year—after the walls and ceilings *(page 36)*, the furniture *(page 66)* and any exposed floor *(page 44)*.

- Keep on hand a well-stocked spot-cleaning kit that includes a supply of clean, white, lint-free cloths and preparations of common solutions in labeled, plastic or glass containers: 1/8 cup of white dishwashing liquid per quart of water; 1/2 cup of clear household ammonia per quart of water; 1/8 cup of white vinegar per quart of water; 3% hydrogen peroxide solution; dry-cleaning fluid.

- Follow cleaning and maintenance instructions for the carpeting supplied by the manufacturer; with an area rug, for example, there is often a tag attached to the back of it.

- Test any cleaning agent and method you use on an inconspicuous spot *(page 59)*—even if you are only dabbing or wiping using a cloth dampened with water.

- Follow the cleaning instructions supplied by the manufacturer for any commercial cleaning product you use.

- To protect a surface from a cleaning agent, use plastic sheeting or a dropcloth. Wipe up any stray or spilled cleaning agent immediately using a clean, white, lint-free cloth.

- Vacuum the carpeting before applying a cleaning agent to it. When you are trying to lift a stain, always start with the mildest cleaning agent recommended, progressing to a stronger cleaning agent only if necessary. Make several attempts to lift a stain with a cleaning agent before abandoning it; allow each application of it to dry thoroughly before repeating an application of it.

- Clean a fresh spill, splash or mark off carpeting as soon as it occurs. To minimize dirt buildup and soiling, spot-vacuum frequently the high-traffic areas of carpeting such as in halls or at doors. Keep a small, portable hand-held vacuum cleaner on hand for quick clean-ups of spills of dry material and for spot-vacuuming of high-traffic areas.

- Do not hesitate to ask for cleaning advice from the carpeting manufacturer or retailer or a cleaning professional.

- Store cleaning agents well out of the reach of children; dispose of any leftover cleaning agent safely.

CLEANING A FRESH SPILL

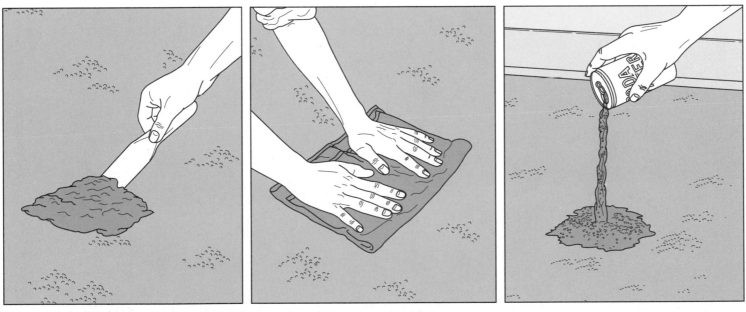

Treating a fresh spill. Clean up a fresh spill on carpeting quickly to prevent it from leaving a stain. For a dry-solid spill, use an old toothbrush to make short, gentle strokes across the carpeting to dislodge it, then vacuum it up. For a semi-liquid spill, use a plastic spatula to scoop up as much of it as possible *(above, left)* without scraping the carpet, then blot up any residue with a clean, white, lint-free cloth or paper towels. For a liquid spill, blot it up by laying a clean, white, lint-free cloth or paper towels on it and pressing down firmly *(above, center)*, soaking up as much of it as possible; repeat with more dry cloths or paper towels until all the liquid is absorbed. If a spill discolors the carpet, prevent a permanent stain by immediately wetting—not soaking—the area with soda water poured from a can *(above, right)*; wait for any fizzing action to stop, then blot up the liquid with a clean, white, lint-free cloth or paper towels.

VACUUMING CARPETING

Adjustment knob

Power nozzle

Vacuuming a wall-to-wall carpet.
To remove loose particles and keep the pile fresh and upright, vacuum the carpet regularly. Prepare to vacuum the carpet by moving small objects and light furniture off it. Empty or change the dust bag of the vacuum cleaner if it is more than half full. With a canister type of vacuum cleaner, use a power-nozzle attachment, adjusting its rotary brushes to the depth of the carpet pile *(inset)*. Starting at a corner of the room and working back to the door, vacuum a small section of the carpet at a time, moving the power-nozzle attachment slowly back and forth in overlapping strokes to agitate the pile *(left)*; make several passes over a high-traffic section. Continue vacuuming the same way, repositioning heavy furniture as necessary. For the edges of the carpet, use the vacuum cleaner with a crevice attachment, ensuring that the suction control flap is closed.

Crevice attachment

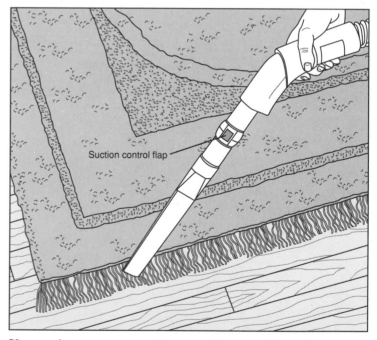

Suction control flap

Vacuuming a stair runner. To remove loose particles and keep the pile fresh and upright, vacuum the stair runner regularly. Empty or change the dust bag of the vacuum cleaner if it is more than half full. With a canister type of vacuum cleaner, use an upholstery attachment. Starting at the top of the stairs and working down them, vacuum the stair runner one riser and tread at a time, moving the upholstery attachment slowly back and forth in overlapping strokes to agitate the pile; make several passes over a high-traffic section. For the edges of the stair runner, use the vacuum cleaner with a crevice attachment *(above)*, ensuring that the suction control flap is closed.

Vacuuming an area rug. To remove loose particles and keep the pile fresh and upright, vacuum the rug regularly. Move furniture off the rug and empty or change the dust bag of the vacuum cleaner if it is more than half full. With a canister type of vacuum cleaner, use a power-nozzle attachment, adjusting its rotary brushes to the depth of the rug pile. Working from end to end of the rug, vacuum a small section at a time, moving the power-nozzle attachment slowly back and forth in overlapping strokes to agitate the pile; make passes parallel to an edge to avoid lifting it. For any fringe, vacuum using a crevice attachment *(above)*, ensuring that the suction control flap is open.

REMOVING A STAIN

STAIN	CLEANING AGENT
Blood	Cool water; solution of 1/2 cup of clear household ammonia per quart of water; solution of 2 tablespoons of enzyme laundry detergent per quart of water; 3% hydrogen peroxide solution
Butter, margarine, oil or grease	Dry-cleaning fluid; solution of 1/8 cup of white dishwashing liquid per quart of water; solution of 1/8 cup of white vinegar per quart of water
Coffee	Solution of 1/8 cup of white dishwashing liquid per quart of water; solution of 1/8 cup of white vinegar per quart of water; if with cream or milk, solution of 2 tablespoons of enzyme laundry detergent per quart of water
Fruit juice or soft drink	Solution of 1/8 cup of white dishwashing liquid per quart of water; solution of 1/2 cup of clear household ammonia per quart of water; solution of 1/8 cup of white vinegar per quart of water
Ink (ballpoint)	Methyl alcohol; dry-cleaning fluid
Milk, cream or ice cream	Solution of 1/8 cup of white dishwashing liquid per quart of water; solution of 1/2 cup of clear household ammonia per quart of water; solution of 1/8 cup of white vinegar per quart of water; solution of 2 tablespoons of enzyme laundry detergent per quart of water
Rust	Lemon juice
Shoe polish or tar	Dry-cleaning fluid
Urine or vomit	Solution of 1/8 cup of white dishwashing liquid per quart of water; solution of 1/2 cup of clear household ammonia per quart of water; solution of 1/8 cup of white vinegar per quart of water; 3% hydrogen peroxide solution
Mildew	3% hydrogen peroxide solution
Unknown origin	Dry-cleaning fluid; solution of 1/8 cup of white dishwashing liquid per quart of water; 3% hydrogen peroxide solution; solution of 1/8 cup of white vinegar per quart of water

1 Choosing a cleaning agent. Remove a stain as soon as you notice it—and be patient; repeated applications of a cleaning agent may be necessary. To help identify a stain, use its color, texture and odor as clues. Following any specific procedures on stain removal recommended by the carpeting manufacturer, consult the chart at left to choose an appropriate cleaning agent. Always start with the mildest cleaning agent suggested for a stain, listed first in the chart; if it does not remove the stain, try the next cleaner suggested, continuing as necessary. When mixing or applying any cleaning agent, wear rubber gloves; when using ammonia or dry-cleaning fluid, work in a well-ventilated room and avoid inhaling any vapor.

2 Testing the cleaning agent. Before starting to clean or remove a stain with a cleaning agent, always test it on an inconspicuous spot of the carpeting to assess its effectiveness. With a cleaning solution, wear rubber gloves and use an eyedropper to apply a few drops of it onto the test spot *(above, left)*; for patterned carpeting, ensure that each of its colors is included in the test spot. Wait several seconds, then use a clean, white, lint-free cloth to press down on the test spot for several seconds, blotting up the cleaning solution *(above,*

right). Allow the test spot to dry thoroughly before assessing the effectiveness of the cleaning solution; for carpeting of pile other than wool, use a hair dryer to speed the drying, if necessary. If the color of the test spot bleeds or comes off onto the cloth or if the pile of the carpeting is damaged, do not use the cleaning solution; try a weaker concentration of it or another cleaning solution *(step 1)*, testing it first. Otherwise, apply the cleaning solution to try and lift the stain *(step 3)*.

REMOVING A STAIN (continued)

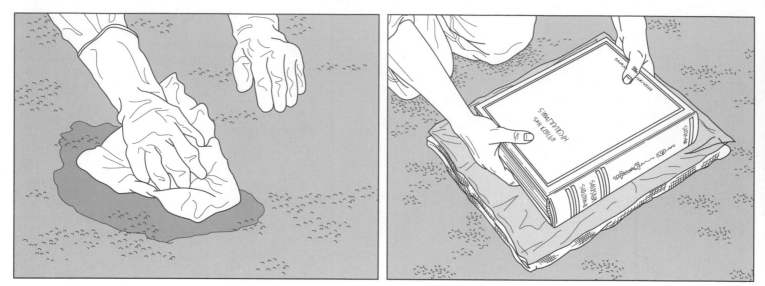

3 **Applying the cleaning agent.** With a cleaning solution, wear rubber gloves to moisten a clean, white, lint-free cloth with it and gently dab the stain *(above, left)*, working from the perimeter to the center; avoid rubbing or scouring the stain. If you cannot blot up the stain, choose another cleaning agent *(step 1)*; otherwise, continue blotting up the stain until you remove most of it, changing to a clean cloth as necessary. To absorb wetness, lay a clean paper towel or cloth down flat and apply moderate pressure on it with the heel of your hand. Change to a clean paper towel or cloth as necessary, absorbing as much of the wetness as possible. To absorb any remaining wetness, lay a clean cloth down flat and cover it with plastic, then weight down the plastic and cloth uniformly with a heavy object *(above, right)*. After several hours, remove the weight, the plastic and the cloth, then gently rub any flattened pile with your fingertips to raise it. Repeat the procedure as necessary to lift the stain.

REMOVING A BURN MARK

Cleaning burned pile. For a deep burn to the base of the pile in a carpet of loop pile, consult a carpet professional; in a carpet of cut pile, try replacing the pile *(step right)*. For a superficial burn to the tips of the pile in a carpet, gently scrape away the charred tips using a stiff-bristled fiber brush or the edge of a knife; or, for a carpet of cut pile, trim off the charred tips with cuticle scissors *(above)*. Vacuum the area of burned pile thoroughly. To remove any discoloration from the remaining pile, wear rubber gloves to mix a solution of 1/8 cup of white dishwashing liquid per quart of water. Test your cleaning solution *(page 59)*, then apply it *(step 3, above)*.

Replacing burned cut-pile. Trim off each damaged tuft of pile at its base using cuticle scissors, then use tweezers to pull replacement tufts of pile out of a remnant or an inconspicuous spot of the carpet. To install the replacement tufts, make a tuft setter; fit a darning needle securely into a hole bored in the end of a wood dowel and use diagonal-cutting pliers to cut off the upper portion of its eye. Coat the exposed backing of the carpet carefully with a latex multipurpose adhesive, then install the replacement tufts one at a time. Fit a tuft on the tuft setter, then jab it into a hole in the backing of the carpet *(above)*, pushing far enough to seat the base of it firmly.

REMOVING CHEWING GUM

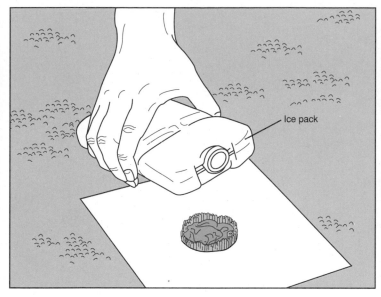

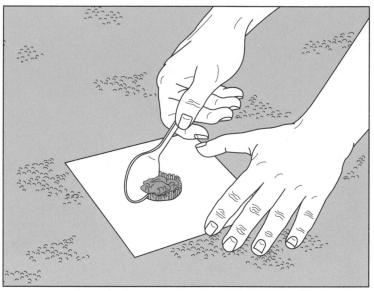

Lifting off chewing gum. To lift chewing gum off the carpet, cut a hole equal to its diameter in the center of a piece of cardboard. Position the cardboard on the carpet with the gum protruding through the hole in it. Apply an ice pack to the gum *(above, left)*, setting it fully on the cardboard; avoid resting it on any carpet at the perimeter of the cardboard. Leave the ice pack in place on the gum, chilling it until it is hard and brittle. Then, remove the ice pack and gently pick the gum off the carpet with a spoon *(above, right)*; if necessary, break it into pieces. To clean any remaining residue off the carpet, wear rubber gloves to apply dry-cleaning fluid following the manufacturer's instructions. Test your cleaning agent *(page 59)*, then apply it *(page 60)*.

PREPARING TO CLEAN CARPETING

1 Testing the cleaning solution. Test any cleaning solution you plan to use on an inconspicuous spot. Wearing rubber gloves, pour a small amount of the cleaning solution into a spray container and mist the test spot with it *(above)*; for patterned carpeting, ensure that each of its colors is included in the test spot. Apply enough of the cleaning solution to wet the test spot without soaking it. Wait several seconds, then gently scrub the test spot using a soft-bristled fiber brush. Allow the test spot to dry for 24 hours and vacuum it. If the color of the test spot bleeds or the pile of the carpeting is damaged, do not use the cleaning solution; try a weaker concentration of it or another cleaning solution, testing it first.

2 Vacuuming the carpet. To remove loose particles and agitate the pile, vacuum the carpeting. Move furniture off the carpeting and empty or change the dust bag of the vacuum cleaner if it is more than half full. With a canister type of vacuum cleaner, use a power-nozzle attachment, adjusting its rotary brushes to the depth of the carpeting pile. Vacuuming a small section of the carpeting at a time, move the power-nozzle attachment slowly back and forth in overlapping strokes. With an area rug, make passes parallel to an edge to avoid lifting it and vacuum any fringe using a crevice attachment, ensuring that the suction control flap is open; roll up the area rug, then unroll it upside down to vacuum its backing the same way *(above)*.

PREPARING TO CLEAN CARPETING (continued)

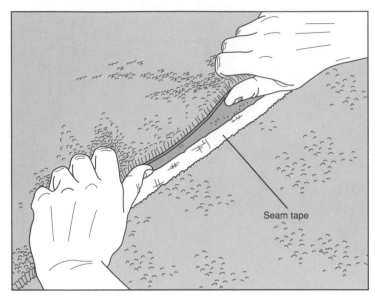

3 **Resecuring lifted edges of a wall-to-wall carpet.** With an area rug, lay it out for cleaning *(step 4)*. With a wall-to-wall carpet, resecure any lifted edges along a seam or split. Use scissors to carefully snip off any frayed backing along the edges. Cut a strip of self-adhesive carpet seam tape 2 inches longer than the edges and peel off its paper backing. Work with a helper, if necessary, to raise the edges and center the tape under them with its adhesive side facing up. Pull one edge toward the other edge and press it down firmly onto the tape. Then, pull the other edge *(above)* until it meets the first edge and press it down firmly onto the tape.

4 **Laying out an area rug for cleaning.** Lay out an area rug for cleaning onto plastic sheeting large enough to extend several inches beyond each edge of it; if necessary, use overlapping sections of plastic sheeting. For a small area rug you plan to hand-clean, lay out plastic sheeting at your cleaning site, then roll up the area rug and unroll it upside down onto the plastic sheeting *(above)*. For a large area rug you plan to deep-clean, fold it back halfway and position plastic sheeting on the floor under it, then unfold it onto the plastic sheeting; use the same procedure to position plastic sheeting on the floor under the other half of the area rug.

DEEP-CLEANING CARPETING

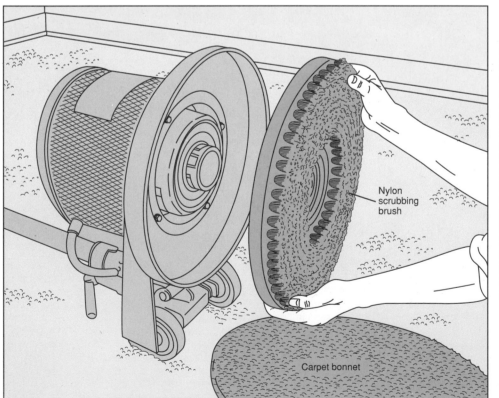

1 **Preparing to use a floor polisher and carpet bonnet.** For an area rug up to 4-by-6 feet, hand-clean it *(page 64)*; otherwise, deep-clean the carpeting. If the carpeting is not heavily soiled, vacuum it *(page 61)* and prepare to use a water-extraction cleaning machine *(step 3)*. If the carpeting is heavily soiled, first scrub it using a floor polisher. Rent a floor polisher with a speed of no more than 180 revolutions per minute at a tool rental agency; ensure that it is equipped with a nylon scrubbing brush and a carpet bonnet. Also buy enough of the shampoo recommended for your carpeting. Prepare enough shampoo to fill a spray container following the manufacturer's instructions, then prepare to clean the carpeting *(page 61)*. To set up the floor polisher, lay it on its side and follow the manufacturer's instructions to install the scrubbing brush *(left)*. Soak the carpet bonnet in water, then wring it out and center it on the scrubbing brush, pressing it firmly against the bristle tips to seat it.

DEEP-CLEANING CARPETING (continued)

2 **Using the floor polisher and carpet bonnet.** Use the floor polisher and carpet bonnet to scrub each heavily-soiled section of the carpeting. Wearing rubber gloves, mist the section with shampoo, wetting but not soaking it. Position the floor polisher at one end of the section and plug it in. With the power cord clear of the carpet bonnet, grip the handle firmly with both hands and turn on the floor polisher—immediately beginning to move it slowly back and forth across the section *(left)*, overlapping passes. When the section is lathered completely, turn off the floor polisher to reposition it. Continue the same way, periodically turning off the floor polisher and tilting it back to inspect the carpet bonnet. When one side of the carpet bonnet is soiled, remove it and turn it over, mounting the other side of it; when both sides of it are soiled, replace it.

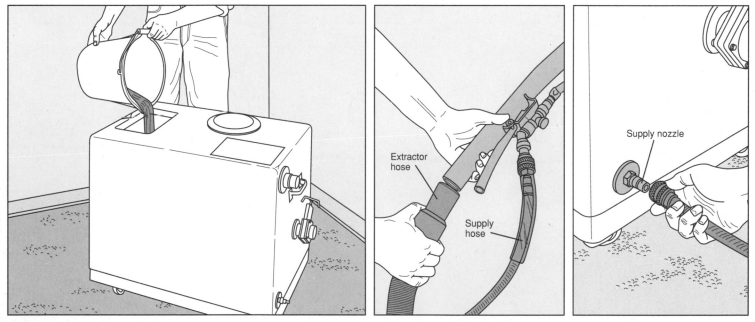

3 **Preparing to use a water-extraction cleaning machine.** Rent a water-extraction cleaning machine with a suitable nozzle at a tool rental agency. Ensure that the cleaning machine is equipped with a sufficient length of hose for the job and buy enough of the shampoo recommended for your carpet. Prepare a small amount of shampoo in a spray container following the manufacturer's instructions, then test it *(page 61)*. Set up the cleaning machine following the manufacturer's instructions, preparing enough shampoo to fill the supply tank; pour in the water *(above, left)*—cold for carpeting of wool, warm for carpeting of a synthetic—then add the shampoo. Add the recommended amount of defoamer to the waste reservoir. Connect one end of the extractor hose and the supply hose to the spray wand *(above, center)*, then the other end of each hose to the appropriate tank nozzle *(above, right)*.

DEEP-CLEANING CARPETING (continued)

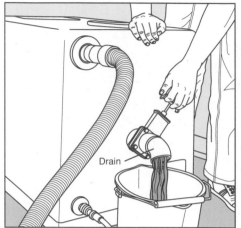

4 **Using the water-extraction cleaning machine.** Starting at a corner of the carpeting, clean one section of it 3 feet square at a time; for a stair runner, clean from the top to the bottom of it one riser and tread at a time. Holding the spray wand firmly, depress the spray trigger and move the nozzle slowly back and forth over the carpeting in overlapping strokes; wet the carpeting without soaking it. To extract the shampoo and dirt, release the spray trigger and move the nozzle back and forth again over the carpeting. Continue the same way *(above)*, overlapping sections slightly. When the supply tank empties, turn off the cleaning machine to empty the waste reservoir *(step 5)*. Refill the supply tank to continue, if necessary.

5 **Emptying the waste reservoir.** Turn off and unplug the cleaning machine, then position a bucket below the drain of the waste reservoir. Open the drain valve following the manufacturer's instructions, filling the bucket *(above)*. Close the drain valve to empty the bucket, continuing the same way until the waste reservoir is empty. When the waste reservoir is empty, wipe the inside of it using a clean cloth. Add defoamer to the waste reservoir to continue, if necessary; otherwise, finish up the cleaning job *(page 65)*.

HAND-CLEANING AN AREA RUG

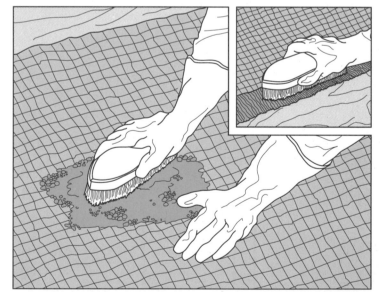

1 **Preparing the area rug.** For an area rug larger than 4-by-6 feet, consider deep-cleaning it *(page 62)*. Otherwise, plan to work outdoors on a sloped surface or on a garage or basement floor near a floor drain, cleaning first the backing and then the pile of the area rug. Prepare to clean the area rug *(page 61)*, mixing in a spray container a cleaning solution of 1/8 cup of white dishwashing liquid per quart of water: cold for an area rug of wool; warm for an area rug of a synthetic. Using a garden hose fitted with a spray nozzle, mist the area rug with water *(above)*, wetting but not soaking it.

2 **Hand-cleaning the area rug.** Wearing rubber gloves and safety goggles, prepare enough of the cleaning solution to fill a bucket and apply it using a soft-bristled fiber brush. Working from one end to the other end of the area rug, start at a corner to hand-clean a small section of it at a time. Soak the brush in the cleaning solution, then shake it thoroughly and gently scrub with it, making circular strokes. Continue the same way *(above)*, changing the cleaning solution when it becomes cloudy. For any fringe, set a clean, white, lint-free cloth under it and brush from its base to its tips *(inset)*.

HAND-CLEANING AN AREA RUG (continued)

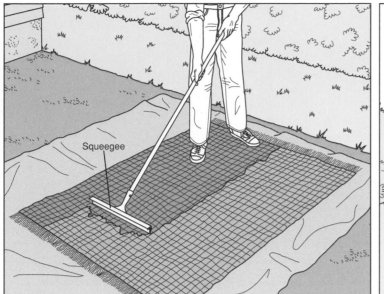

3 **Rinsing the area rug.** Using a garden hose fitted with a spray nozzle, rinse the area rug thoroughly with water, then use a heavy-duty squeegee to squeeze out the water and any remaining cleaning solution. Working from the high point to the low point of the area rug, steady it and apply firm pressure to push the squeegee across a section of it at a time. Continue the same way, overlapping passes *(above, left)*; work back and forth across the area rug as nec-

essary to squeeze out as much moisture as possible. Turn the area rug over to repeat the entire procedure on the other side of it, misting *(step 1)*, hand-cleaning *(step 2)* and rinsing its pile. When the area rug is clean, hang it up *(above, right)* out of direct sunlight and allow it to drip until its backing is dry to the touch—this may take 48 hours. Then, put back the area rug and finish up the cleaning job *(steps below)*.

FINISHING UP A CLEANING JOB

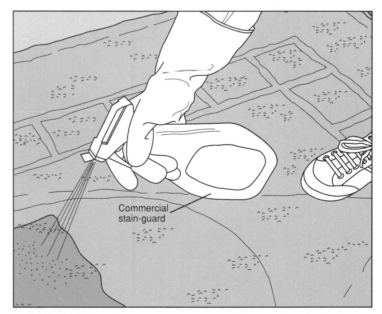

Drying the carpeting. To speed the drying of the carpeting, raise the pile by brushing against it with a long-handled brush. Allow the carpeting to dry to the touch—this may take 24 hours. If the corner of an area rug starts to curl, cover it with a clean, white, lint-free cloth and lay plastic sheeting on the cloth, then weight it down with a heavy object *(above)*. When the carpeting is dry to the touch, move back any furniture you removed. To prevent the legs of furniture from staining slightly-damp carpeting, slip plastic sheeting under them *(inset)*; leave it in place until the carpeting is completely dry.

Treating the carpeting. If the carpeting is not factory-treated with a stain-guard, apply a commercial stain-guard to help keep it from soiling and staining. Buy a commercial spray stain-guard of a type recommended for your carpeting and follow the manufacturer's instructions to apply it; most types can be applied while the carpeting is still wet or after it is completely dry. Wearing rubber gloves, work from one end to the other end of the carpeting, spraying a small section of it at a time evenly with the stain-guard *(above)*; use a slow, steady, back-and-forth sweeping motion.

FURNITURE

Your furniture helps to define the living environment of your home—usually a major investment of dollars. And few elements of your home are as vulnerable as the furniture to the rigors of everyday life: spills; wet glasses on table tops; sticky fingers; shoes reposed on upholstery. Even if the best of living habits are practiced in your home, the furniture rarely escapes all mishaps. Refer to the Troubleshooting Guide (below) for procedures on cleaning and stain removal for your furniture; to the Cleaning Tips (page 67) for basic guidelines. Consult Tools & Techniques (page 116) for information on cleaning supplies and techniques.

Clean a fresh spill off the furniture as soon as it occurs (page 67). To maintain and help prevent soiling of the furniture, vacuum or dust regularly; accord greatest frequency to materials most difficult to rid of stains. Light-cleaning of most furniture is easy; however, always test your cleaning agent (page 68). With patience and care, many stains and blemishes can be removed from furniture; upholstery of vinyl or especially of leather is a notable exception, typically requiring the cleaning services of an upholstery professional. Always check for and follow any cleaning and maintenance instructions for the furniture supplied by its manufacturer.

TROUBLESHOOTING GUIDE

PROBLEM	PROCEDURE
FABRIC UPHOLSTERY	
Fresh spill	Treat fresh spill on fabric upholstery (p. 67) □○; protect fabric with commercial stain-guard
Dust or lint	Clean fabric upholstery (p. 69) □○
Soiling	Deep-clean fabric upholstery (p. 69) ◒●▲; protect fabric with commercial stain-guard
Stain	Remove fabric-upholstery stain (p. 77) □◒; protect fabric with commercial stain-guard
VINYL UPHOLSTERY	
Fresh spill	Treat fresh spill on vinyl upholstery (p. 67) □○; protect vinyl with commercial stain-guard
Dust	Vacuum vinyl upholstery using upholstery attachment
Soiling	Clean vinyl upholstery (p. 70) □◒; protect vinyl with commercial stain-guard
Stain	Remove vinyl-upholstery stain (p. 76) □◒; protect vinyl with commercial stain-guard
LEATHER UPHOLSTERY	
Fresh spill	Treat fresh spill on leather upholstery (p. 67) □○
Dust	Vacuum leather upholstery using upholstery attachment
Soiling	Clean leather upholstery (p. 71) □◒
Stain	Remove leather-upholstery stain (p. 76) ◒◒
WICKER	
Fresh spill	Treat fresh spill on wicker (p. 67) □○; protect wood (p. 75) □○
Dust or soiling	Clean wicker (p. 71) □◒; protect wood (p. 75) □○
Blemish	Remove wood blemish (p. 75) ◒◒; protect wood (p. 75) □○
WOOD	
Fresh spill	Treat fresh spill on wood (p. 67) □○; protect wood (p. 75) □○
Dust or soiling	Clean wood (p. 73) □◒; protect wood (p. 75) □○
Blemish	Remove wood blemish (p. 75) ◒◒; protect wood (p. 75) □○
MIRRORS AND GLASS	
Dust or smudge	Clean mirror or glass (p. 72) □○
PLASTICS AND LAMINATES	
Dust or smudge	Clean plastic or laminate (p. 73) □○
MATTRESSES	
Fresh spill	Treat fresh spill on mattress (p. 67) □○; guard mattress with mattress protector
Dust, lint or odor	Freshen mattress (p. 72) □○
Soiling or stain	Guard mattress from further soiling and stains with mattress protector

DEGREE OF DIFFICULTY: □ Easy ◒ Moderate ■ Complex
ESTIMATED TIME: ○ Less than 1 hour ◒ 1 to 3 hours ● Over 3 hours   ▲ Special tool required

CLEANING TIPS

• Establish a weekly and seasonal household-maintenance routine; in general, clean the furniture of a room after the walls and ceiling (page 36) and before the carpet (page 56) or floor (page 44).

• Keep on hand a well-stocked cleaning kit that includes a supply of clean, white, lint-free cloths and preparations of common solutions in labeled, plastic or glass containers: 1/8 cup of white dishwashing liquid per quart of water; 1/8 cup of white vinegar per quart of water; 2 tablespoons of enzyme laundry detergent per quart of water; 1/2 cup of clear household ammonia per quart of water; 3% hydrogen peroxide solution.

• Test any cleaning agent you use on an inconspicuous spot (page 68)—even if the cleaning agent is only water.

• Follow cleaning and maintenance instructions for the furniture supplied by the manufacturer. With upholstery, for example, there is often a cleaning tag—usually attached to the bottom of a cushion or the furniture. If the cleaning tag is marked W or WS, you can "steam"-clean the upholstery using a water-extraction cleaning machine; if it is marked S, X or otherwise, have the upholstery cleaned by an upholstery professional.

• To protect a surface from a cleaning agent, use a dropcloth or plastic sheeting. Wipe up any stray or spilled cleaning agent immediately with a clean, white, lint-free cloth.

• Vacuum the furniture before applying a cleaning agent to it. When you are trying to lift a stain, always start with the mildest cleaning agent recommended, progressing to a stronger cleaning agent only if necessary. Make several attempts to lift a stain with a cleaning agent before abandoning it; allow each application of it to dry thoroughly before repeating an application of it.

• Resist the temptation to clean overzealously; soaking instead of dampening with a cleaning agent and scrubbing instead of dabbing can make a stain larger—and more difficult to remove.

• Do not hesitate to ask for cleaning advice from the furniture manufacturer or retailer or a cleaning professional. To help with the identification of a type of upholstery, for example, take a cushion or arm cover with you.

• Store cleaning agents well out of the reach of children; dispose of any leftover cleaning agent safely.

CLEANING A FRESH SPILL

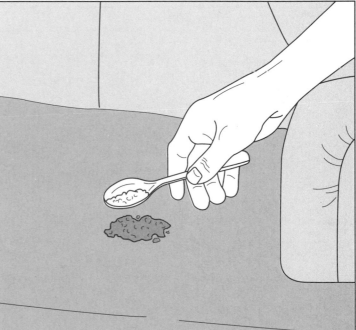

Treating a fresh spill. Treat a fresh spill quickly to prevent it from leaving a stain. Lift off a semi-solid using a spoon, working carefully from the edges toward the center of the spill to keep from spreading it. Wick up a liquid using the corner of a folded paper towel, touching it gently to the center of the spill (above, left); change to a fresh corner or paper towel as necessary, wicking up as much of the spill as possible. Blot up remaining residue from the spill with a fresh paper towel, laying it flat and applying moderate pressure with the heel of your hand; change to a fresh paper towel as necessary, blotting up as much of the spill as possible. Absorb remaining wetness from the spill by sprinkling it with a thin layer of powder (above, right): cornstarch or talcum powder for a light-colored fabric or leather; fuller's earth otherwise. Allow the powder to sit for 1 minute, then remove it using a vacuum cleaner with a crevice attachment. Continue as necessary to absorb remaining wetness.

REMOVING A STAIN

STAIN	CLEANING AGENT
Blood	Cool water; solution of 1/2 cup of clear household ammonia per quart of water; solution of 2 tablespoons of enzyme laundry detergent per quart of water; 3% hydrogen peroxide solution
Butter, margarine, oil or grease	Dry-cleaning fluid; solution of 1/8 cup of white dishwashing liquid per quart of water; solution of 1/8 cup of white vinegar per quart of water
Chewing gum	Apply ice pack until gum hard and brittle, then pick it off using spoon; remove any remaining residue using dry-cleaning fluid
Coffee	Solution of 1/8 cup of white dishwashing liquid per quart of water; solution of 1/8 cup of white vinegar per quart of water; if with cream or milk, solution of 2 tablespoons of enzyme laundry detergent per quart of water
Fruit juice or soft drink	Solution of 1/8 cup of white dishwashing liquid per quart of water; solution of 1/2 cup of clear household ammonia per quart of water; solution of 1/8 cup of white vinegar per quart of water
Milk, cream or ice cream	Solution of 1/8 cup of white dishwashing liquid per quart of water; solution of 1/2 cup of clear household ammonia per quart of water; solution of 1/8 cup of white vinegar per quart of water; solution of 2 tablespoons of enzyme laundry detergent per quart of water
Perspiration	Solution of 1/2 cup of clear household ammonia per quart of water; solution of 1/8 cup of white dishwashing liquid per quart of water; solution of 1/2 cup of household laundry bleach per quart of water
Urine or vomit	Solution of 1/8 cup of white dishwashing liquid per quart of water; solution of 1/2 cup of clear household ammonia per quart of water; solution of 1/8 cup of white vinegar per quart of water; 3% hydrogen peroxide solution
Mildew	3% hydrogen peroxide solution
Unknown origin	Dry-cleaning fluid; solution of 1/8 cup of white dishwashing liquid per quart of water; 3% hydrogen peroxide solution; solution of 1/8 cup of white vinegar per quart of water

Choosing a cleaning agent. Remove a stain as soon as you notice it—and be patient; repeated applications of a cleaning agent may be necessary. To help identify a stain, use its color, texture and odor as clues. Following any specific procedures on stain removal recommended by the furniture manufacturer, consult the chart at left to choose an appropriate cleaning agent. Always start with the mildest cleaning agent suggested for a stain, listed first in the chart; if it does not remove the stain, try the next cleaning agent suggested, continuing as necessary. When using any cleaning agent, wear rubber gloves; when using ammonia or dry-cleaning fluid, work in a well-ventilated room and avoid inhaling any vapor.

TESTING A CLEANING AGENT

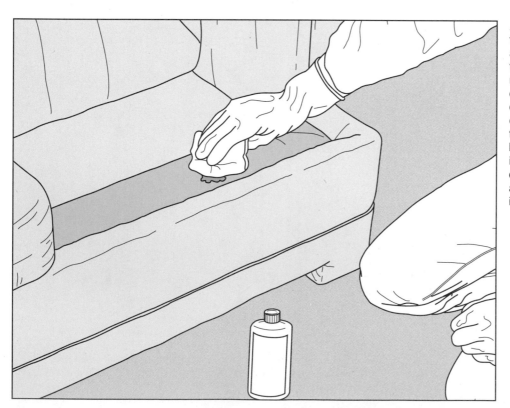

Assessing a cleaning agent. Before starting to clean or remove a stain with a cleaning agent, always test it on an inconspicuous spot of the furniture to assess its effectiveness. Wearing rubber gloves, moisten a clean, white, lint-free cloth with the cleaning agent and dab it lightly onto the test spot *(left)*; for fabric upholstery, ensure that each of its colors is included in the test spot. Allow the test spot to dry thoroughly before assessing the effectiveness of the cleaning agent. If the color of the test spot bleeds or comes off onto the cloth, do not use the cleaning agent; try a milder form of it or a different cleaning agent, testing first on an inconspicuous spot.

CLEANING FABRIC UPHOLSTERY

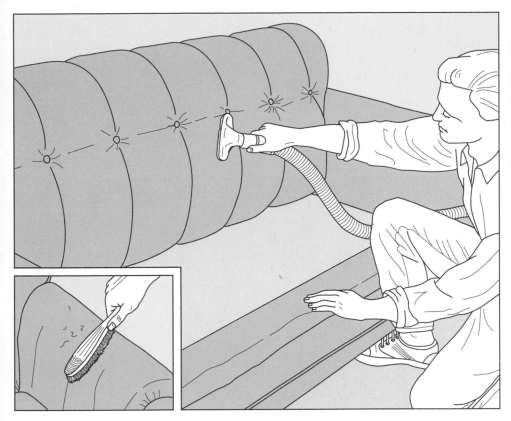

Vacuuming dust and lint off the upholstery. Vacuum fabric upholstery regularly to remove dust and lint, helping to keep it from soiling. Take off any cushion and set it aside. Clean panel by panel across the furniture using an upholstery attachment, keeping it flat and applying moderate pressure *(left)*; clean each side of any cushion the same way. For crevices and seams, clean with a crevice attachment. Put back any cushion you removed; to help distribute wear, turn it over or reverse its orientation each time you clean, if possible. To pick up stubborn lint or pet hair, brush gently with a lint brush *(inset)*; or, wrap a strip of masking tape around your fingers with its sticky side facing out and dab lightly with it.

DEEP-CLEANING FABRIC UPHOLSTERY

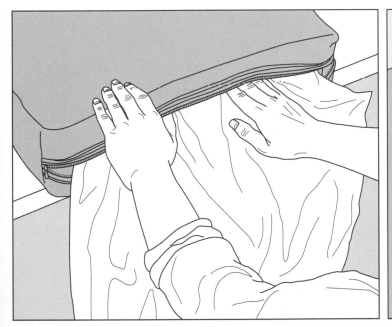

Pretreating solvent

1 Preparing to "steam"-clean the upholstery. Vacuum the upholstery *(step above)*, then check it for a cleaning tag—usually attached to the bottom of a cushion or the furniture. If the cleaning tag is marked W or WS, "steam"-clean the upholstery using a water-extraction cleaning machine; if it is marked S, X or otherwise, have the upholstery cleaned by a professional. Rent a water-extraction cleaning machine at a tool rental center; also buy enough pretreating solvent, upholstery shampoo and defoamer. Work in a well-ventilated room,

spreading a dropcloth on the floor and setting the furniture on it. Unzip the upholstery of each cushion and check the padding for stains. To keep a stain on the padding from seeping back through the upholstery, slide a plastic trash bag between them *(above, left)*. Smooth the plastic to eliminate wrinkles, then rezip the upholstery and set each cushion aside on the dropcloth. Lightly mist the upholstery with the pretreating solvent *(above, right)*, spraying only enough to slightly moisten it. Allow the pretreating solvent to soak into the upholstery for about 5 minutes.

DEEP-CLEANING FABRIC UPHOLSTERY (continued)

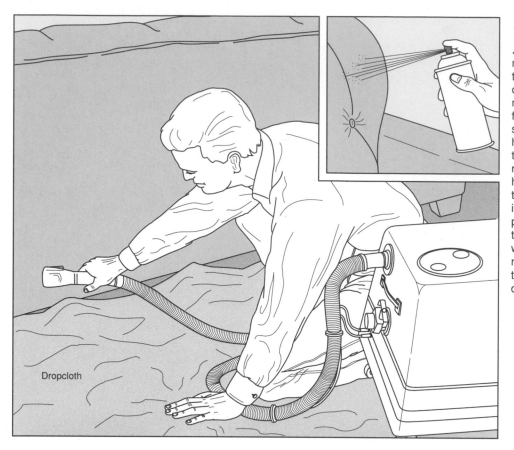

Dropcloth

2 **"Steam"-cleaning the upholstery.**
Wearing rubber gloves, follow the instructions for the water-extraction cleaning machine to mix the upholstery shampoo, then test it *(page 68)*. Add the recommended amount of defoamer to the waste reservoir. Turn on the machine and clean from end to end across the furniture. Apply the shampoo by depressing the spray trigger while slowly drawing the vacuum head across the upholstery *(left)*; avoid soaking the upholstery. To extract the shampoo and dirt, release the spray trigger and move the vacuum head back and forth across the upholstery. Allow the upholstery to dry for at least 8 hours, standing any cushion on an edge and repositioning it periodically; use an exhaust fan to help speed the drying. If the upholstery is not factory-treated with a stain-guard, buy a stain-guard of a type recommended on the cleaning tag and follow the manufacturer's instructions to apply it evenly on the upholstery *(inset)*.

ACLEANING VINYL UPHOLSTERY

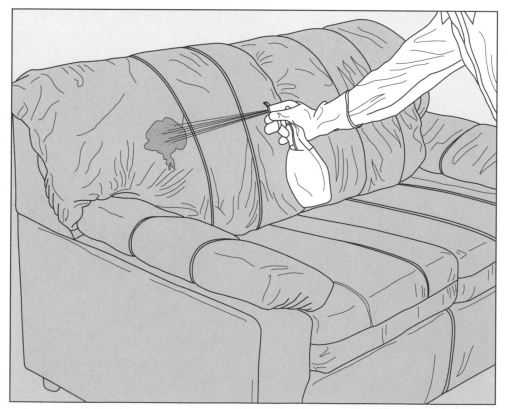

Cleaning and protecting the upholstery.
If necessary, unzip the upholstery of a cushion and check the back of it to ensure that it is vinyl; if there is a suede finish on the back of it, clean it as you would any leather upholstery *(page 71)*. Otherwise, wear rubber gloves to mix a solution of 1/8 cup of white dishwashing liquid per quart of water, then test it *(page 68)*. Pour the solution into a spray container and lightly mist the upholstery with it *(left)*, then wipe it off using a clean, white, lint-free cloth. To remove an adhered material such as candle wax, wet the upholstery around it with the solution, then gently pick it off using a plastic spatula and wipe the upholstery dry. If the upholstery is not factory-treated with a stain-guard, buy a stain-guard of a type recommended for vinyl and follow the manufacturer's instructions to apply it evenly on the upholstery.

CLEANING LEATHER UPHOLSTERY

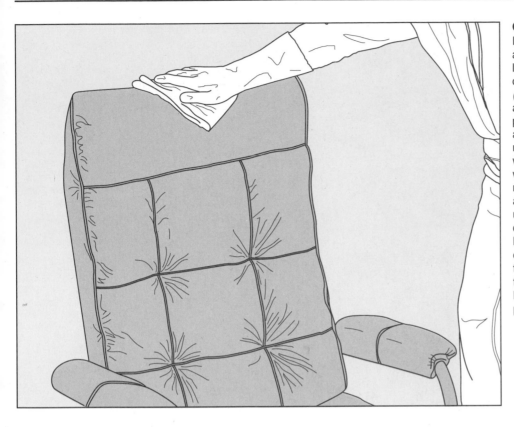

Cleaning and preserving the upholstery. If necessary, unzip the upholstery of a cushion and check the back of it to ensure that it is leather; if there is no suede finish on the back of it, clean it as you would any vinyl upholstery *(page 70)*. Otherwise, wear rubber gloves to mix a solution of 1/8 cup of white dishwashing liquid per quart of water, then test it *(page 68)*. Gently apply the solution to the upholstery using a moist sponge; wring it thoroughly before wiping with it. Wipe the upholstery dry using a clean, white, lint-free cloth. To remove an adhered material such as candle wax, wet the upholstery around it with the solution, then gently pick it off using a plastic spatula and wipe the upholstery dry. To help preserve the upholstery, apply a light, even coat of mink oil on it with a clean cloth *(left)*, following the manufacturer's instructions. Do not apply a commercial stain-guard to the upholstery; its chemicals can damage the leather over time. Have the upholstery cleaned periodically by a professional.

CLEANING WICKER

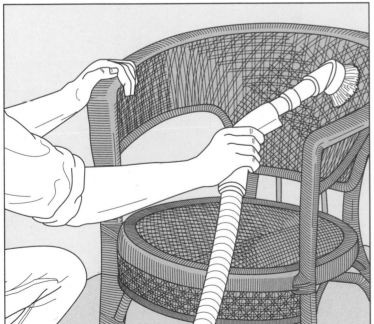

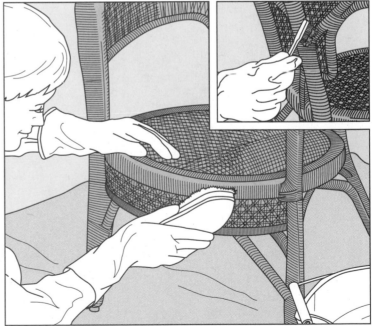

Vacuuming and washing the wicker. Spread a dropcloth on the floor and set the furniture on it. Vacuum dust and dirt off the wicker using a soft brush attachment *(above, left)*, working back and forth in the direction of the weave. Wear rubber gloves to mix a solution of 1/8 cup of white dishwashing liquid per quart of water, then test it *(page 68)*. Gently apply the solution to the wicker using a clean, white, lint-free cloth; moisten it, then wring it thoroughly before wiping with it. Rinse the wicker carefully before it dries using a clean cloth dampened with water, then wipe it dry using another cloth. To remove an adhered material such as candle wax, wet the wicker around it with the solution, then gently pick it off using a plastic spatula; rinse the wicker and wipe it dry. For heavily-soiled spots, use a soft-bristled fiber brush; dampen it, then shake it thoroughly before scrubbing lightly in the direction of the weave *(above, right)*. On a spot that is hard to reach, use a toothbrush the same way *(inset)*. Rinse the wicker again and dry it thoroughly.

FRESHENING A MATTRESS

Vacuuming and turning a mattress.
Vacuum a mattress and box spring regularly to remove dust and particles, helping to keep them from soiling. Strip linen off the mattress, then vacuum the top of it using an upholstery attachment. Working with a helper, raise the mattress *(left)* and stand it on one edge on the box spring. With your helper holding the mattress steady, vacuum the bottom of it and as much of the box spring as possible *(inset)*; to vacuum the rest of the box spring, slide the raised mattress to the center of it. Turn the mattress over and rotate it, reversing its orientation to help distribute wear. Do not attempt to remove a stain from the mattress; use a mattress protector to prevent further staining. Put clean linen onto the mattress.

CLEANING MIRRORS AND GLASS

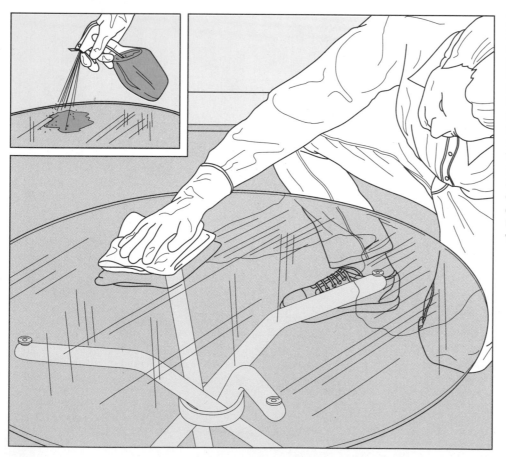

Lifting fingerprints and smudges. Clear the surface, then wear rubber gloves to mix a solution of 1/8 cup of white vinegar or 1/2 cup of clear household ammonia per quart of water. Pour the solution into a spray container, then lightly mist the surface with it *(inset)*; avoid getting any solution on an adjacent wood surface, wiping it off immediately with a clean cloth. Wipe the surface using a crumpled sheet of newspaper or a clean, white, lint-free cloth, rubbing vigorously until it is dry. To remove an adhered material such as candle wax, wet the surface around it with the solution, then gently scrape it off using a razor blade tool and wipe the surface dry. Viewing the surface at an angle, polish it until there are no streaks using a clean, dry, white, lint-free cloth *(left)*.

CLEANING PLASTICS AND LAMINATES

Lifting fingerprints and smudges. Clear the surface, then wear rubber gloves to mix a solution of 1/8 cup of white dishwashing liquid per quart of water. Apply the solution to the surface using a moist sponge or cloth, wringing it thoroughly before rubbing with it *(left)*; avoid getting any solution on an adjacent wood surface, wiping it off immediately with a clean cloth. Wipe the surface dry using a clean, white, lint-free cloth. To remove an adhered material such as candle wax, wet the surface around it with the solution, then gently scrape it off using a plastic spatula and wipe the surface dry. Viewing the surface at an angle, polish it until there are no streaks using a clean, dry, white, lint-free cloth.

CLEANING WOOD

1 Dusting the wood. Clean the wood regularly to remove dust and particles that can damage the finish. Clear the surface, then dust it from end to end along the wood grain using a feather duster; avoid using a cloth or other tool that can grind particles into the finish. Sweep the duster lightly along the surface *(above)* using a slow, smooth, wiping motion; apply only enough pressure to just touch the surface, collecting dust and particles from it. Move away from the furniture to shake out the duster into a trash bag.

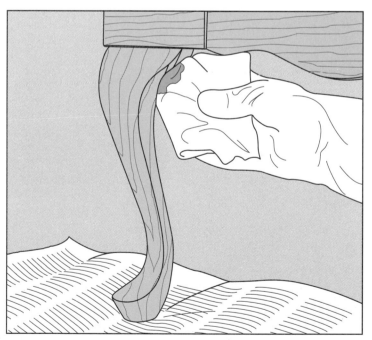

2 Identifying the type of finish. Work in a well-ventilated room to identify the type of finish applied to the furniture. Wearing rubber gloves, moisten a clean, white, lint-free cloth with mineral spirits and dab a corner of it lightly onto a small, inconspicuous spot of the finish—at the top on the back of a leg, for example *(above)*. If the color of the test spot bleeds or comes off onto the cloth, clean the furniture as you would any penetrating finish *(step 4)*; otherwise, clean it as you would any surface finish *(step 3)*.

CLEANING WOOD (continued)

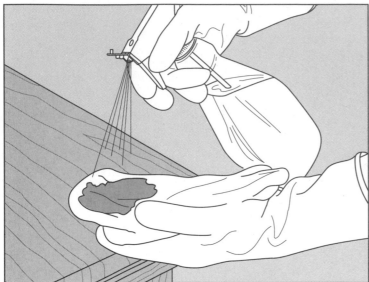

3 **Cleaning a surface finish.** For light-cleaning, apply a commercial liquid furniture polish following the manufacturer's instructions. Wearing rubber gloves, pour the polish into a spray container, then dampen a clean, white, lint-free cloth with it *(above, left)*. Wipe the surface with the cloth, working on a section of it at a time in the direction of the wood grain. As the cloth dries, rub the section of the surface vigorously, buffing it until it shines. Continue the same way, changing to a clean cloth as necessary. For deep-cleaning, mix a solution of 1 tablespoon of white dishwashing liquid per quart of warm water, then whip it using an eggbeater to create as much foam as possible. Soak a clean, white, lint-free cloth with the solution *(above, right)* and scrub the surface vigorously, working on a section of it a time in the direction of the wood grain. Wipe the surface dry using a clean cloth. After deep-cleaning, wait 1 to 2 days, then protect the finish *(page 75)*.

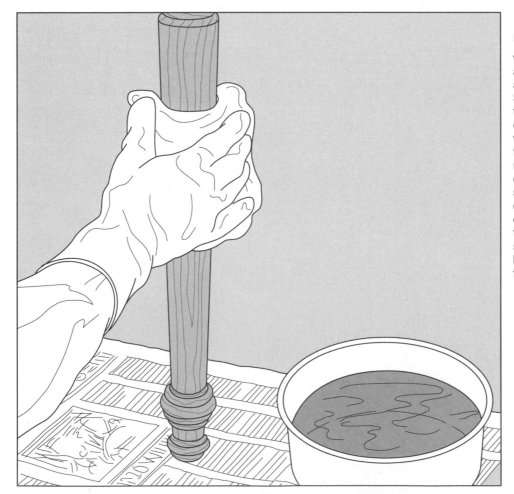

4 **Cleaning a penetrating finish.** For light-cleaning, protect the finish *(page 75)*. For deep-cleaning, work in a well-ventilated room and wear rubber gloves to mix a solution of equal parts of boiled linseed oil and turpentine in a metal or glass container. Soak a clean, white, lint-free cloth with the solution and scrub the surface vigorously, working on a section of it at a time in the direction of the wood grain *(left)*. Allow the solution to soak in for about 5 minutes, then wipe the surface dry using a clean cloth. Continue the same way, changing to a clean cloth as necessary. If the surface is still not clean, increase the proportion of turpentine in the solution and repeat the procedure. After deep-cleaning, wait 1 to 2 days, then protect the finish. **Caution:** To prevent spontaneous combustion, hang cloths used with boiled linseed oil and turpentine outdoors to dry, then wash them thoroughly before storing them.

PROTECTING WOOD

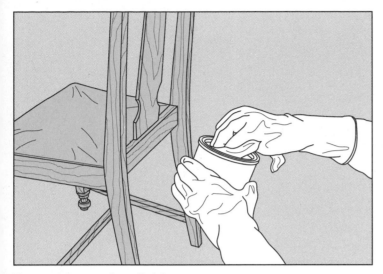

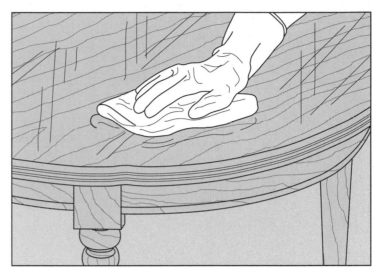

Protecting a surface finish. Identify the type of finish *(page 73)*. To protect a surface finish, dust and clean it *(page 74)*; if it is in poor condition, deep-clean it, then apply a commercial furniture paste wax following the manufacturer's instructions. Working in a well-ventilated room, wear rubber gloves to fold a clean, white, lint-free cloth into a small pad and dip into the wax *(above)*. Wipe a thin coat of the wax evenly onto the surface, working on a small section of it at a time in the direction of the wood grain. Fold another cloth into a pad slightly larger than your hand and rub the section of the surface vigorously, buffing it until it shines. Continue, changing to clean cloths as necessary.

Protecting a penetrating finish. Identify the type of finish *(page 73)*. To protect a penetrating finish, apply boiled linseed oil; if it is in poor condition, first dust and deep-clean it *(page 74)*. Working in a well-ventilated room, wear rubber gloves to soak a clean, white, lint-free cloth with the oil. Rub the oil onto the surface, working on a small section of it at a time in the direction of the wood grain *(above)*; continue until the oil does not soak in. Fold another cloth into a pad slightly larger than your hand and rub the section of the surface vigorously until it is dry. Continue, changing to clean cloths as necessary. **Caution:** To prevent spontaneous combustion, hang cloths used with boiled linseed oil outdoors to dry, then wash them thoroughly before storing them.

REMOVING WOOD BLEMISHES

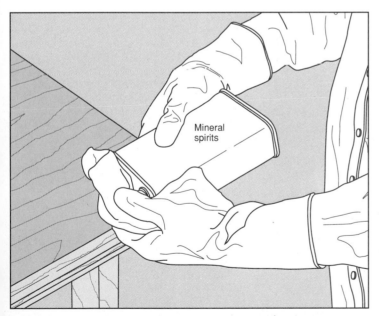

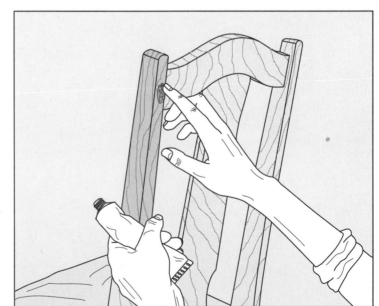

1 Dissolving the blemish. Working in a well-ventilated room, wear rubber gloves to moisten a clean, white, lint-free cloth with mineral spirits *(above)*. Use a corner of the cloth to gently rub the blemish in the direction of the wood grain, then buff the surface dry with a clean cloth. If the blemish dissolves, protect the finish *(steps above)*. Otherwise, identify the type of finish *(page 73)*. For a blemish in a surface finish, abrade with toothpaste *(step 2)*; for a blemish in a penetrating finish, abrade with steel wool *(step 4)*.

2 Abrading the blemish with toothpaste. Apply a small amount of regular, white toothpaste to the blemish with your fingertip and rub it gently in the direction of the wood grain *(above)*. After 10 strokes, wipe off the toothpaste with a clean, white, lint-free cloth dampened with water. If the blemish disappears, buff the surface dry with a clean cloth and protect the finish *(step above, left)*. Otherwise, repeat the procedure up to 10 times before abrading with rottenstone *(step 3)*; stop if the finish begins to lighten in color.

REMOVING WOOD BLEMISHES (continued)

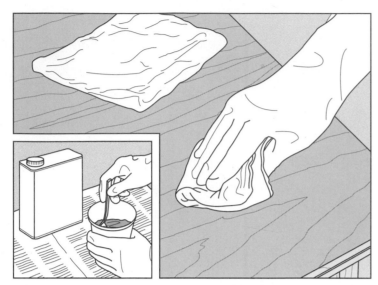

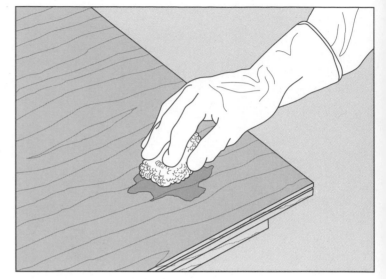

3 **Abrading the blemish with rottenstone.** Wearing rubber gloves, mix a paste of rottenstone and mineral spirits in a container *(inset)*. Apply a small amount of paste to the blemish with your fingertip, then use a clean, white, lint-free cloth to rub it gently in the direction of the grain *(above)*. After 10 strokes, wipe off the paste using a clean cloth dampened with mineral spirits. If the blemish disappears, buff the surface dry with a clean cloth and protect the finish *(page 75)*. Otherwise, repeat the procedure up to 10 times before abrading with steel wool *(step 4)*; stop if the finish begins to lighten in color.

4 **Abrading the blemish with steel wool.** Wearing rubber gloves, pour a small amount of mineral oil onto the blemish, then use a pad of super-fine (grade 4/0) steel wool to gently rub it in the direction of the grain *(above)*; keep the blemish lubricated with mineral oil. After 10 strokes, wipe off the mineral oil using a clean, white, lint-free cloth dampened with mineral spirits. If the blemish disappears, buff the surface dry with a clean cloth and protect the finish *(page 75)*. Otherwise, repeat the procedure as many times as necessary for the blemish to disappear; stop if the finish begins to lighten in color.

REMOVING VINYL- AND LEATHER-UPHOLSTERY STAINS

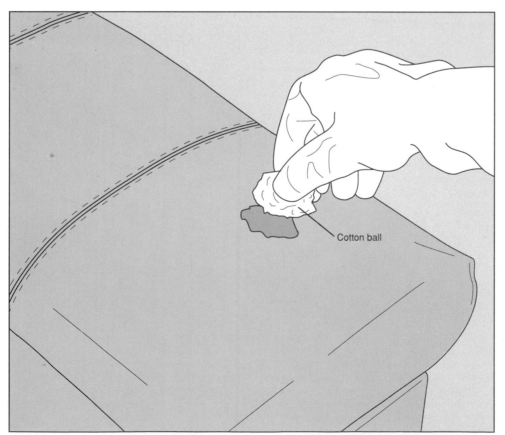

Cotton ball

Lifting a stain. Removing a stain is often impossible without damaging the upholstery; for most stains, you should consult an upholstery professional. Choose a cleaning agent cautiously and always test it *(page 68)*; do not try using a cleaning agent that is solvent-based—such as dry-cleaning fluid. For a stain on vinyl upholstery, you can try a 3% hydrogen peroxide solution. Wearing rubber gloves, moisten a ball of cotton with the solution, then test it by setting the cotton on an inconspicuous spot for 1 minute; if the color of the test spot is not affected, repeat the procedure on the stain *(left)*. Wipe the upholstery using a clean, white, lint-free cloth moistened with a solution of 1/8 cup of white dishwashing liquid per quart of water, then rinse it using a clean cloth dampened with water. Wipe the upholstery dry with another clean cloth. For a stain on leather upholstery, you can try rubbing gently with a clean gum eraser; if the color of the upholstery starts to lighten, clean your hands and rub them together to produce skin oil, then rub it into the upholstery.

REMOVING FABRIC-UPHOLSTERY STAINS

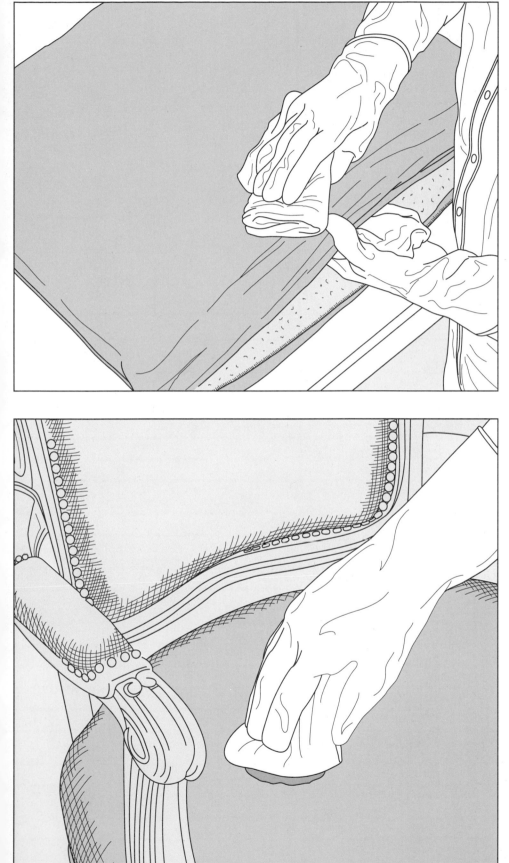

Lifting a stain from the back. If the back of the upholstery is not accessible or is sealed with a latex coating, lift the stain from the front of it *(step below)*. Otherwise, choose a cleaning agent appropriate for the stain and test it *(page 68)*. Wear rubber gloves to mix a solution in a container, then moisten a clean, white, lint-free cloth with it. Fold the cloth into a pad and press it against the back of the stain, working from the edges toward the center; hold a dry, folded cloth against the front of the stain to help absorb it *(left)*. If the upholstery is of sturdy fabric, rub the stain gently; otherwise, only dab it. Refold or change the cloths as soon as they become stained. When the stain disappears, use the same technique to rinse the upholstery with cool water, then blot it dry with another cloth.

Lifting a stain from the front. If the back of the upholstery is accessible and is not sealed with a latex coating, lift the stain from the back of it *(step above)*. Otherwise, choose a cleaning agent appropriate for the stain and test it *(page 68)*. Wear rubber gloves to mix a solution in a container, then moisten a clean, white, lint-free cloth with it. Fold the cloth into a pad and press it against the front of the stain *(left)*, working from the edges toward the center; hold it in place only for a few seconds at a time, pressing a dry, folded cloth against the stain to help absorb it. If the upholstery is of sturdy fabric, rub the stain gently; otherwise, only dab it. Refold or change the cloths as soon as they become stained. When the stain disappears, use the same technique to rinse the upholstery with cool water, then blot it dry with another cloth.

FIREPLACES AND WOOD STOVES

A crackling fire in the fireplace of the living room or the wood stove of the family room is a legendary element of our homeowner culture—a symbol of energy self-sufficiency as well as a practical means of reducing heating bills. Keeping the fireplace or wood stove clean, however, is an imperative. An ash-filled or soot-covered fireplace or wood stove cannot work efficiently, making it more expensive to use; more important it is a source of dust and particles that can be a potential fire hazard and a health threat.

The best way to prevent a buildup of ash, soot and creosote in a fireplace or wood stove is to operate it properly, following safe burning practices. Ensure that you know how to use any damper, doors or fire screen on the fireplace or wood stove correctly. Never burn plastics, waxy or colored paper, household refuse or painted or pressure-treated wood in a fireplace or wood stove; the smoke created can be toxic and dangerous levels of creosote (gummy resin deposits) inside it can result. At least once each year, have your chimney and the firebox of your fireplace or wood stove professionally cleaned; if necessary, also inspected.

Proper use and maintenance of a fireplace or wood stove can eliminate hazards and reduce discoloring or damaging of its surfaces. Refer to the Troubleshooting Guide *(below)* for procedures on cleaning and stain removal for your fireplace or wood stove; to the Cleaning Tips *(page 79)* for basic guidelines and general strategy. Consult Tools & Techniques *(page 116)* for information on cleaning supplies and techniques.

Remove ashes from your fireplace or wood stove regularly *(page 79)*. If dirt, soot or staining becomes a problem, you can clean the exterior surfaces of cast iron or steel on your wood stove *(page 80)*; the brick or stone facing and hearth of your fireplace or wood stove *(page 83)*. Also ensure that you clean the doors, fire screen and accessories of your fireplace or wood stove *(page 81)*. Always wear the safety gear recommended for the job: work gloves and a dust mask to remove ashes; rubber gloves and safety goggles to apply a solvent with a brush. To prevent damage to your fireplace or wood stove, always test your cleaning agent and method; if necessary, change to a milder agent or gentler technique.

TROUBLESHOOTING GUIDE

PROBLEM	PROCEDURE
FIREPLACE	
Firebox filled with ashes	Remove ashes from fireplace (p. 79) □○
Insert exterior dirty, sooty or stained	Clean insert exterior as you would wood-stove exterior (p. 80) □◗
Glass doors dirty, sooty or stained	Clean glass doors (p. 81) □○
Fire screen dirty, sooty or stained	Clean fire screen (p. 81) □○
Andiron, poker, grate or other accessory dirty, sooty or stained	Clean accessory (p. 81) □○
Brick or stone dirty or sooty	Clean dirt and soot off brick or stone (p. 82) □◗
Brick or stone creosote-caked (gummy resin deposits)	Clean creosote off brick or stone (p. 82) □◗; follow safe practices in using fireplace
Brick or stone deposit-encrusted or stained	Clean encrusted deposits and stains off brick or stone (p. 83) □◗
Flue or damper dirty, sooty or creosote-caked (gummy resin deposits)	Call professional chimney sweep; follow safe practices in using fireplace
WOOD STOVE	
Firebox or ashbox filled with ashes	Remove ashes from wood stove (p. 80) □○
Exterior dirty, sooty or stained	Clean wood-stove exterior (p. 80) □◗
Glass doors dirty, sooty or stained	Clean glass doors (p. 81) □○
Fire screen dirty, sooty or stained	Clean fire screen (p. 81) □○
Andiron, poker, grate or other accessory dirty, sooty or stained	Clean accessory (p. 81) □○
Brick or stone dirty or sooty	Clean dirt and soot off brick or stone (p. 82) □◗
Brick or stone creosote-caked (gummy resin deposits)	Clean creosote off brick or stone (p. 82) □◗; follow safe practices in using wood stove
Brick or stone deposit-encrusted or stained	Clean encrusted deposits and stains off brick or stone (p. 83) □◗
Pipe or damper dirty, sooty or creosote-caked	Call professional chimney sweep; follow safe practices in using wood stove

DEGREE OF DIFFICULTY: □ Easy ▭ Moderate ■ Complex
ESTIMATED TIME: ○ Less than 1 hour ◗ 1 to 3 hours ● Over 3 hours

CLEANING TIPS

● Establish a weekly and seasonal household-maintenance routine; in general, remove the ashes from your fireplace or wood stove at least every 10 uses and clean it thoroughly at least once each year—before cleaning the walls and ceiling *(page 36)*, furniture *(page 66)* and carpet *(page 56)* or floor *(page 44)* of the room.

● Whenever you are using the fireplace or wood stove, follow safe burning practices—also making cleaning it easier. Burn only well-aged, dry wood.

● Whenever the fireplace or wood stove is not in use, keep the damper closed.

● Keep on hand a well-stocked spot-cleaning kit that includes a supply of clean, white, lint-free cloths and commercial polishes.

● Follow the cleaning instructions supplied by the manufacturer for any commercial cleaning product you use.

● Test any cleaning agent and method you use on an inconspicuous spot of the surface—even if you are only dabbing or wiping using a cloth dampened with water.

● To protect a surface from a cleaning agent, use a dropcloth. Wipe up any stray or spilled cleaning agent immediately with a clean, white, lint-free cloth.

● Remove the ashes from a fireplace or wood stove and vacuum it before applying a cleaning agent to it. When you are trying to lift a stain, always start with the mildest cleaning agent recommended, progressing to a stronger cleaning agent only if necessary. Make several attempts to lift a stain with a cleaning agent before abandoning it; allow each application of it to dry thoroughly before repeating an application of it.

● Store cleaning agents well out of the reach of children; dispose of any leftover cleaning agent safely.

REMOVING ASHES

Dump door

1 Removing ashes from a fireplace. Wait at least two days after a fire before removing the ashes from a wood stove *(step 2)* or fireplace. Cover the hearth and floor in front of the fireplace with a dropcloth and move furniture out of the way. Wearing work gloves and a dust mask, close the damper and set aside any fire screen, grate or andiron. For a fireplace with no ashpit, carefully sweep up the ashes in the firebox using a fireplace broom and shovel *(left)*, depositing them into a metal bucket; work slowly to avoid scattering them. For a fireplace with an ashpit, open the dump door in the bottom of the firebox *(inset)* and use the broom and shovel to push the ashes through it; locate the ashpit clean-out door outdoors or in the basement and shovel the ashes out of the ashpit into a metal bucket. Vacuum the firebox to remove remaining ashes. Safely dispose of the ashes collected *(step 3)*.

REMOVING ASHES (continued)

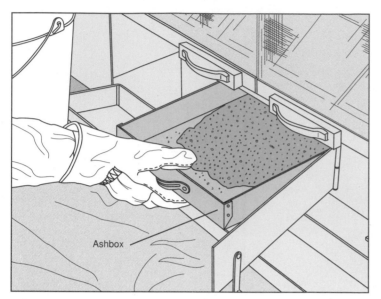

2 **Removing ashes from a wood stove.** Wait at least two days after a fire before removing the ashes. Cover the floor in front of the stove with a dropcloth and move furniture out of the way. Wearing work gloves and a dust mask, slide the ashbox out of the stove *(above)* and empty it into a metal bucket. If the stove has no ashbox, open the doors and remove any grate, then sweep up the ashes in the firebox using a broom and shovel, depositing them into a metal bucket. Vacuum the firebox and any ashbox to remove remaining ashes. Safely dispose of the ashes collected *(step 3)*.

Ashbox

3 **Safely disposing of ashes.** After vacuuming ashes out of the firebox and any ashbox, immediately remove the vacuum-cleaner bag from the vacuum cleaner and discard it outdoors away from the house in a metal trash can for disposal with your other household refuse *(inset)*. For a metal bucket filled with loose ashes, seal it tightly with a metal cover and store it outdoors away from the house for at least three days, then empty the ashes out of it into a trash can *(above)* for disposal with your other household refuse; stand well back from it to avoid inhaling any particles.

CLEANING A WOOD-STOVE EXTERIOR

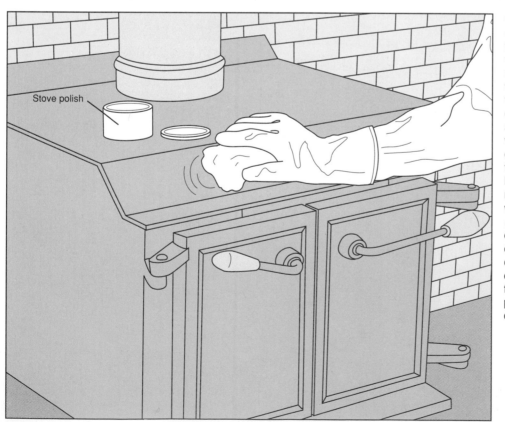

Stove polish

Cleaning the exterior surfaces. Let the exterior surfaces of the stove cool completely, then clean dust and particles off them using a vacuum cleaner and a soft brush attachment. To remove soot or rust from cast iron or steel, wear work gloves and rub the surface gently using very-fine (grade 2/0) steel wool. Sweep particles off the surface using a soft-bristled fiber brush and smooth it using super-fine (grade 4/0) steel wool, then sweep it again and wipe it with a clean, dry, white, lint-free cloth. Restore the surface using a commercial paste stove polish following the manufacturer's instructions. Wearing rubber gloves, load a clean, white, lint-free cloth with polish and rub it vigorously onto the surface *(left)*. To remove soot from enamel, brass or chrome, wear rubber gloves to apply a solution of 1/8 cup of white dishwashing liquid per quart of warm water using a clean, white, lint-free cloth. If necessary, apply a commercial product following the manufacturer's instructions: fireplace glass cleaner for enamel; polish for brass or chrome.

CLEANING DOORS, SCREENS AND ACCESSORIES

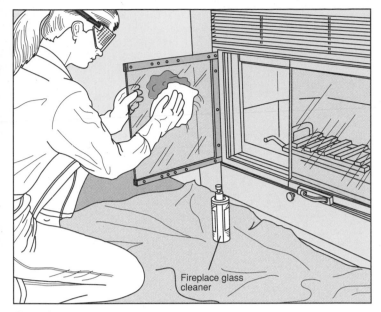

Cleaning glass doors. Let the doors cool completely, then lay a dropcloth on the floor below them. Wearing rubber gloves and safety goggles, clean the doors using a commercial fireplace glass cleaner or spray oven cleaner following the manufacturer's instructions. Mist the doors with the cleaner and let it sit for the time specified, then use a clean, white, lint-free cloth dampened with water to wipe it off *(above)*; dislodge encrusted particles with a razor-blade tool. Then, apply a solution of 1/8 cup of white vinegar per quart of water to the doors using a clean cloth. Wipe the doors dry with a crumpled sheet of newspaper or a clean cloth, rubbing vigorously to remove streaks.

Cleaning a fire screen. Let the screen cool completely, then stand it upright onto a dropcloth spread out on the floor. To clean dust and particles off the screen, vacuum each side of it thoroughly using a soft brush attachment *(above)*. Wearing rubber gloves and safety goggles, wash the screen using a solution of 1/8 cup of white dishwashing liquid per quart of water. Lay the screen down flat on its side and apply the solution to it using a soft-bristled fiber brush, scrubbing gently to dislodge encrusted particles. Wipe the screen using a clean, white, lint-free cloth dampened with water, then dry it thoroughly with a clean, dry cloth.

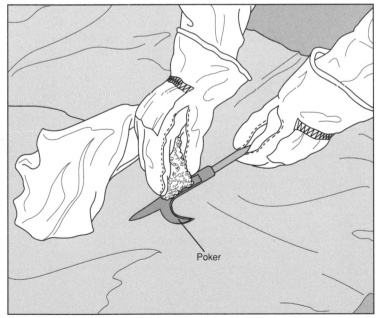

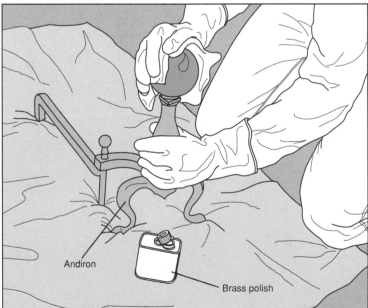

Cleaning accessories. Let the accessory cool completely, then set it down onto a dropcloth spread out on the floor. Wearing rubber gloves and safety goggles, wash the accessory using a solution of 1/8 cup of white dishwashing liquid per quart of water. Apply the solution to the accessory using a soft-bristled fiber brush, scrubbing gently to dislodge encrusted particles. Wipe the accessory using a clean, white, lint-free cloth dampened with water, then dry it thoroughly with a clean, dry cloth. To remove stubborn soot or rust from a poker of cast iron or steel, wear work gloves and rub the surface gently using very-fine (grade 2/0)

steel wool. Sweep particles off the surface using a soft-bristled fiber brush and smooth it using super-fine (grade 4/0) steel wool *(above, left)*, then sweep it again and wipe it with a clean, dry, white, lint-free cloth. Restore the surface using a commercial paste stove polish following the manufacturer's instructions. To remove stubborn soot from a brass stand of an andiron, apply a commercial polish for brass following the manufacturer's instructions. Wearing rubber gloves, load a clean, white, lint-free cloth with polish and rub it vigorously onto the surface *(above, right)*.

CLEANING BRICK AND STONE

Cleaning off dirt and soot. Let the surface cool completely, then lay a dropcloth on the floor below it. Clean dust and particles off the surface with a vacuum cleaner and a soft brush attachment. Wearing rubber gloves and safety goggles, mix a solution of 1/2 cup of white dishwashing liquid per gallon of water in a plastic bucket; for a surface other than marble, add 2 teaspoons of household laundry bleach per gallon of water. To apply the cleaning solution, use a stiff-bristled fiber brush. Test your cleaning solution and method on an inconspicuous spot of the surface, letting it dry for at least 10 minutes; if necessary, mix a milder cleaning solution or use a gentler cleaning technique. To clean off the dirt and soot, soak the surface with water using a sponge *(inset)*, then apply the cleaning solution, soaking the brush and shaking it thoroughly before scrubbing with it *(left)*; to reach tight spots, use a toothbrush the same way. Rinse the surface thoroughly with water using the same technique.

Cleaning off creosote. Let the surface cool completely, then lay a dropcloth on the floor below it. Clean dust and particles off the surface with a vacuum cleaner and a soft brush attachment. To clean deposits of creosote off the surface, use a commercial creosote cleaner recommended for the material of the surface following the manufacturer's instructions. Test your cleaner on an inconspicuous spot of the surface, allowing it to sit before brushing it off; if the test spot is damaged, try another method to remove the deposits and any stain *(page 83)*. Otherwise, wear rubber gloves and safety goggles to soak the surface thoroughly with hot water using a sponge, then apply the cleaner and let it sit for the time specified by the manufacturer. Gently scrub the surface using a stiff-bristled, natural-fiber brush *(left)*, rinsing it in water to clean it. Rinse the surface thoroughly with warm water using the sponge and let it dry for 24 hours. If necessary, repeat the procedure.

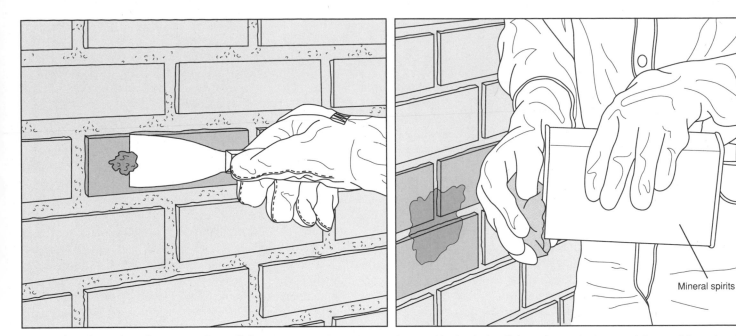

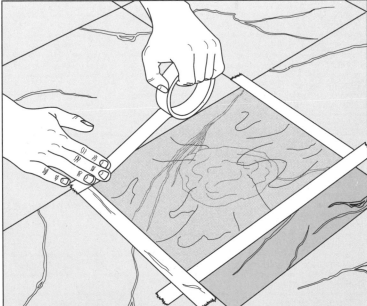

Removing deposits of encrusted particles. To remove a stubborn deposit of encrusted particles from a surface, use a putty knife. Wearing work gloves and safety goggles, gently work the edge of the putty knife under the deposit *(above, left)*; apply moderate pressure and use a slight scraping motion to dislodge it. To soften the deposits or clean remaining residue off the surface, work in a well-ventilated room and wear rubber gloves to apply a chemical solvent such as mineral spirits. Test the solvent by wiping a small amount of it on an inconspicuous spot of the sur-

face and letting it dry; if the test spot is damaged, try a milder solvent. Otherwise, dampen a clean, white, lint-free cloth with the solvent *(above, right)*, then gently dab the surface using a corner of it; avoid using a rubbing or wiping motion. Rinse the surface using a clean cloth dampened with water, then blot it dry with another cloth. Continue the same way, refolding or changing cloths as they become stained. If necessary, use a pad of super-fine (grade 4/0) steel wool to apply the solvent, rubbing the surface gently with it.

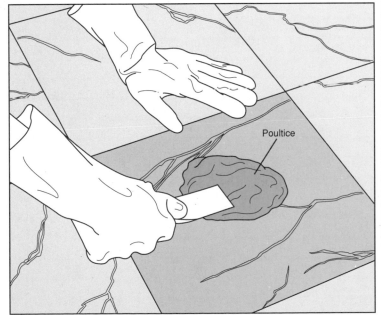

Removing stains. To lift a stubborn stain from a surface, use a poultice. Wearing rubber gloves, prepare a poultice of a liquid ingredient and a dry ingredient: cornstarch or talcum powder for a light-colored surface; fuller's earth otherwise. For the liquid ingredient, use household laundry bleach if the surface is of marble or granite; a citrus-based solvent otherwise. Mix the poultice in a clean container into a thick, uniform paste that is the consistency of putty, adding a small amount of the dry ingredient and pouring in the liquid ingredient a little at a time. Test your poultice on an inconspicuous spot of the surface, allowing it to dry before brushing it

off; if the test spot is damaged, try a poultice of a milder liquid ingredient. Otherwise, apply a thick, even coat of the poultice onto the surface *(above, left)*. Cover the poultice with plastic sheeting and seal the edges of it with masking tape *(above, right)*, then allow the poultice to dry—this may take 24 hours. When the poultice is dry, gently sweep it off the surface using a soft-bristled fiber brush. Remove traces of the poultice from the surface by wiping it using a clean, white, lint-free cloth dampened with water, then allow it to dry. If necessary, repeat the procedure.

BATHROOMS AND KITCHEN

The bathrooms and kitchen of a home are subjected to more daily abuse than any other room in it; fortunately, they are usually the easiest rooms to maintain, their special surfaces designed for quick, efficient cleaning. Refer to the Troubleshooting Guide *(below)* for procedures on cleaning the special surfaces of your bathrooms and kitchen. For a wall, ceiling or floor of a material that typically can be found in other rooms of the home, consult the chapters entitled Walls And Ceilings *(page 36)* and Floors *(page 44)*; for your refrigerator, range and other appliances, consult the chapter entitled Appliances *(page 92)*. For basic guidelines and general strategy on cleaning and stain removal for a bathroom or the kitchen, read the Cleaning Tips *(page 85)*. Consult Tools & Techniques *(page 116)* for information on cleaning supplies and equipment.

While the cleaning of a bathroom or the kitchen is rarely a difficult job, time, patience and orderliness are necessary to do it well. With a well-planned cleaning strategy for your bathrooms and kitchen, you can hold the upper hand in the never-ending war against dirt and grime that must be waged in these rooms. And with cleaning conquests in your bathrooms and kitchen, you can often curtail the frequency and scale of cleaning campaigns needed in other rooms of your home.

Adopt the practice of "cleaning as you go" for your bathrooms and kitchen, cleaning spills, splashes and marks off surfaces as soon as they occur; if an ounce of prevention is better than a pound of cure, then the little chores of keeping them clean are preferable to the major job of getting them clean. As well as spot-cleaning, thorough weekly-cleaning of the special surfaces of the bathrooms and kitchen typically is necessary: the sink *(page 88)*, bathtub *(page 88)*, shower doors *(page 89)* and toilet *(page 89)* of a bathroom; the sink *(page 86)*, countertops and cabinets *(page 86)*, and butcher block *(page 87)* of the kitchen. Thankfully, most of the ceramic tiles, laminates and acrylics, porcelain, fiberglass, metals and other materials of the special surfaces of the bathrooms and kitchen can be cleaned the same way—as often as is needed.

Spot- and weekly-cleaning of your bathrooms and kitchen can reduce the staining of their special surfaces, but is unlikely to eliminate it. Knowledge about the material of a special surface simplifies removing stains *(page 90)*—and reduces the risk of damage. Save the maintenance instructions supplied by the manufacturer for the material of the special surfaces of your bathrooms and kitchen. Never hesitate to ask for cleaning advice from the material manufacturer or retailer or a cleaning professional.

TROUBLESHOOTING GUIDE

PROBLEM	PROCEDURE
KITCHEN	
Sink dirty or grimy	Clean everyday dirt and grime off sink *(p. 86)* □○
Sink stained	Remove stain from sink *(p. 90)* □○
Countertop or cabinet dirty or grimy	Clean everyday dirt and grime off countertop or cabinet *(p. 86)* □○
Countertop or cabinet stained	Remove stain from countertop or cabinet *(p. 90)* □○
Wood butcher block dirty or grimy	Clean wood butcher block *(p. 87)* □○
Ceramic tile dirty or grimy	Clean everyday dirt and grime off ceramic tiles *(p. 87)* □○
Ceramic tile stained	Remove stain from ceramic tiles *(p. 90)* □○
BATHROOM	
Sink dirty or grimy	Clean everyday dirt and grime off sink *(p. 88)* □○
Sink stained	Remove stain from sink *(p. 90)* □○
Countertop or cabinet dirty or grimy	Clean everyday dirt and grime off countertop or cabinet *(p. 86)* □○
Countertop or cabinet stained	Remove stain from countertop or cabinet *(p. 90)* □○
Bathtub dirty or grimy	Clean everday dirt and grime off bathtub *(p. 88)* □○
Bathtub stained	Remove stain from bathtub *(p. 90)* □○
Shower door dirty or grimy	Clean shower doors and tracks *(p. 89)* □○
Shower door stained	Remove stain from shower door *(p. 90)* □○
Toilet dirty or grimy	Clean toilet *(p. 90)* □○
Toilet stained	Remove stain from toilet *(p. 90)* □○
Ceramic tile dirty or grimy	Clean everyday dirt and grime off ceramic tiles *(p. 87)* □○
Ceramic tile stained	Remove stain from ceramic tiles *(p. 90)* □○

DEGREE OF DIFFICULTY: □ Easy ◪ Moderate ■ Complex
ESTIMATED TIME: ○ Less than 1 hour ◖ 1 to 3 hours ● Over 3 hours

CLEANING TIPS

• Establish a weekly and seasonal household-maintenance routine that includes your bathrooms and kitchen; in general, clean special surfaces such as countertops and cabinets, the sink, the toilet, the bathtub, and the shower doors at least every week—after cleaning of the walls and ceilings *(page 36)* and before cleaning of the floors *(page 44)* or appliances *(page 92)*.

• Keep on hand a well-stocked spot-cleaning kit that includes a supply of clean, white, lint-free cloths, sponges, white scrubbing pads and a commercial all-purpose spray cleaner. Keep tools to clean toilet bowls separate; do not use them on another surface.

• Avoid "tub ring" by adding bubble bath or water softener to bath water; to prevent mildew, let air circulate around wet surfaces.

• Test any cleaning agent and method you use on an inconspicuous spot of the surface—even if you are only dabbing or wiping using a cloth dampened with water.

• Follow the cleaning instructions supplied by the manufacturer for any commercial cleaning product you use.

• Clean a fresh spill, splash or mark off a surface as soon as it occurs. To minimize dirt buildup and soiling, spot-clean frequently around the high-traffic surfaces of the bathrooms and kitchen—the countertops and cabinets, for example.

• To protect a surface from a cleaning agent, use a dropcloth or plastic sheeting. Wipe up any stray or spilled cleaning agent immediately with a clean, white, lint-free cloth.

• When you are trying to lift a stain from a surface, always start with the cleaning agent recommended, progressing to a stronger cleaning agent only if necessary. Make several attempts to lift a stain with a cleaning agent before abandoning it; dry each application of it thoroughly before repeating an application of it.

• Disinfect toilet bowls at least twice each year with a commercial toilet-bowl cleaner following the manufacturer's instructions; if necessary, use a green scrubbing pad to remove stubborn stains.

• Store cleaning agents well out of the reach of children; dispose of any leftover cleaning agent safely.

TESTING A CLEANING AGENT AND METHOD

Testing the cleaning agent. Always test a cleaning agent on an inconspicuous spot of the surface. Wearing rubber gloves, moisten a clean, white, lint-free cloth with the cleaning agent and dab it lightly onto the test spot *(above)*. Wait several minutes, then wipe the test spot dry with a clean cloth. If the test spot becomes discolored, streaked or otherwise damaged, try a milder form of the cleaning agent or a different cleaning agent, testing it first.

Testing the cleaning method. Always test your cleaning method on an inconspicuous spot of the surface. With a white scrubbing pad, for example, wear rubber gloves to load it with the cleaning agent and scrub lightly *(above)*, gradually increasing your pressure. If the test spot is damaged, try scrubbing more gently or change to a cleaning tool or method that is less abrasive. With a sponge, for example, try rubbing lightly, gradually increasing your pressure.

CLEANING A KITCHEN SINK

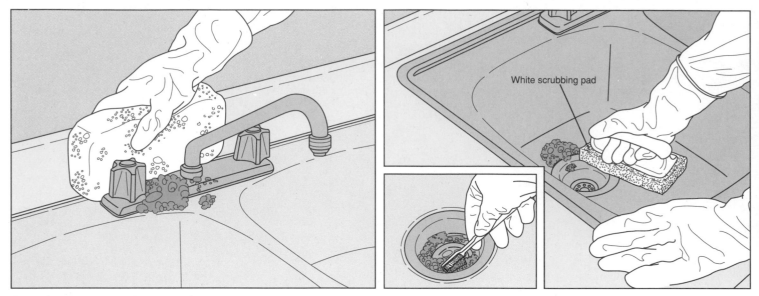

Cleaning everyday dirt and grime. Clear off the countertop around the sink, then clean the faucets and the sink using an all-purpose spray cleaner and a sponge. Test your cleaning agent and method *(page 85)*. Wearing rubber gloves, mist the faucets and the sink with the cleaner, then dampen the sponge with water and wipe using it. Starting at the perimeter of the sink, clean first the faucets *(above, left)*, then the remaining edges and the inside of the sink. For stubborn dirt and grime, scrub gently with a white scrubbing pad *(above, right)*, applying more cleaner as necessary. For the drain, the base of the faucets or other surfaces hard to reach, scrub gently with an old toothbrush *(inset)*. Rinse the faucets and the sink using a clean sponge dampened with water, then wipe them dry with a clean, white, lint-free cloth.

CLEANING COUNTERTOPS AND CABINETS

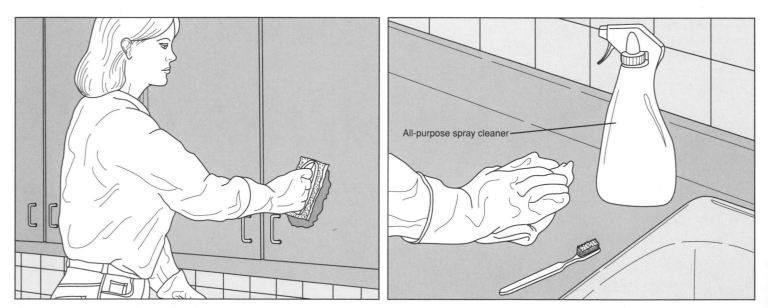

Cleaning everyday dirt and grime. Clear off the countertops and shut the doors and drawers of the cabinets, then clean them using an all-purpose spray cleaner and a sponge. Test your cleaning agent and method *(page 85)*. Wearing rubber gloves, mist the countertops and the cabinets with the cleaner, then dampen the sponge with water and wipe using it. Working from top to bottom, clean first the upper cabinets, then the countertops and the lower cabinets. For stubborn dirt and grime, scrub gently with a white scrubbing pad *(above, left)*, applying more cleaner as necessary. For the edges around a sink, a handle or hinge or other surfaces hard to reach, scrub gently with an old toothbrush. Rinse the countertops and the cabinets using a clean sponge dampened with water, then wipe them dry with a clean, white, lint-free cloth *(above, right)*.

CLEANING A WOOD BUTCHER BLOCK

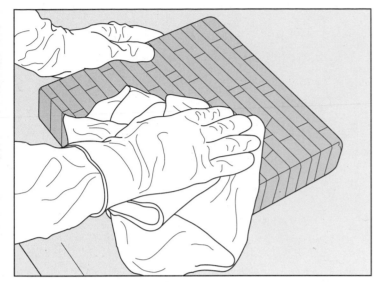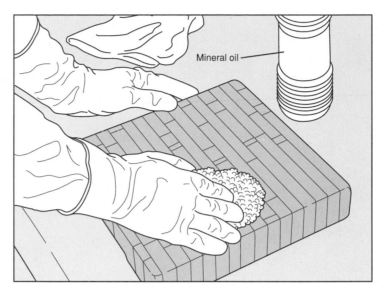

Mineral oil

1 **Cleaning and disinfecting the wood.** Wearing rubber gloves, clean the block using a solution of 2 teaspoons of dishwashing liquid per quart of warm water. Soak a clean, white, lint-free cloth with the solution, then wring it and rub the block *(above)* in the direction of the grain. Rinse the block with water, holding it at an angle under a faucet or wiping it with a clean, moist sponge. Wipe the block dry using a clean, dry cloth. Disinfect the block using a solution of 2 tablespoons of household laundry bleach per quart of water, applying it with a clean, damp cloth. Rinse and dry the block again.

2 **Sealing the wood with mineral oil.** Soak a clean, white, lint-free cloth with mineral oil and rub the block with it in the direction of the grain. When the block is saturated with oil, wear rubber gloves to scrub it using super-fine (grade 4/0) steel wool *(above)* or a clean white scrubbing pad; make a slight circular motion. Allow the oil to soak into the block for about 30 minutes, then wipe off any excess with a clean cloth. Rinse the block with water and wipe it dry with a clean cloth. Stand the block on end until you need it; after using it, wipe it with a clean cloth dampened with water.

CLEANING CERAMIC TILES

Cleaning everyday dirt and grime. Working in a well-ventilated room, wear rubber gloves to clean the tiles using an all-purpose spray cleaner; or, use a commercial tile cleaner following the manufacturer's instructions. Working from top to bottom along the tiles, clean a section 3 feet wide at a time. Mist the section with the cleaner, then rub it in a slight circular motion using a sponge dampened with water. Continue the same way *(above, left)*, rinsing the sponge in water and wringing it as necessary. For stubborn dirt and grime, scrub gently with a white scrubbing pad, applying more cleaner as necessary. Rinse the tiles with water, applying it with a clean, moist sponge; in the bathtub or shower, apply it with the shower nozzle, if possible. Wipe the tiles dry using a clean, white, lint-free cloth; in the bathtub or shower, dry the tiles using a squeegee, drawing its blade from top to bottom in slightly overlapping passes *(above, right)* and wiping its blade with a clean cloth.

CLEANING A BATHROOM SINK

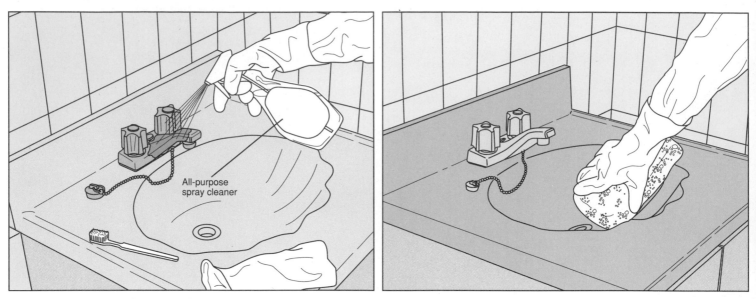

Cleaning everyday dirt and grime. Clear off the countertop around the sink, then clean the faucets and the sink using an all-purpose spray cleaner and a sponge. Test your cleaning agent and method *(page 85)*. Wearing rubber gloves, mist the faucets and the sink with the cleaner *(above, left)*, then dampen the sponge with water and wipe using it. Starting at the perimeter of the sink, clean first the faucets, then the remaining edges and the inside of the sink. For stubborn dirt and grime, scrub gently with a white scrubbing pad, applying more cleaner as necessary. For the drain, the base of the faucets or other surfaces hard to reach, scrub gently with an old toothbrush. Rinse the faucets and the sink using a clean sponge dampened with water *(above, right)*, then wipe them dry with a clean, white, lint-free cloth.

CLEANING A BATHTUB

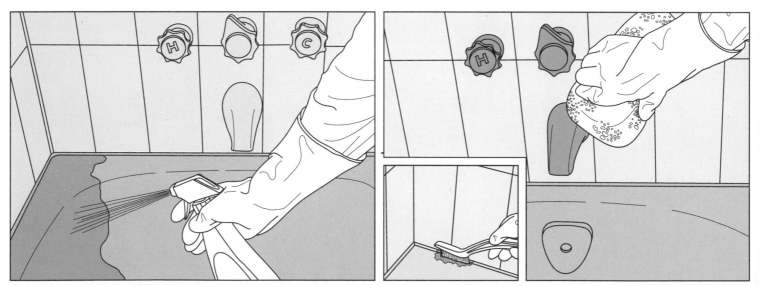

Cleaning everyday dirt and grime. Clear off the edges at the perimeter of the bathtub, then clean the faucets and the bathtub using an all-purpose spray cleaner and a sponge. Test your cleaning agent and method *(page 85)*. Wearing rubber gloves, mist the faucets and the bathtub with the cleaner *(above, left)*, then dampen the sponge with water and wipe using it. Starting at the perimeter of the bathtub, clean first the faucets *(above, right)*, then the edges, walls and bottom of the bathtub. For stubborn dirt and grime, scrub gently with a white scrubbing pad, applying more cleaner as necessary. For the edges of the bathtub, the drain, the base of the faucets or other surfaces hard to reach, scrub gently with a tile grout brush *(inset)* or old toothbrush. Rinse the faucets and the bathtub using a clean sponge dampened with water, then wipe them dry with a clean, white, lint-free cloth.

CLEANING SHOWER DOORS

1 **Cleaning the door tracks.** Dislodge particles from the tracks using a stiff-bristled fiber brush *(above)* if they are metal; a sponge if they are fiberglass or acrylic. Vacuum particles out of the tracks with a crevice attachment. Protect the floor around the bathtub or shower stall with a dropcloth, then clean the tracks using an all-purpose spray cleaner. Wearing rubber gloves, mist the tracks with cleaner, then scrub them using the brush or sponge; for corners hard to reach, scrub using an old toothbrush. Rinse the tracks with water, using the shower nozzle, if possible, or a spray container for pressure.

2 **Cleaning the door panes.** Clean the panes using an all-purpose spray cleaner and a clean, white, lint-free cloth. Test your cleaning agent and method *(page 85)*. Wearing rubber gloves, work from top to bottom of the panes, misting with the cleaner and wiping with the cloth *(above)*. For stubborn dirt and grime, scrub gently with a white scrubbing pad, applying more cleaner as necessary. For edges hard to reach, scrub gently with an old toothbrush. Rinse the panes with water using a clean, moist sponge or the shower nozzle, if possible. Wipe the panes and the tracks dry using a clean cloth.

CLEANING A TOILET

All-purpose spray cleaner

1 **Cleaning the tank, seat cover, seat and base.** Clear off the top of the toilet tank, then clean the tank, seat cover, seat and base using an all-purpose spray cleaner and a sponge. Test your cleaning agent and method *(page 85)*. Wearing rubber gloves, mist the tank *(above, left)*, seat cover, seat and base with the cleaner, then dampen the sponge with water and wipe using it. Starting at the top of the toilet, clean first the tank, then each side of the seat cover and the seat *(above, right)*, and the base. For stubborn dirt and grime, scrub gently with a white scrubbing pad, applying more cleaner as necessary. For edges or corners hard to reach, scrub gently with an old toothbrush. Rinse the tank, seat cover, seat and base using a clean sponge dampened with water, then wipe them dry with a clean, white, lint-free cloth.

CLEANING A TOILET (continued)

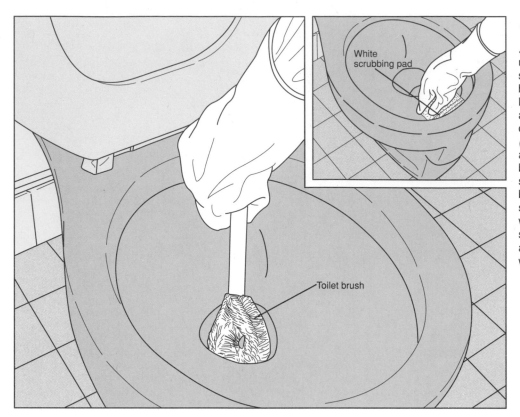

2 Cleaning the bowl. Empty a bucket of water into the bowl, forcing it to drain. Wearing rubber gloves, mist the rim and upper edges of the bowl with an all-purpose spray cleaner, then squirt the inside of the bowl with a commercial toilet-bowl cleaner following the manufacturer's instructions. Wait about 15 minutes, then scrub the surfaces of the bowl vigorously using a toilet brush *(left)*—including the bottom of the rim as well as the water inlet and water outlet. For stubborn dirt and grime, scrub gently with a white scrubbing pad (used specifically only for the bowl) *(inset)*, applying more cleaner as necessary. Rinse the bowl by flushing the toilet and wiping the rim and upper edges of it using a sponge dampened with water. Wipe the rim and upper edges of the bowl dry with a clean, white, lint-free cloth.

REMOVING STAINS

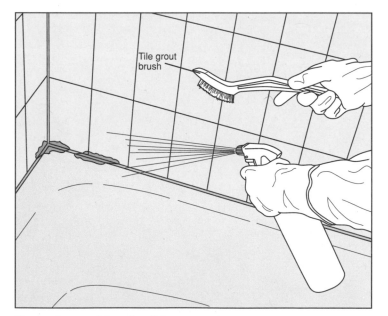

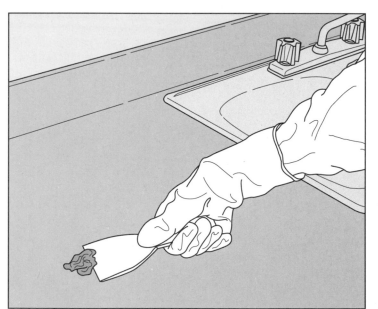

Removing mold and mildew. Working in a well-ventilated room, wear rubber gloves and safety goggles to mix a solution of 1 cup of household laundry bleach per quart of warm water in a spray container. Scrub the surface with the cleaning solution using a tile grout brush, old toothbrush or white scrubbing pad. Test your cleaning solution and method *(page 85)*. Mist the surface with the cleaning solution *(above)* and let it sit for about 10 minutes, then scrub with the brush or pad. Rinse the surface with water, applying it with a clean, moist sponge. Wipe the surface dry using a clean, white, lint-free cloth.

Removing gum, wax or adhesive. For gum or wax, apply an ice pack until the material is brittle, then gently scrape it off the surface using a plastic spatula *(above)*. For a sticker or other adhesive-backed material, work in a well-ventilated room and wear rubber gloves to apply a citrus-based solvent to the surface with a clean, white, lint-free cloth. Test your cleaning solvent and method *(page 85)*. Soak the cloth with the solvent, then wring it out and gently rub the surface with it. Rinse the surface with water, applying it with a clean, moist sponge. Wipe the surface dry using a clean, white, lint-free cloth.

REMOVING STAINS (continued)

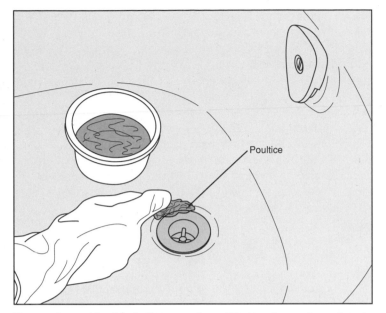

Removing embedded dirt or grime. Working in a well-ventilated room, wear rubber gloves to prepare a poultice of cornstarch or talcum powder and a liquid ingredient: household laundry bleach for a surface of marble or fiberglass; a citrus-based solvent otherwise. Mix the poultice in a clean container into a thick, uniform paste that is the consistency of putty. Test your poultice, letting it dry before removing it *(page 85)*. Apply a thick, uniform coat of the poultice to the surface with your finger *(above)* and allow it to dry. When the poultice is dry, gently lift it off the surface with a plastic spatula. Rinse the surface thoroughly with water, applying it with a clean, moist sponge. Wipe the surface dry using a clean, white, lint-free cloth.

Removing rust. Working in a well-ventilated room, wear rubber gloves to clean the surface. For a surface of metal, apply a chemical solvent such as acetone using a clean, white, lint-free cloth. Test your cleaning solvent and method *(page 85)*. Soak the cloth with the solvent, then wring it out; fold it into a small pad or use a corner of it to gently rub the surface *(above)*. If necessary, apply pressure through the cloth with a finger. Rinse the surface thoroughly with water, applying it with a clean, moist sponge. Wipe the surface dry using a clean cloth. For a surface of marble or fiberglass, apply a commercial rust poultice recommended for the material following the manufacturer's instructions, then rinse the surface and dry it.

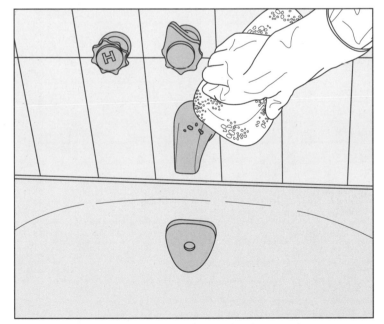

Removing soap scum. Wearing rubber gloves, clean the surface using a commercial degreasing spray cleaner, scrubbing with a sponge or white scrubbing pad. Test your cleaning solution and method *(page 85)*. Working from top to bottom of the surface, mist it with the cleaner. Let the cleaner sit for the time specified, then dampen the sponge or pad with water and scrub with it *(above)*. Rinse the surface with water, applying it with a clean, moist sponge. Wipe the surface dry using a clean, white, lint-free cloth.

Removing hard water spots. Wear rubber gloves to mix a solution of 1 cup of white vinegar per quart of warm water in a bowl and apply it with a clean, white, lint-free cloth. Test your cleaning solution and method *(page 85)*. Soak the cloth with the solution, then wring it out; fold it into a small pad or use a corner of it to gently rub the surface. If necessary, apply pressure through the cloth with a finger. Rinse the surface with water, applying it with a clean, moist sponge *(above)*. Wipe the surface dry using a clean cloth.

APPLIANCES

Your household appliances are the veritable workhorses of your home, their surfaces and working parts exposed to relentless use and abuse; consequently, they demand continual cleaning to keep them looking bright and shiny—and operating smoothly. In the kitchen, major appliances such as the range, the refrigerator and the dishwasher as well as most small appliances are quickly dirtied by sticky spills, greasy cooking fumes, moisture and dust. In the laundry room, your clothes washer is prone to buildups of detergent and mineral deposits; both it and the clothes dryer are vulnerable to clogging from lint and to mildew. The appliances of the heating and cooling systems in your home are also prone to all kinds of cleaning problems: dust and greasy dirt can clog a furnace filter or a baseboard heater; mineral deposits and bacterial growth can become problems with vaporizers, humidifiers and air conditioners. In the living room, family room and bedrooms, dust and grit collect in the contours and recesses of your electronic video, audio and computer equipment.

Perform quick cleanups of your household appliances on a regular basis, denying dust, dirt and deposits the chance to accumulate—and saving yourself time and elbow grease when you undertake a thorough cleaning of each appliance. Clean grease drops and spills off your range or microwave oven when they occur. Clean the filter of your dishwasher and the lint trap of your clothes washer and clothes dryer after each use of the appliance. Wipe sticky smudges and fingerprints off the toaster, the refrigerator doors, the control buttons of the blender and your electronic equipment the moment you spot them. Consult the owner's manual for each appliance of your home; follow the manufacturer's recommendations to develop a maintenance routine for it. Refer to the Troubleshooting Guide *(below)* for procedures on the thorough cleaning of typical household appliances; to the Cleaning Tips *(page 93)* for basic cleaning guidelines. Consult Tools & Techniques *(page 116)* for general information on cleaning supplies and techniques.

Before undertaking a thorough cleaning of any household appliance, take the time to prepare for the job properly. Gather together your cleaning agents and tools; protect surfaces from cleaning agents by covering them with dropcloths or plastic sheeting. Ensure that you turn off and unplug an appliance or shut off power to it *(page 93)* before beginning to clean it. If you need to move a large appliance to gain access to the back of it, work carefully to avoid injuring yourself *(page 124)*. Follow the owner's manual instructions for an appliance if you need to disassemble it for cleaning; keep track of all the parts you remove for reassembly. To prevent any inadvertent damage to an appliance you are cleaning, always test your cleaning agent and method on an inconspicuous spot of the surface; if necessary, change to a milder cleaning agent or a gentler cleaning technique. Avoid dripping a cleaning solution into the internal mechanical or electrical parts of any appliance. Make sure that the surfaces of any appliance you clean are thoroughly dry before you reassemble and use the appliance.

TROUBLESHOOTING GUIDE

PROBLEM	PROCEDURE
Electric range dirty	Clean control panel *(p. 94)* □○, rangetop *(p. 94)* □◒, oven *(p. 96)* □◒ and drawer *(p. 98)* □○
Gas range dirty	Clean control panel *(p. 94)* □○, rangetop *(p. 95)* ◪◒, oven *(p. 96)* ◪◒ and drawer *(p. 98)* ◪◒
Range hood dirty	Clean range hood *(p. 98)* □○
Microwave oven dirty	Clean microwave oven *(p. 103)* □○
Small appliance dirty	Clean small appliance *(p. 103)* □○
Refrigerator dirty	Clean refrigerator *(p. 99)* ◪○
Dishwasher dirty	Clean dishwasher *(p. 100)* ◪○
Clothes washer dirty	Clean clothes washer *(p. 101)* ◪○
Clothes dryer dirty	Clean clothes dryer *(p. 102)* □○
Electronic equipment dirty	Clean electronic equipment *(p. 104)* ◪○
Vaporizer dirty	Clean vaporizer *(p. 105)* □○
Portable humidifier dirty	Clean portable humidifier *(p. 105)* □○
Central humidifier dirty	Clean central humidifier *(p. 107)* ◪◒
Furnace filter dirty	Clean filter element *(p. 107)* □○; clean electronic filter and cell *(p. 108)* ◪◒
Window air conditioner dirty	Clean window air conditioner *(p. 108)* ◪◒
Central air conditioner dirty	Clean central air conditioner *(p. 109)* ◪◒
Heat pump dirty	Clean heat pump *(p. 109)* ◪◒
Baseboard heater dirty	Clean baseboard heater *(p. 109)* □○

DEGREE OF DIFFICULTY: □ Easy ◪ Moderate ■ Complex
ESTIMATED TIME: ○ Less than 1 hour ◒ 1 to 3 hours ● Over 3 hours

CLEANING TIPS

● Establish a household-maintenance routine that includes the cleaning of each appliance. Follow any maintenance schedule supplied by the manufacturer of an appliance and accord the greatest cleaning priority to your most-often-used appliances.

● Turn off and unplug an appliance or shut off power to it before you clean it *(steps below)*.

● Follow any specific cleaning and stain-removal tips for an appliance supplied by the manufacturer; check the owner's manual and any tags or labels on the appliance.

● Plan an effective cleaning strategy for each appliance; in general, work from the top to the bottom of it and from the interior surfaces to the exterior surfaces, letting one part soak with cleaning solution while you apply cleaning solution to another part.

● Follow the cleaning instructions supplied by the manufacturer for any commercial cleaning product you use.

● Test any cleaning agent and method you use on an inconspicuous spot of the surface—even if you are only dabbing or wiping using a cloth dampened with water.

● Allow the cleaning solution to do most of the work in cleaning an appliance; soak parts of the appliance with the cleaning solution to loosen and dissolve stubborn deposits or films before you start your rubbing and scrubbing.

● Clean a fresh spill off the surface of an appliance the moment it occurs. To minimize grease and grime buildup, spot-clean frequently the working surfaces of appliances using a clean, white, lint-free cloth dampened with an all-purpose cleaner; wipe them dry with another cloth, buffing vigorously until they shine.

● To protect a surface from a cleaning solution, use a dropcloth or plastic sheeting. Wipe up any stray or spilled cleaning solution immediately with a clean, white, lint-free cloth.

● When you are cleaning an appliance, always start with the cleaning solution recommended, progressing to a stronger cleaning solution only if necessary. Make several attempts to wash the surface with a cleaning solution before abandoning it; wipe each application of it dry thoroughly before repeating an application of it.

● Store cleaning agents well out of the reach of children; dispose of any leftover cleaning agent safely.

SHUTTING OFF POWER

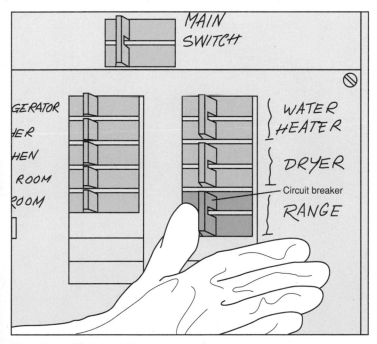

Shutting off electricity. If possible, unplug the appliance; otherwise, shut off electricity to it at the main service panel. If the area around the main service panel is damp, stand on a dry board or wear dry rubber boots. Wearing heavy rubber gloves, work only with one hand and do not touch anything metal. At a circuit breaker panel, find the circuit breaker for the circuit and flip it to OFF *(above)*; to restore electricity, flip it fully to OFF, then to ON. At a fuse panel, find the plug fuse or fuse block for the circuit and remove it; to restore electricity, reinstall it.

Shutting off gas. Read the manufacturer's instructions for the appliance. Find the shutoff valve on the supply pipe to the appliance and close it by turning the handle perpendicular to the supply pipe *(above)*. If there is no shutoff valve on the supply pipe to the appliance, shut off the main gas supply. To restore the gas supply, open the valve by turning the handle parallel to the supply pipe, then relight each pilot on the appliance. If you cannot relight a pilot or there is a strong odor of gas, immediately close the shutoff valve and call for service.

CLEANING THE RANGE CONTROL PANEL

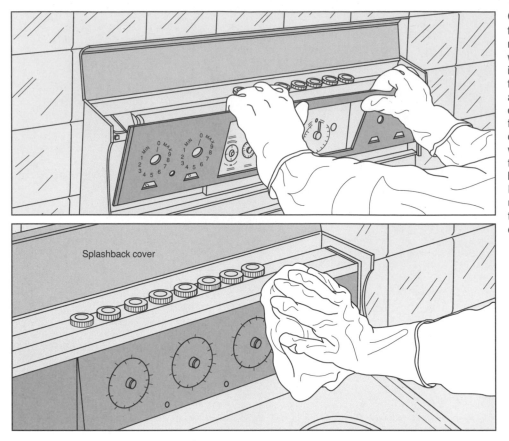

Splashback cover

Cleaning the control panel. Shut off power to the range *(page 93)*. Wearing rubber gloves, mix a solution of an all-purpose cleaner and hot water. Remove the control knobs and soak them in the solution, then scrub them using an old toothbrush. Rinse the control knobs with water and wipe them dry using a clean, white, lint-free cloth. Raise the splashback cover to clean the faceplate. If the faceplate is removable, take it off *(left, top)* and soak it in the solution; otherwise, wipe it using a clean cloth moistened with the solution. If necessary, gently scrub off stubborn deposits using a white scrubbing pad. Rinse the faceplate with water and wipe it dry using another cloth *(left, bottom)*. Reassemble the control panel and close the splashback cover before restoring power to the range.

CLEANING THE RANGETOP: ELECTRIC RANGE

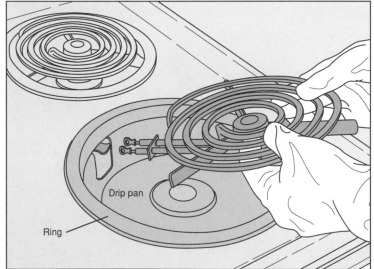

Drip pan

Ring

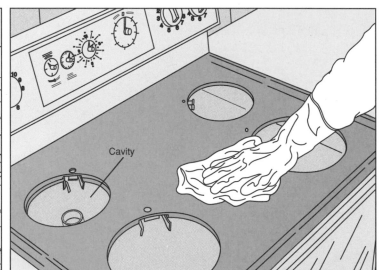

Cavity

Cleaning the rangetop. Shut off power to the range *(page 93)*. Wearing rubber gloves, mix a solution of an all-purpose cleaner or a commercial degreaser and hot water. Diassemble each burner for cleaning: pulling out a plug-in element *(above, left)*; raising a wired element to lift out the drip pan and the element ring. Soak the drip pans and the element rings in the solution, then scrub them using a white scrubbing pad. Rinse the drip pans and the element rings with water and wipe them dry with a clean, white, lint-free cloth. Wipe the elements using a clean cloth dampened with water; gently scrub

stubborn deposits off them using a pad of extra-fine (grade 3/0) steel wool. To clean the rangetop cavity, raise the rangetop or work through the burner openings. Vacuum the cavity with a crevice attachment, then wipe the base of it using a clean cloth moistened with solution. Rinse the base of the cavity using a sponge dampened with water and wipe it dry with another cloth; gently scrub off stubborn deposits using a white scrubbing pad. Wash, rinse and dry the rangetop surface the same way, buffing it until it shines *(above, right)*. Reassemble the rangetop before restoring power to the range.

CLEANING THE RANGETOP: GAS RANGE

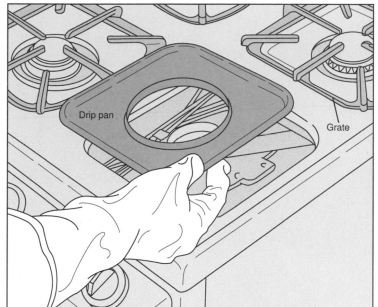

Drip pan

Grate

1 Cleaning the rangetop. Shut off power to the range *(page 93)*. Wearing rubber gloves, mix a solution of an all-purpose cleaner or a commercial degreaser and hot water. Disassemble each burner, lifting out the burner grate and the drip pan *(above, left)*. Soak the drip pans in the solution, then scrub them using a white scrubbing pad. Rinse the drip pans with water and wipe them dry using a clean, white, lint-free cloth. Wipe the burner grates using a clean cloth dampened with water; gently scrub stubborn deposits off them using a pad of

extra-fine (grade 3/0) steel wool. To clean the rangetop cavity, raise the rangetop or work through the burner openings. Vacuum the cavity with a crevice attachment *(above, right)*, then wipe the base of it using a clean cloth moistened with solution. Rinse the base of the cavity using a sponge dampened with water and wipe it dry with another cloth; gently scrub off stubborn deposits using a white scrubbing pad. Wash, rinse and dry the rangetop surface the same way, buffing it until it shines.

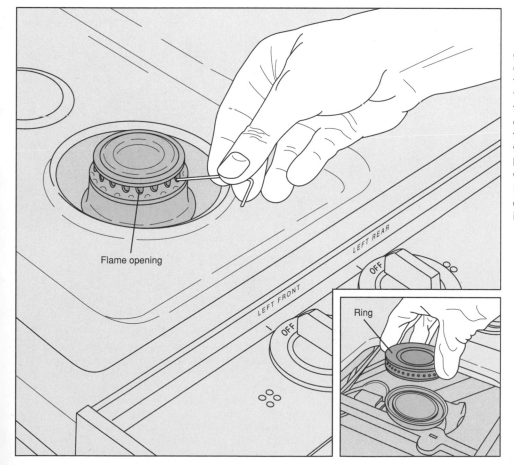

Flame opening

LEFT REAR

LEFT FRONT

OFF

OFF

OFF

Ring

2 Cleaning the burners. Wearing rubber gloves, mix a solution of an all-purpose cleaner or a commercial degreaser and hot water, then clean the burners one at a time. With an older model of range, the top ring of the burner may be removable *(inset)* for soaking in the solution. Otherwise, wipe the top ring and the base of the burner using a clean, white, lint-free cloth moistened with solution; gently scrub off stubborn deposits using a white scrubbing pad. Rinse the top ring and the base of the burner using a sponge dampened with water and dry them with another cloth. Reinstall the top rings if you removed them. To clean each flame opening of a top ring, gently it a thin wire or a sewing pin into it *(left)*.

CLEANING THE RANGETOP: GAS RANGE (continued)

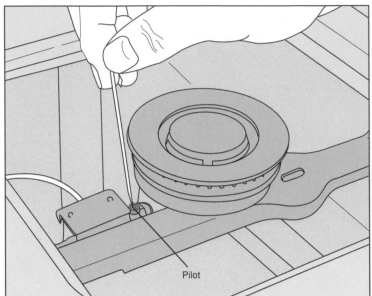

Pilot

Igniter

3 **Cleaning the pilots or igniters.** To clean the pilots or igniters, raise the rangetop or work through the burner openings. Clean the pilots or igniters one at a time, removing any metal shields obstructing access to the top of them. To clean a pilot, carefully insert a sharp wooden toothpick into its opening *(above, left)*; gently wiggle the toothpick, being careful not to enlarge or deform the open-

ing. To clean an igniter, gently wipe it using a dry cotton swab *(above, right)*; rub off any stubborn film or deposit using another cotton swab dampened with a solution of an all-purpose cleaner or a commercial degreaser and water. Put back any metal shields you removed and reassemble the rangetop before restoring power to the range.

CLEANING THE RANGE OVEN

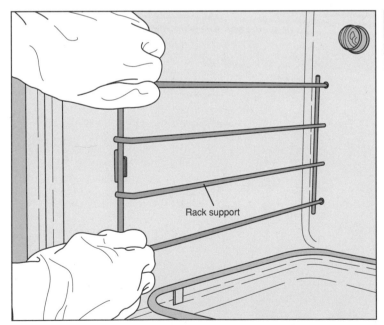

Rack support

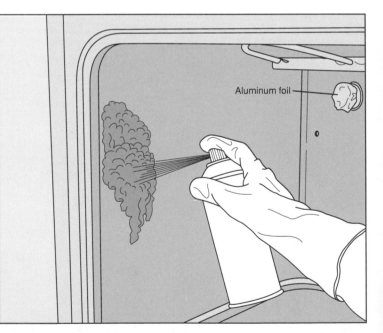

Aluminum foil

1 **Preparing to clean the oven.** Shut off power to the range *(page 93)* and set a bowl of clear household ammonia inside the oven a few hours before cleaning it; the fumes help to soften deposits. Wearing rubber gloves, remove the bowl of ammonia, then mix a solution of 2 tablespoons of clear household ammonia and a small amount of an all-purpose cleaner per gallon of warm water. **Caution:** Do not use an all-purpose cleaner containing chlorine. Take the racks and drip pans out of the oven, then remove each rack support *(above, left)*. Soak the racks, drip pans and rack supports in the solution,

then wipe them using a clean, white, lint-free cloth moistened with solution; scrub off stubborn deposits using a white scrubbing pad. Rinse the racks, drip pans and rack supports using a sponge dampened with water, then wipe them dry with another cloth. Sweep loose particles out of the oven using a whisk broom, then remove the light bulb and cover the socket with aluminum foil. Working in a well-ventilated room, wear safety goggles to apply a commercial spray oven cleaner to each interior surface of the oven *(above, right)*, coating it generously. Close the oven door and let the cleaner sit for the time specified by the manufacturer.

CLEANING THE RANGE OVEN (continued)

Hinge

2 **Cleaning the oven.** For greatest access to the interior surfaces of the oven, remove the oven door, if possible. In general, open the oven door to its first stop, then grip each side of it and brace it with your knee, lifting straight up to pull it off its hinges *(above, left)*. Set the oven door interior-side up onto a dropcloth on the floor. Working from the top to the bottom of the oven, wipe each interior surface in turn using a clean, white, lint-free cloth dampened with water *(above, right)*; scrub off stubborn deposits using a white scrubbing pad.

Rinse the interior surfaces using a sponge soaked with warm water and wipe them dry with another cloth. Clean the interior side of the oven door the same way. To clean residue off the window of the oven door, apply a solution of 1/8 cup of white vinegar per quart of water using a clean cloth. Wipe the window dry with a crumpled sheet of newspaper or another cloth, rubbing vigorously until it is streak-free. For a gas range, clean the oven burner *(step 3)*. Otherwise, reassemble the oven before restoring power to the range.

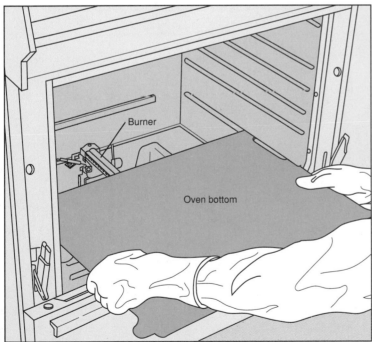

Burner

Oven bottom

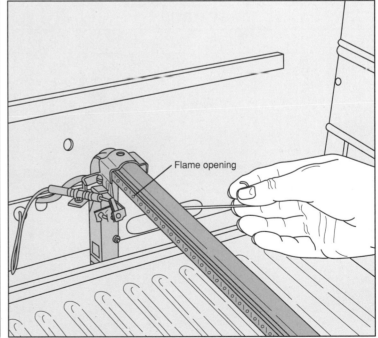

Flame opening

3 **Cleaning a gas oven burner.** Detach and slide out the oven bottom *(above, left)*, then detach and lift out any baffle under it obstructing access to the burner. Vacuum the burner chamber using a crevice attachment. Wearing rubber gloves, mix a solution of an all-purpose cleaner or a commercial degreaser and hot water. Wipe the surfaces of the burner and the burner chamber using a clean, white, lint-free cloth moistened with solution; scrub off stubborn deposits

using a white scrubbing pad. Rinse the surfaces of the burner and the burner chamber using a sponge dampened with water and wipe them dry with another cloth. To clean each flame opening of the burner, carefully insert a thin wire or a sewing pin into it *(above, right)*; gently wiggle the wire or pin, being careful not to enlarge or deform the opening. Reassemble the oven before restoring power to the range.

CLEANING THE RANGE DRAWER

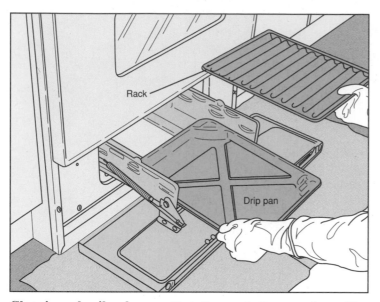

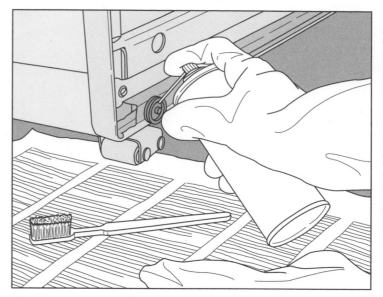

Cleaning a broiler drawer. Shut off power to the range *(page 93)*. Wearing rubber gloves, mix a solution of 2 tablespoons of clear household ammonia and a little non-chlorine all-purpose cleaner per gallon of hot water. Remove the rack and drip pan *(above)*, then soak them in the solution. Wearing safety goggles, apply a commercial spray oven cleaner to the drawer interior; let it sit for the time specified by the manufacturer. Wipe the rack, drip pan and drawer interior using a clean, white, lint-free cloth; scrub off deposits with a white scrubbing pad. Rinse the rack, drip pan and drawer interior using a sponge dampened with water and wipe them dry with another cloth. Reassemble the drawer before restoring power to the range.

Cleaning a storage drawer. Empty the drawer, then slide it out as far as possible and lift the front of it clear of the tracks to remove it. Wearing rubber gloves, mix a solution of 2 tablespoons of clear household ammonia and a little non-chlorine all-purpose cleaner per gallon of hot water. Wipe the drawer surfaces using a clean, white, lint-free cloth moistened with the solution; scrub off deposits with a white scrubbing pad. Rinse the drawer surfaces using a sponge dampened with water and wipe them dry with another cloth. Scrub the drawer tracks using an old toothbrush dampened with the solution. To keep the drawer from sticking or squeaking, spray the track mechanisms with a recommended lubricant *(above)* before reinstalling it.

CLEANING THE RANGE HOOD

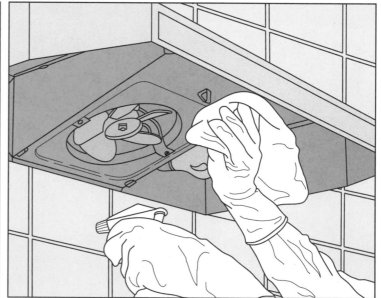

Cleaning the range hood. Shut off power to the range hood *(page 93)*. Wearing rubber gloves, detach the filter and lift it off the range hood *(above, left)*. If the filter is of aluminum, soak it in a solution of an all-purpose cleaner and hot water; if it is of charcoal, replace it if it is dirty. Mist the surfaces of the range hood using a commercial spray degreaser and let it sit for several minutes, then wipe them using a clean, white, lint-free cloth *(above, right)*; scrub off stubborn deposits with a white scrubbing pad. Wipe the fan blades using a clean cloth moistened with the degreaser. Rinse any soaked filter, the surfaces of the range hood and the fan blades using a sponge dampened with water, then wipe them dry with another cloth. Reassemble the range hood before restoring power to it.

CLEANING THE REFRIGERATOR

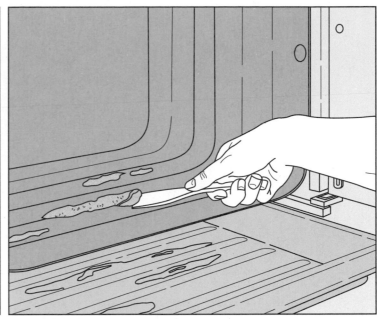

1 **Defrosting and cleaning the freezer compartment.**
Unplug the refrigerator, then clear the freezer and refrigerator compartments. If the refrigerator is not frost-free, leave its doors open and place dropcloths on the floor around it until the freezer compartment defrosts; to speed the process, set pots of boiling water in the freezer and refrigerator compartments. As any tray or drawer accumulates water, remove it *(above, left)* to empty it, then reinstall it. Carefully dislodge pieces of ice using a plastic spatula *(above, right)*—never a sharp metal tool. When the freezer compartment is defrosted, remove

the pots of water. Wearing rubber gloves, mix a solution of 2 tablespoons of clear household ammonia and a little all-purpose cleaner per gallon of warm water. **Caution:** Do not use an all-purpose cleaner containing chlorine. Working from top to bottom of the freezer compartment, wipe its interior surfaces using a clean, white, lint-free cloth moistened with the solution. Gently scrub off stubborn deposits with a white scrubbing pad; on surfaces hard to reach, scrub using an old toothbrush. Rinse the interior surfaces using a sponge dampened with water and wipe them dry with another cloth.

Gasket

2 **Cleaning the refrigerator compartment.** Wearing rubber gloves, lift the shelves, drawers and other accessories out of the refrigerator compartment, then soak them in the solution. Working from top to bottom of the refrigerator compartment, wipe its interior surfaces using a clean, white, lint-free cloth moistened with the solution *(left)*. Scrub off stubborn deposits with a white scrubbing pad; on surfaces hard to reach, scrub using an old toothbrush. Rinse the interior surfaces using a sponge dampened with water and wipe them dry with another cloth. Wash, rinse and dry the shelves, drawers and other accessories the same way. Clean stubborn dirt off the door gasket using a clean cloth moistened with a solution of 3 teaspoons of citrus-based solvent per gallon of water, rubbing it vigorously *(inset)*.

CLEANING THE REFRIGERATOR (continued)

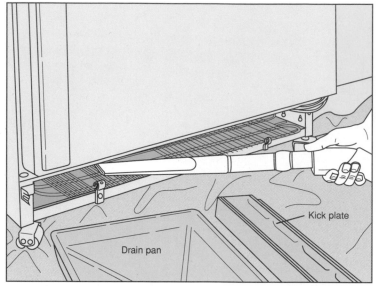

3 **Cleaning the condenser coils and the compressor.**
Remove the kick plate from the front of the refrigerator and lift out the drain pan behind it. Clean the ground-level condenser coils using a vacuum cleaner and a crevice attachment *(above, left)*; gently scrub off stubborn deposits with a bottle brush. Wipe the drain pan using a clean, white, lint-free cloth moistened with the solution, rinse it using a sponge dampened with water and wipe it dry using another cloth. Reinstall the drain pan and the kick plate. Move the refrigerator out from the wall to clean the rear-mounted condenser coils,

vacuuming them with the crevice attachment and scrubbing stubborn deposits off them using the bottle brush *(above right)*. Clean the compressor below the condenser coils the same way, then move the refrigerator back against the wall. Working from top to bottom of the refrigerator, wipe its exterior surfaces using another cloth moistened with the solution, then rinse them using the sponge dampened with water and dry them with another cloth, buffing vigorously until they shine. Reassemble the freezer and refrigerator compartments before plugging the refrigerator back in.

CLEANING THE DISHWASHER

Cleaning the dishwasher. Take the filter out of the bottom of the dishwasher and remove the spray arm. Wearing rubber gloves, rinse the filter under running water; dislodge stubborn deposits by scrubbing it with an old toothbrush *(above, left)*. Clean the spray arm the same way; gently push out any debris clogging its holes with a stiff wire. Working from top to bottom of the dishwasher, wipe its interior and exterior surfaces in turn using a clean, white, lint-free cloth moistened with an all-purpose cleaner. Rinse the interior and exterior surfaces using a

sponge dampened with water, then dry them with another cloth *(above, right)*, buffing vigorously until they shine. Clean stubborn dirt off the door gasket using a clean cloth moistened with a solution of 3 teaspoons of citrus-based solvent per gallon of water, rubbing it vigorously. Reinstall the filter and the spray arm. To deodorize the dishwasher and prevent bacterial growth, fill the soap dispenser with 3 to 4 tablespoons of the citrus-based solvent, then run the dishwasher through a full wash cycle.

CLEANING THE CLOTHES WASHER

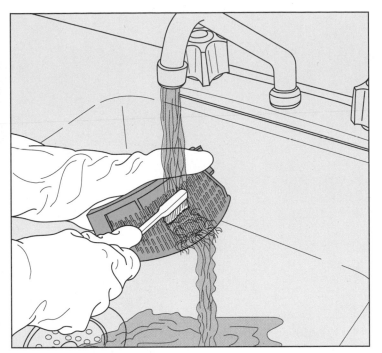

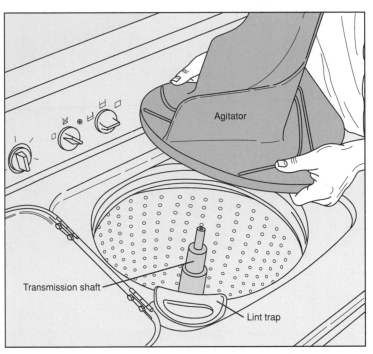

1 **Cleaning the lint trap.** Unplug the clothes washer, then remove the lint trap from it. For a card-type lint trap such as the one shown, pull it out of its cavity in the rim of the opening in the washer top. For a basket-type lint trap, lift it off the top of the agitator. Wearing rubber gloves, rinse the screen of the lint trap under running water; scrub encrusted particles off it using an old toothbrush (above). Then, reinstall the lint trap in the clothes washer.

2 **Cleaning the agitator.** Remove the agitator, detaching it and lifting it off the transmission shaft (above). Wearing rubber gloves, rinse the agitator under running water; scrub encrusted particles off it using an old toothbrush. Wipe the transmission shaft using a clean, white, lint-free cloth dampened with water, then wipe it dry with another cloth. Dab a little petroleum jelly on the top of the transmission shaft to prevent corrosion. Then, reinstall the agitator.

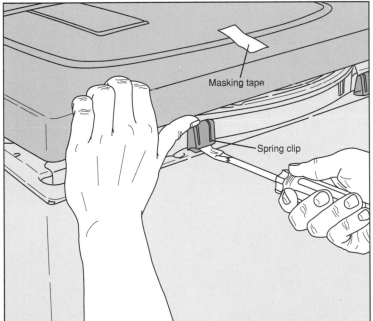

3 **Cleaning under the washer top.** Tape the lid of the clothes washer shut with masking tape. Wrap the blade of a screwdriver with a strip of masking tape, then use it to release the spring clips securing the washer top (above, left). Wearing rubber gloves, mix a solution of 2 tablespoons of an all-purpose cleaner per gallon of hot water. Raising the washer top, wipe the surfaces under it using a clean, white, lint-free cloth moistened with solution (above, right); scrub off encrusted particles with a green scrubbing pad. Rinse the surfaces using a sponge dampened with water and wipe them dry with another cloth. Resecure the washer top and remove the tape from the lid. Working from top to bottom of the clothes washer, wipe its exterior surfaces using a clean cloth moistened with an all-purpose cleaner or a commercial degreaser. Rinse the exterior surfaces using the sponge dampened with water and wipe them dry with another cloth, buffing vigorously until they shine. Then, plug the clothes washer back in.

CLEANING THE CLOTHES DRYER

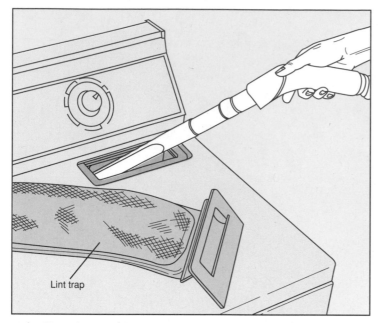

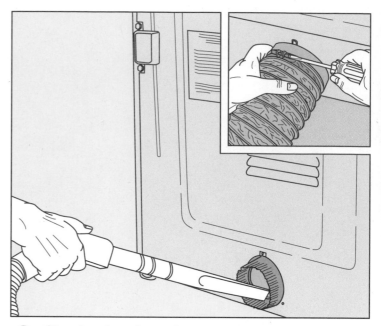

1 Cleaning the lint trap. Unplug the clothes dryer, then remove the lint trap from it. For a lint trap such as the one shown, pull it by its handle out of its cavity in the dryer top. Gently peel any lint off the screen of the lint trap using your fingers, then clean fine particles of dust off it using a vacuum cleaner and a crevice attachment; also vacuum its cavity in the dryer top *(above)*. Then, reinstall the lint trap into its cavity in the clothes dryer.

2 Cleaning the exhaust duct. Move the clothes dryer to gain access to the back of it; for a gas type, call a professional to disconnect it. Loosen the hose clamp securing the exhaust hose on the back of the dryer and pull the exhaust hose off the exhaust duct. Using a vacuum cleaner and a crevice attachment, clean the exhaust duct *(above)* and the free end of the exhaust hose. Reinstall the exhaust hose and tighten the hose clamp *(inset)*.

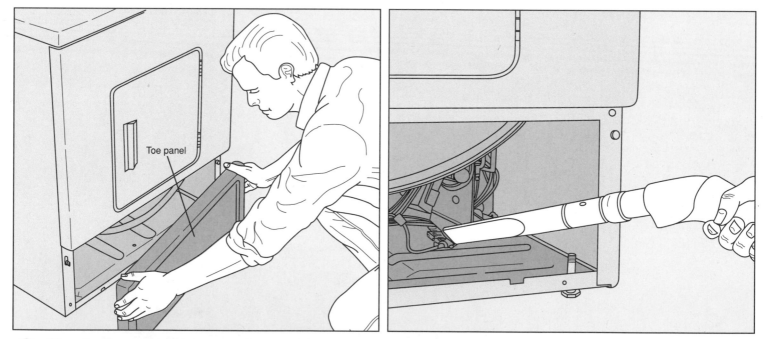

3 Cleaning the motor. Gain access to the motor following the manufacturer's instructions for the clothes dryer, taking the toe panel off the front of it *(above, left)* or the back plate off the back of it. Using a vacuum cleaner and a crevice attachment, clean the motor and the surfaces around it *(above, right)*; if necessary, light the bottom of the clothes dryer with a flashlight. Reinstall the toe panel or back plate and reposition the clothes dryer; have a gas type reconnected. Wearing rubber gloves, work from top to bottom of the clothes dryer to wipe its exterior surfaces using a clean, white, lint-free cloth moistened with an all-purpose cleaner or a commercial degreaser; scrub off stubborn deposits with a green scrubbing pad. Rinse the exterior surfaces using a sponge dampened with water and wipe them dry with another cloth, buffing vigorously until they shine. Plug the clothes dryer back in.

CLEANING THE MICROWAVE OVEN

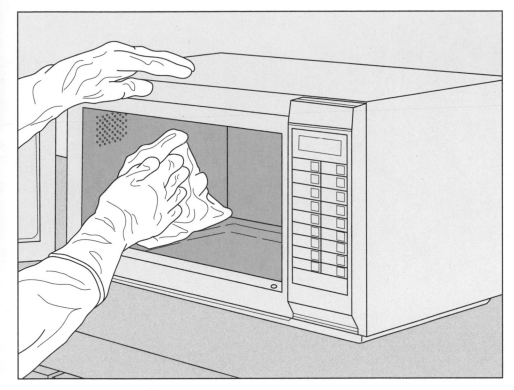

Cleaning the oven. Wash any glass tray in a solution of dishwashing liquid and water. Boil water in a heat-resistant glass container for 5 minutes inside the oven to soften encrusted deposits on its interior surfaces; do not use an abrasive cleaner or tool. Turn off the oven and unplug it. Wearing rubber gloves, work from top to bottom of the oven to wipe its interior surfaces using a clean, white, lint-free cloth moistened with a solution of dishwashing liquid and water. Rinse the interior surfaces using a sponge dampened with water and wipe them dry with another cloth *(left)*. Vacuum the exterior air vents using a crevice attachment, then wash, rinse and dry the exterior surfaces, buffing them vigorously with a cloth until they shine; scrub stubborn deposits off them with a white scrubbing pad or an old toothbrush. To deodorize the oven, wipe its interior surfaces using a clean cloth moistened with a solution of 4 tablespoons of sodium bicarbonate (baking soda) per quart of water; rinse them with the sponge and wipe them dry with another cloth. Or, boil a solution of 4 teaspoons of lemon juice per cup of water in a heat-resistant glass container for 5 minutes inside the oven.

CLEANING SMALL APPLIANCES

TIPS FOR SMALL APPLIANCES

• Follow specific cleaning and maintenance instructions supplied by the manufacturer for an appliance.

• After each use of an appliance, wash its detachable parts and wipe clean its exterior surfaces.

• Do not clean any appliance part in the dishwasher unless specifically instructed by the manufacturer—the heat may damage the part.

• Turn off and unplug an appliance before cleaning it; let it cool. Plug an appliance back in only when it is completely dry.

• Never submerge an appliance in water to clean it.

• Handle the sharp blade of an appliance carefully to prevent cutting yourself while cleaning it.

• Avoid wetting the internal mechanical and electrical parts of an appliance when you clean it.

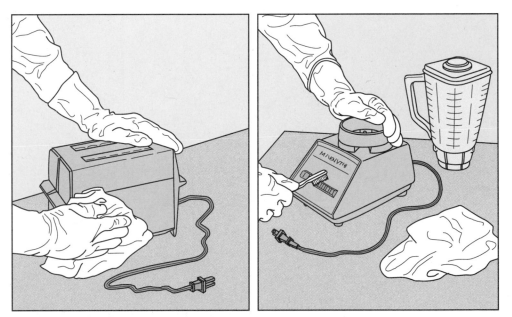

Cleaning a small appliance. Turn off and unplug the appliance, then disassemble it for cleaning following the manufacturer's instructions. Wearing rubber gloves, clean washable parts you removed using a solution of dishwashing liquid and water. Working from top to bottom of the appliance, wipe its exterior surfaces using a clean, white, lint-free cloth moistened with an all-purpose cleaner or a solution of 2 tablespoons of dishwashing liquid per gallon of warm water *(above, left)*; scrub off stubborn deposits with an old toothbrush *(above, right)* or a white scrubbing pad. Rinse the exterior surfaces using a clean cloth dampened with water and wipe them dry with another cloth, buffing vigorously until they shine. Plug the appliance back in.

CLEANING ELECTRONIC EQUIPMENT

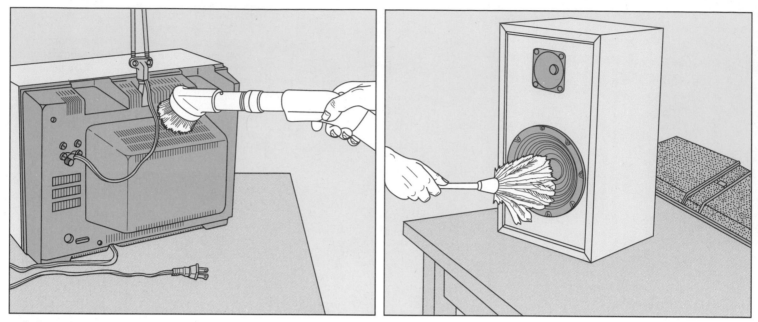

1 **Dusting surfaces.** Turn off the equipment and unplug it, then turn it on to drain any capacitor of its electrical charge. Clean dust and particles off exterior surfaces such as vents and grilles using a vacuum cleaner and a soft brush attachment *(above, left)*; work carefully to avoid scratching them. For the recesses around control knobs and other spots hard to reach, use a can of compressed air—available at an electronic or photographic equipment supplier. Wearing safety goggles, fit the can with its extension tube, then insert the tube into the recess and spray a short burst of air, blowing out dust and particles. For delicate surfaces such as speaker cones, brush gently using a feather duster *(above, right)*.

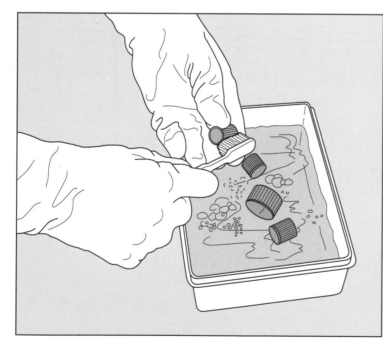

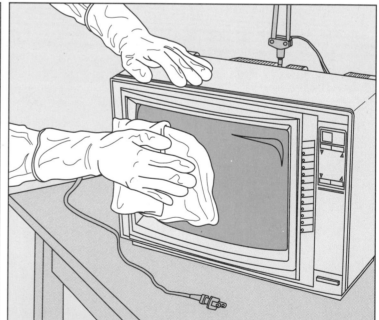

2 **Cleaning washable parts and surfaces.** To clean washable plastic or metal parts and surfaces, wear rubber gloves to mix a solution of 2 tablespoons of dishwashing liquid per gallon of water. Follow the manufacturer's instructions for the equipment to remove detachable parts such as control knobs for soaking in the solution and to wipe other parts and surfaces using a clean, white, lint-free cloth dampened with the solution. If necessary, gently scrub off deposits using an old toothbrush *(above, left)* or a white scrubbing pad. Rinse the parts and surfaces using a clean cloth dampened with water, then dry them thoroughly with another cloth. To clean the screen of a television or a computer monitor, use a commercial anti-static spray cleaner—available at an electronic or computer equipment supplier. Follow the manufacturer's instructions to mist the screen with the cleaner, then wipe it using a clean, white, lint-free cloth *(above, right)*. Restore the anti-static coating to the screen after every few cleanings using a commercial screen conditioner following the manufacturer's instructions. Reinstall the parts removed and turn off the equipment before plugging it back in.

CLEANING A VAPORIZER

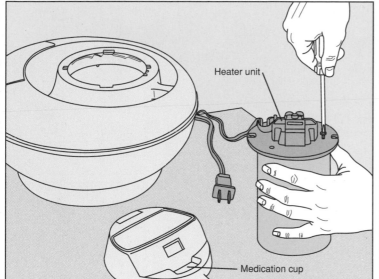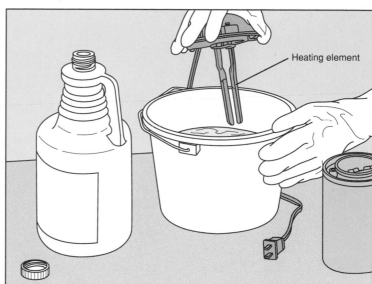

Cleaning the reservoir and the heater unit. Unplug the vaporizer, then remove the heater unit from the reservoir. Wearing rubber gloves, mix a solution of 1/4 cup of laundry bleach and a few squirts of dishwashing liquid per gallon of warm water. Fill the reservoir halfway with solution and reinstall the heater unit. Gently agitate the vaporizer, thoroughly swishing the solution around inside it. Remove the heater unit to empty the reservoir, then wipe the interior of the reservoir and the shaft of the heater unit using a clean, white, lint-free cloth dampened with the solution. Wipe the medication cup using a clean cloth dampened with rubbing alcohol. Rinse the reservoir, heater unit and medication cup thoroughly with water. Disassemble the heater unit following the manufacturer's instructions for the vaporizer *(above, left)* to check for mineral deposits on the heating element. To clean mineral deposits off the heating element, soak it overnight in a container of white vinegar *(above, right)*, taking care not to wet any electrical terminal or wire. If necessary, gently scrub off stubborn mineral deposits using an old toothbrush. Rinse the heating element with water and dry it with a clean cloth. Reassemble the heating unit and reinstall it in the reservoir.

CLEANING A PORTABLE HUMIDIFIER

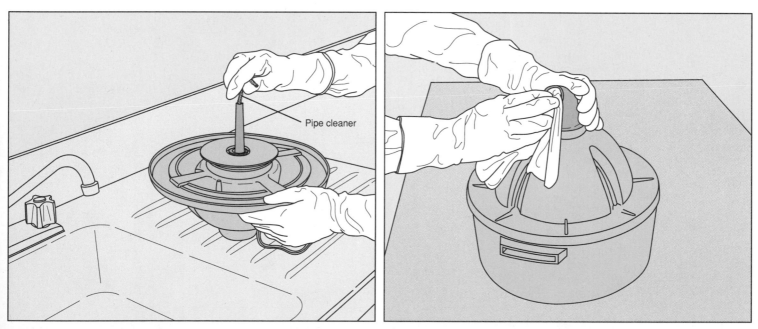

Cleaning a cool-mist humidifier. Unplug the humidifier, then take the top off it. Wearing rubber gloves, mix a solution of 1/4 cup of laundry bleach and a few squirts of dishwashing liquid per gallon of warm water. Wipe the interior of the reservoir and the top using a clean, white, lint-free cloth dampened with the solution; scrub the intake tube using a pipe cleaner soaked with the solution *(above, left)*. Fill the reservoir halfway with solution and reinstall the top, then block the mist outlet with a cloth *(above, right)*. Plug in the humidifier and let it run for 1 hour, keeping the mist from escaping. Unplug the humidifier and remove the top to empty the reservoir, then fill it with water and repeat the procedure. Rinse the interior of the reservoir and the top using a clean cloth dampened with water, then dry them with another cloth. Allow the humidifier to sit for 24 hours before using it again.

CLEANING A PORTABLE HUMIDIFIER (continued)

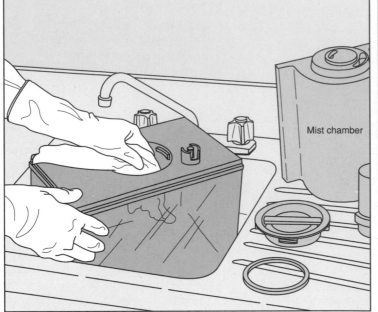

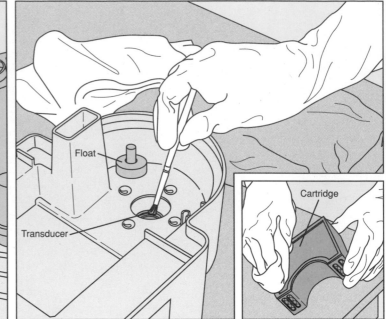

Cleaning an ultrasonic humidifier. Unplug the humidifier, then disassemble it for cleaning following the manufacturer's instructions. Wear rubber gloves to mix a cleaning solution recommended by the humidifier manufacturer. Wipe the surfaces of the reservoir *(above, left)*, the mist chamber, the directional nozzle and any gaskets or covers using a clean, white, lint-free cloth dampened with the solution, then rinse them thoroughly with water and wipe them dry using another cloth. Fill the reservoir with solution and let it sit for 1 hour, then empty it. Gently scrub the transducer *(above, right)* and the float using a soft-bristled artist's brush soaked with the solution. Rinse the transducer, the float and the reservoir thoroughly with water, then wipe them dry using a clean cloth. Clean the demineralization cartridge by gently wiping it using a clean cloth dampened with warm water *(inset)*—not the solution. Reassemble the humidifier before using it again.

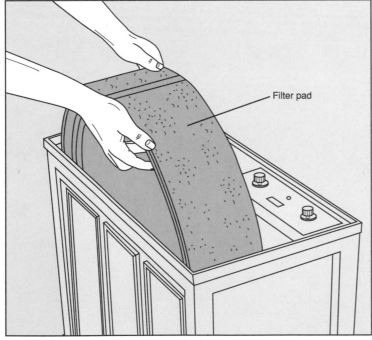

Cleaning a drum-type console humidifier. Turn off and unplug the humidifier, then disassemble it for cleaning following the manufacturer's instructions. Remove the cover and lift out the drum *(above, left)*, then detach the filter pad from it and take out the reservoir. Soak the filter pad in a solution of 2 quarts of white vinegar per gallon of water until any mineral deposits are dissolved, then rinse it thoroughly with water and wring it almost dry; if stubborn mineral deposits remain, buy a new filter pad. Wearing rubber gloves, mix a solution of 1/2 cup of laundry bleach and 2 tablespoons of dishwashing liquid per gallon of water. Wipe the surfaces of the reservoir *(above, right)*, the drum and the cover using a clean, white, lint-free cloth dampened with the solution. If necessary, scrub off stubborn mineral deposits using a green scrubbing pad soaked with white vinegar. Rinse the reservoir, the drum and the cover thoroughly with water, then wipe them dry using another cloth. Reassemble the humidifier before plugging it back in.

CLEANING A CENTRAL HUMIDIFIER

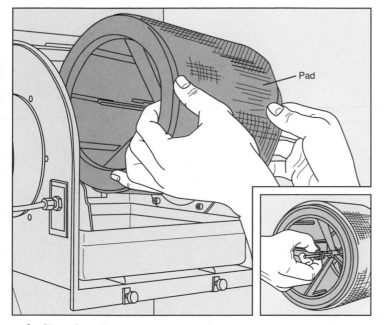

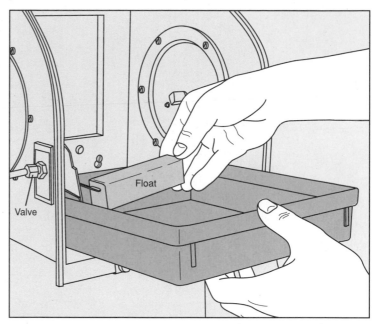

1 **Cleaning the evaporator pad.** Shut off power to the heating and cooling system *(page 93)*, then disassemble the humidifier for cleaning following the manufacturer's instructions. Remove the cover and lift out the drum *(above)*, then pull the retaining clip off its shaft *(inset)* to separate it and free the pad. Soak the pad in a solution of 2 quarts of white vinegar per gallon of water until any mineral deposits are dissolved, then rinse it thoroughly with water and wring it almost dry; if stubborn mineral deposits remain, buy a new pad.

2 **Cleaning the evaporator tray.** With the water supply valve turned off, lift the float and pull out the tray *(above)*. Soak the tray in a solution of 2 quarts of white vinegar per gallon of water for a few hours, then wipe it using a clean, white, lint-free cloth. If necessary, scrub off stubborn mineral deposits using a green scrubbing pad. Rinse the tray thoroughly with water, then wipe it dry using another cloth. Reassemble the humidifier and turn on the water supply valve before restoring power to the heating and cooling system.

CLEANING A FURNACE FILTER

Cleaning a filter element. Turn off the furnace and shut off power to it *(page 93)*. Remove the filter element following the manufacturer's instructions for the furnace, sliding it out of its slot between the return duct and the blower *(left)* or removing the access panel to pull it out of the furnace interior. Hold the filter element up to a strong light to inspect it for dirt. If the light is nearly or completely blocked by the filter element, replace it if it is of fiberglass; wash it if it is of metal or plastic using a garden hose fitted with a high-pressure nozzle, then let it drip dry. Install the filter element and put back any access panel removed before restoring power to the furnace and turning it back on.

CLEANING A FURNACE FILTER (continued)

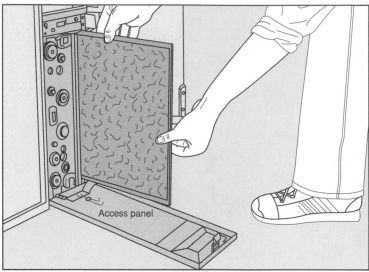

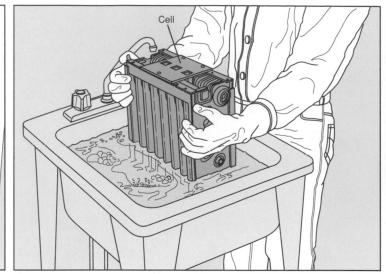

Cleaning an electronic filter and cell. Turn off the furnace and shut off power to it *(page 93)*. Remove the filter and cell following the manufacturer's instructions for the furnace; wait for any time specified to allow for discharging. Open the access panel, then pull the filter out of its sleeve *(above, left)* and slide the cell out of its cavity. Wearing rubber gloves, soak the filter in a solution of 2 tablespoons of dishwasing liquid per gallon of water; soak the cell in a solution of 2 table- spoons of dishwasher detergent per gallon of warm water *(above, right)*. After about 30 minutes, remove the filter and the cell from their solutions, then rinse them thoroughly with water and let them dry. Clean the cavity and sleeve of the furnace using a vacuum cleaner and a crevice attachment, then reinstall the cell and the filter. Close the access panel before restoring power to the furnace and turning it back on.

CLEANING A WINDOW AIR CONDITIONER

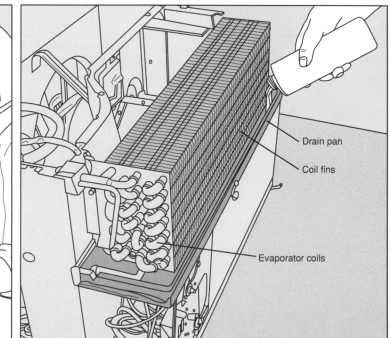

Cleaning the air conditioner. Turn off and unplug the air conditioner, then disassemble it for cleaning following the manufacturer's instructions. Remove the front panel *(above, left)* and unfasten any retaining clips to lift out the filter. Wearing rubber gloves, mix a solution of 1/2 cup of laundry bleach per gallon of warm water. Soak the filter in the solution for about 30 minutes, then rinse it thoroughly with water *(inset)* and let it dry. Work with a helper to set the air conditioner onto a drop-cloth on a sturdy work surface. Remove the housing, then clean the condenser and evaporator coils and coil fins using a vacuum cleaner and a soft brush attachment. To clean any drain pan, plug the drain hole and place a bucket under it. Slowly fill the drain pan with solution *(above, right)* and let it sit for about 30 minutes, then unplug the drain hole to drain it. If mineral deposits remain on the filter or the drain pan, repeat the procedure using a solution of 2 quarts of white vinegar per gallon of warm water until they dissolve. Reassemble and reinstall the air conditioner before plugging it back in.

CLEANING A CENTRAL AIR CONDITIONER OR HEAT PUMP

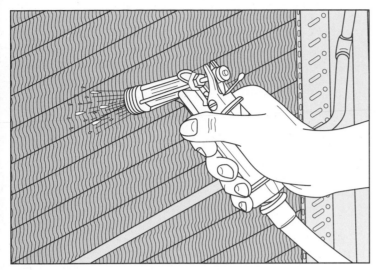

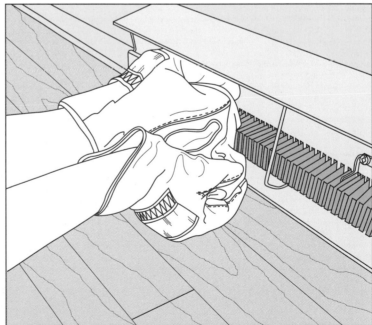

Evaporator coils

Drain pan

1 **Cleaning the condenser unit.** Shut off power to the condenser unit *(page 93)* and disassemble it for cleaning following the manufacturer's instructions, usually by removing the top panel, the side panel and the coil guard. Wash dirt and particles off the condenser fins using a garden hose fitted with a high-pressure nozzle, spraying first outward from inside the unit, then inward from outside the unit *(above)*. If necessary, gently scrub off stubborn particles using a soft-bristled brush, stroking in the direction of the fins. If the fins are heavily coated with grease, have them professionally steam-cleaned. Reassemble the condenser unit before restoring power to it.

2 **Cleaning the evaporator unit.** Shut off power to the furnace *(page 93)* and follow the manufacturer's instructions to gain access to the evaporator coils, usually by removing the side panels. Wearing rubber gloves, wash dirt and particles off the evaporator coils by scrubbing them gently using a soft-bristled brush soaked with water, then let them dry. To clean the drain pan, fill it with water using a garden hose *(above)* and add 1/2 cup of laundry bleach, then let it empty; if mineral deposits remain, repeat the procedure using a commercial scale remover following the manufacturer's instructions. Reinstall the side panels before restoring power to the furnace.

CLEANING A BASEBOARD HEATER

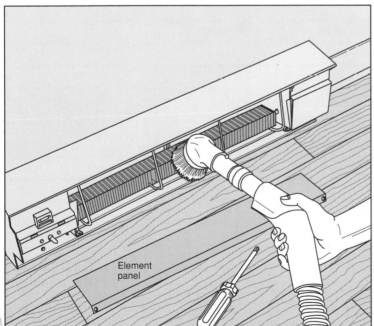

Element panel

Cleaning the heater. Turn off the heater and shut off power to it *(page 93)*, then follow the manufacturer's instructions to remove the element panel. Clean dust and particles off the fins of the heating element using a vacuum cleaner and a soft brush attachment *(above, left)*; if necessary, dislodge stubborn particles by scrubbing gently in the direction of the fins with a soft-bristled brush. Wearing work gloves, carefully wipe the fins using a clean, white, lint-free cloth dampened with

a solution of 2 tablespoons of dishwashing liquid per quart of water *(above, right)*. Rinse the fins using a clean cloth dampened with water, then wipe them dry with another cloth. Clean the exterior surfaces of the heater the same way; if necessary, gently scrub off stubborn particles using a white scrubbing pad. Reinstall the element panel before restoring power to the heater.

FIXTURES

Of the wide variety of fixtures that can be found in the typical home, few present a serious cleaning challenge. General dusting or vacuuming on a routine basis is usually the only cleaning task needed for common household fixtures such as window draperies, blinds and shades, table lamps and ceiling- or wall-mounted light fixtures, and ceiling fans. Often, the biggest challenge in the cleaning of household fixtures can be finding the motivation; since the payoff earned for its performance is usually less than the price paid for its neglect, there can be a temptation to shirk the cleaning of fixtures in favor of the cleaning of other surfaces more immediately gratifying and visually rewarding: the furniture, the carpets, the floors or the windows, for example.

However, while the general dusting or vacuuming of your household fixtures on a routine basis may go quietly unnoticed to others, keep in mind that their long-term attractiveness and functioning can depend on it. The dust that can accumulate on a fixture is a magnet for airborne particles of dirt, grease and other matter, a combination that inevitably leads to the soiling or staining of surfaces and the malfunctioning of mechanical parts. Refer to the Troubleshooting Guide (below) for procedures on the cleaning of typical household fixtures. For basic guidelines and strategy on cleaning household fixtures, read the Cleaning Tips (page 111). Consult Tools & Techniques (page 116) for general information on cleaning supplies and techniques.

Window draperies are among the greatest dust traps in the home, the weave of their fabric readily collecting and holding dust; include the dusting or vacuuming of them at least once a month (page 112) as part of your cleaning strategy for each room of your home. Accord similar attention to window blinds of fabric (page 112), plastic or aluminum (page 113) and window shades of vinyl or paper (page 113), all equally as attractive to dust. Likewise dust or vacuum the table lamps (page 114) and light fixtures (page 114), as well as any ceiling fan (page 115). Follow any specific cleaning instructions supplied by the manufacturer for your household fixtures; often, there is a tag attached to the back of window draperies, blinds or shades.

As a rule, wash your window draperies, blinds and shades once every year, preferably in early spring before opened windows stir up dust trapped indoors during the winter. Some draperies can be washed in the clothes washer; others must be dry-cleaned. Horizontal blinds of plastic or aluminum often are easily taken down for washing outdoors; blinds of fabric or vertical blinds of plastic or aluminum can be washed in place. Treat soiled spots or stains as soon as they are detected, testing your cleaning agent and method (page 111); delicate material such as paper usually can be cleaned with an art gum eraser or a "dry"-cleaning pad. Never hesitate to ask for cleaning advice from the fixture manufacturer or retailer or a cleaning professional.

TROUBLESHOOTING GUIDE

PROBLEM	PROCEDURE
WINDOW DRAPERY	
Dust	Clean everyday dust off drapery (p. 112) □○
Soiling or stain	Treat soiled or stained spot of drapery (p. 112) □◐
WINDOW BLINDS	
Dust	Clean everyday dust off fabric blinds (p. 112) □○; clean everyday dust off plastic or aluminum blinds (p. 113) □○
Soiling or stain	Treat soiled or stained spot of fabric blinds (p. 112) □◐; wash soiled or stained plastic or aluminum blinds (p. 113) □◐
WINDOW SHADE	
Dust	Clean everyday dust off fabric, vinyl or paper shade (p. 113) □○
Soiling or stain	Treat soiled or stained spot of fabric, vinyl or paper shade (p. 113) □◐
TABLE LAMP	
Dust or soiling	Clean lamp shade and base (p. 114) □○
LIGHT FIXTURE	
Dust or soiling	Clean fixture with standard globe and base (p. 114) □○; clean crystal-ornamented chandelier (p. 114) □○
CEILING FAN	
Dust or soiling	Clean ceiling fan (p. 115) □○

DEGREE OF DIFFICULTY: □ Easy ◪ Moderate ■ Complex
ESTIMATED TIME: ○ Less than 1 hour ◐ 1 to 3 hours ● Over 3 hours

CLEANING TIPS

• Establish a weekly and seasonal household-maintenance routine; in general, dust or vacuum the fixtures of each room at least once every month—before the furniture *(page 66)* and the carpet *(page 56)* or the floor *(page 44)*.

• Before vacuuming a fixture, set up the vacuum cleaner properly. Empty or change the dust bag if it is more than half full. Ensure that all attachments are clean and unclogged.

• Follow cleaning and maintenance instructions for the fixture supplied by the manufacturer; with window draperies, blinds or shades, for example, there is often a tag attached to the back.

• Keep on hand a well-stocked spot-cleaning kit that includes a supply of clean, white, lint-free cloths and commercial spot removers such as "dry"-cleaning pads.

• Follow the cleaning instructions supplied by the manufacturer for any commercial cleaning product you use.

• Test any cleaning agent and method you use on an inconspicuous spot of the surface—even if you are only dabbing or wiping using a cloth dampened with water.

• To protect a surface from a cleaning agent, use a dropcloth or plastic sheeting. Wipe up any stray cleaning agent immediately with a clean, white, lint-free cloth.

• When you are trying to lift a stain, always start with the mildest cleaning agent recommended, progressing to a stronger cleaning agent only if necessary. Make several attempts to lift a stain with a cleaning agent before abandoning it; allow each application of it to dry thoroughly before repeating an application of it.

• Do not hesitate to ask for cleaning advice from the manufacturer, retailer or installer of the fixture or a cleaning professional.

• Store cleaning agents well out of the reach of children; dispose of any leftover cleaning agent safely.

TESTING A CLEANING AGENT AND METHOD

Testing the cleaning agent. Always test a cleaning agent on an inconspicuous spot. Wearing rubber gloves, moisten a clean, white, lint-free cloth with the cleaning agent solution and dab it lightly onto the test spot *(above)*; ensure that each color of a fabric is included. Allow the test spot to dry thoroughly. If the test spot bleeds, discolors or otherwise is damaged, try a milder form of the cleaning agent or a different cleaning agent, testing it first.

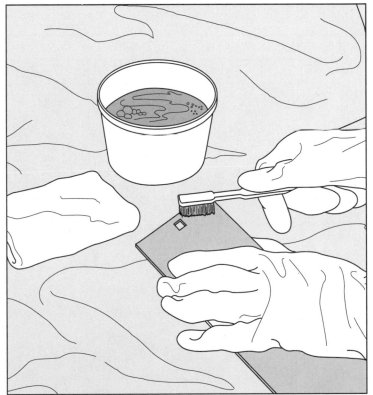

Testing the cleaning method. Always test your cleaning method on an inconspicuous spot. With a toothbrush, for example, wear rubber gloves to load it with the cleaning agent, then try gently scrubbing with it *(above)*, gradually increasing your pressure. If the test spot is damaged, try scrubbing more gently or change to a cleaning tool or method that is less abrasive. With a cloth, for example, try rubbing lightly; if the test spot is damaged, try wiping gently or using a dabbing motion.

CLEANING WINDOW DRAPERIES

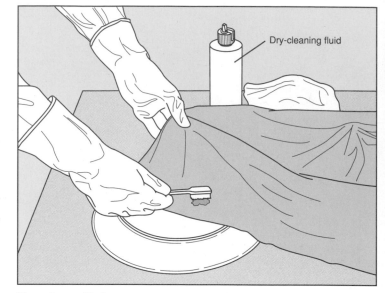

Dry-cleaning fluid

Vacuuming everyday dust. Close the draperies and clean panel by panel across them using an upholstery attachment. Fit the vacuum cleaner with an extension arm and open the suction control flap, then start at a top corner of the draperies and draw the upholstery attachment slowly down them. When the upholstery attachment reaches eye level, lift it off the draperies to reposition it at the top of them and make another pass, overlapping the first pass slightly. After vacuuming the top of the draperies, remove the extension arm to vacuum from eye level to the bottom of the draperies the same way *(above)*.

Treating soiled spots. Check the draperies for a cleaning label; some types can be washed in a clothes washer. Otherwise, take down the draperies and set them on a work surface, placing a plate upside down under the stain. Wearing rubber gloves, tamp the stain using an old toothbrush moistened with dry-cleaning fluid. Test your cleaning agent and method *(page 111)*. Moisten the toothbrush with the dry-cleaning fluid, then gently tamp the stain *(above)*; avoid any scrubbing motion. Blot the stain using a clean, white, lint-free cloth. Continue tamping and blotting the same way until the stain is removed.

CLEANING WINDOW BLINDS: FABRIC

Vacuuming everyday dust. Close the blinds and adjust the vanes for greatest access to one side of them. Clean the tracks and the vanes using a vacuum cleaner and a soft brush attachment; fit the vacuum cleaner with an extension arm, if necessary. Start at the top of each vane and draw the brush attachment slowly down to the bottom of it, steadying it with one hand *(above)*. After vacuuming one side of each vane, adjust the vanes for greatest access to the other side of them, then vacuum the other side of each vane.

Treating soiled spots. Check the blinds for a cleaning label; some types require special cleaning procedures. Otherwise, wear rubber gloves to try removing the stain using a solution of 1/8 cup of white dishwashing liquid per quart of water and a clean, white, lint-free cloth. Test your cleaning agent and method *(page 111)*. Moisten the cloth with the solution and wring it, then gently wipe the surface *(above)*; avoid any scrubbing motion. Rinse the surface using another cloth dampened with water and let it dry.

CLEANING WINDOW BLINDS: PLASTIC OR ALUMINUM

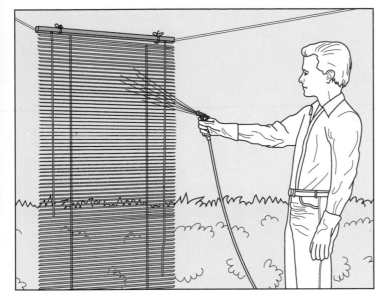

Dropcloth

Cleaning horizontal blinds. Clean dust off the blinds using a feather duster or a vacuum cleaner and a soft brush attachment, adjusting the vanes in turn for greatest access to each side of them. To wash the blinds, take them down and hang them outdoors on a sturdy rope tied between two trees. Wearing rubber gloves, mist each side of the blinds with water using a garden hose fitted with a spray nozzle *(above)*. Mix a solution of 1/8 cup of white dishwashing liquid per quart of water and apply it to the blinds using a soft-bristled fiber brush. Rinse the blinds with water using the garden hose and let them dry.

Cleaning vertical blinds. Clean dust off the blinds using a feather duster or a vacuum cleaner and a soft brush attachment, adjusting the vanes in turn for greatest access to each side of them. To wash the blinds, wear rubber gloves to mix a solution of 1/8 cup of white dishwashing liquid per quart of water. Using a dropcloth to catch drips, apply the solution to the blinds with a clean, white, lint-free cloth. Moisten the cloth with the solution and wring it, then wipe from top to bottom in turn along each side of the vanes *(above)*. Rinse the blinds using a clean cloth dampened with water and let them dry.

CLEANING WINDOW SHADES: FABRIC, VINYL OR PAPER

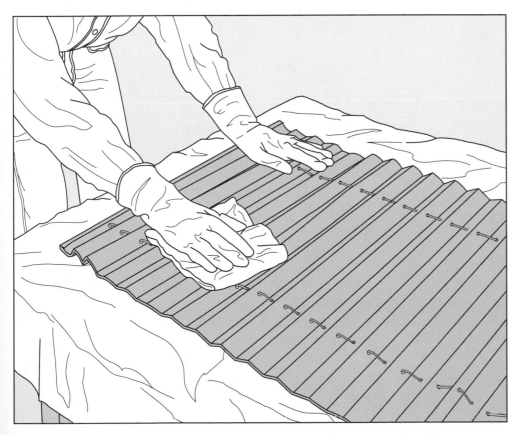

Cleaning a roller or pleated shade.
Clean dust off the shade using a vacuum cleaner and a soft brush attachment. To wash the shade or treat a soiled spot on it, take it down and set it on a work surface; if necessary, protect the work surface with a dropcloth. For a shade of fabric or vinyl, wear rubber gloves to mix a solution of 1/8 cup of white dishwashing liquid per quart of water and apply it using a clean, white, lint-free cloth. For a shade of fabric, test your cleaning agent and method *(page 111)*. Moisten the cloth with the solution and wring it, then wipe from end to end in turn along each side of the shade *(left)*. Rinse the shade using a clean cloth dampened with water and let it dry. For a shade of paper, rub gently using an art gum eraser or a draftsman's "dry"-cleaning pad—a powder-filled, eraser-type pad for artwork, available at a stationery or art supply store. Remove traces of the eraser or pad using a soft-bristled brush.

CLEANING TABLE LAMPS

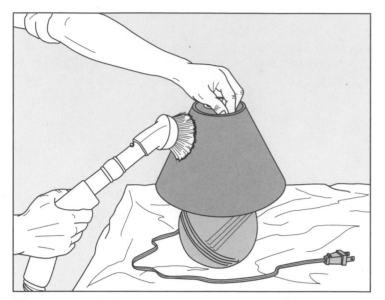

Cleaning the shade. Turn off and unplug the lamp. Steadying the shade by its frame, clean dust off it using a vacuum cleaner and a soft brush attachment *(above)* or a feather duster. To wash the shade, wear rubber gloves to mix a solution of 1/8 cup of white dishwashing liquid per quart of water and apply it using a dampened, clean, white, lint-free cloth. For a soiled spot on the shade, rub gently using an art gum eraser or a draftsman's "dry"-cleaning pad—a powder-filled, eraser-type pad. Test your cleaning agent and method *(page 111)*. Rinse off solution using a clean cloth dampened with water. Remove traces of eraser or pad using a soft-bristled brush.

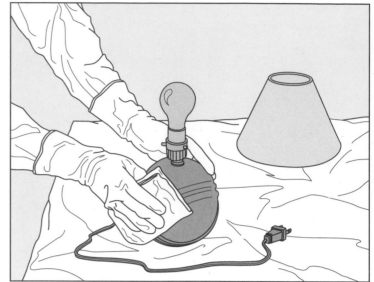

Cleaning the base. Turn off and unplug the lamp, then clean dust off the base using a vacuum cleaner and a soft brush attachment or a feather duster. To wash the base, wear rubber gloves to mix a solution of 1/8 cup of white dishwashing liquid per quart of water. Take the shade off the base and apply the solution with a clean, white, lint-free cloth, moistening and wringing it before wiping with it *(above)*; work carefully to avoid wetting the bulb or other electrical parts. Rinse the base using a clean cloth dampened with water, then dry it with another cloth. If necessary, polish the base using a commercial polish recommended for the material.

CLEANING LIGHT FIXTURES

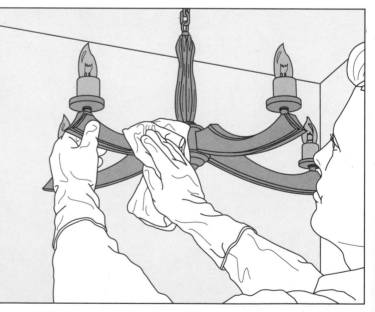

Cleaning standard globes and bases. Turn off the fixture and let it cool. Using a stepladder *(page 122)* to reach comfortably and safely, wear safety goggles to gently clean dust off the fixture with a feather duster; steady the fixture with one hand, if necessary. To wash standard globes and bases, wear rubber gloves to mix a solution of 1/8 cup of white dishwashing liquid per quart of water and apply it using a clean, white, lint-free cloth. Remove each globe for washing in the solution

(above, left) and to wash the base; moisten the cloth with the solution and wring it before wiping the base with it *(above, right)*, working carefully to avoid wetting any bulb or other electrical parts. Rinse each globe and the base using a clean cloth dampened with water, then dry them with another cloth. If necessary, polish the base using a commercial polish recommended for the material.

CLEANING LIGHT FIXTURES (continued)

Cleaning crystal-ornamented chandeliers. Turn off the fixture and let it cool. Using a stepladder *(page 122)* to reach comfortably and safely, wear safety goggles to gently clean dust off the fixture with a feather duster *(above, left)*. To wash a crystal-ornamented chandelier without disassembling it, wear rubber gloves to mix a solution of 1 1/2 cups of methyl alcohol per quart of water in a spray container; or, use a commercial chandelier spray cleaner following the manufacturer's instructions. Cover each bulb using a plastic bag and a rubber band.

Protect surfaces below the chandelier with a dropcloth or plastic sheeting. Mist the chandelier with the solution *(above, right)*, then wipe its surfaces in turn using a clean, white, lint-free cloth; vigorously buff each crystal until it shines, being careful not to tug on it. Continue the same way, dampening a cloth with solution to apply more of it and changing to clean cloths as needed. If necessary, polish the base or other surface using a commercial polish recommended for the material.

CLEANING CEILING FANS

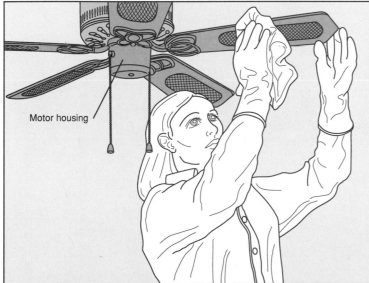

Motor housing

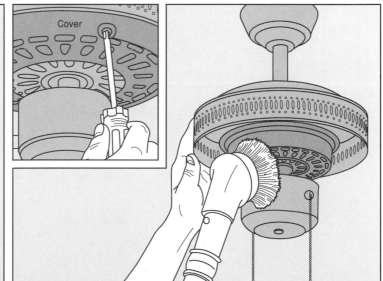

Cover

Cleaning everyday dust and dirt. Clean the blades and other exterior surfaces every month and the interior of the motor housing each season. Turn off the fan and shut off electrical power to it at the service panel. To clean the blades and other exterior surfaces, mix a solution of 1/8 cup of white dishwashing liquid per quart of water; for blades of wood, use a commercial liquid polish for wood following the manufacturer's instructions. Using a stepladder *(page 122)* to reach comfortably and safely, moisten a clean, white, lint-free cloth with the solution, then wipe the blades *(above, left)* and other exterior surfaces

in turn; work carefully to avoid wetting any electrical parts. Rinse the blades and other exterior surfaces using a clean cloth dampened with water and wipe them dry with another cloth. If necessary, polish any exterior surface using a commercial polish recommended for the material. To clean the interior of the motor housing, follow the manufacturer's instructions to remove the blades and take the cover off the motor housing *(inset)*. Vacuum the interior of the motor housing with a vacuum cleaner and a soft brush attachment *(above, right)*; wipe any surface of the motor housing that is hard to reach with a dry cloth.

TOOLS & TECHNIQUES

This chapter introduces the basic tools that are used for home cleaning and stain removal *(below)*, as well as special equipment that you may need to obtain at a tool rental center *(page 118)*. "Green"-cleaning tips *(page 118)* are provided to help you minimize the amount of toxic waste that can be generated by cleaning and stain removal, respecting the health of the environment as well as of your family and you. The cleaning and stain removal chart *(page 119)* is designed for quick-reference in choosing a cleaning agent suited to the job from the wide array of products available.

For the best results in cleaning and stain removal, always use the tool and cleaning agent recommended for the job—and be sure to apply the cleaning agent and use the tool correctly. Wear the proper safety gear: rubber gloves or work gloves to protect your hands; safety goggles to protect your eyes; a respirator to prevent the inhalation of toxic vapors; a dust mask to prevent the inhalation of particles. Take the time to care for your tools, reusing them whenever possible; clean your tools properly after each use and store them in a cool, dry location *(page 120)*. Dispose of or store cleaning agents safely *(page 121)*.

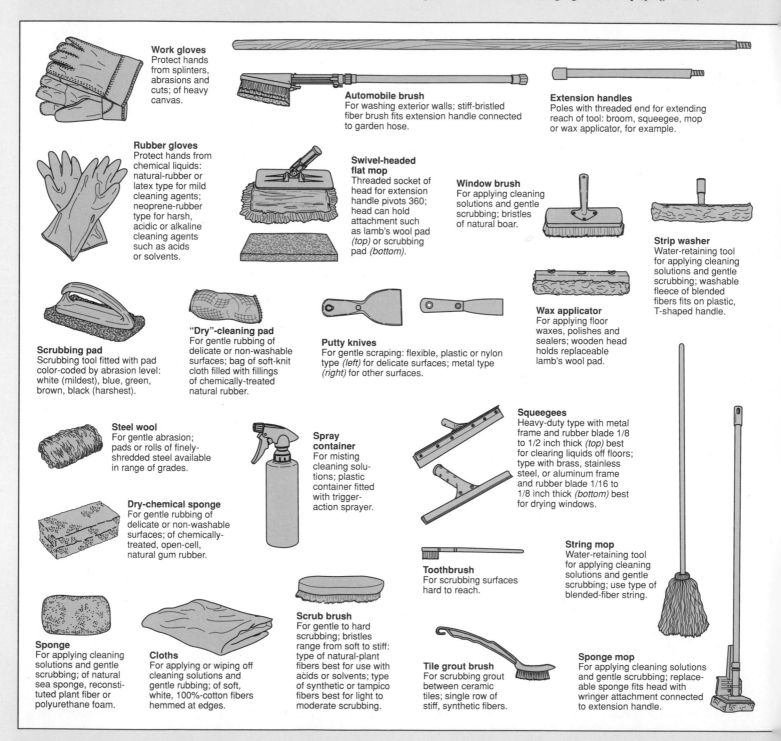

Work gloves
Protect hands from splinters, abrasions and cuts; of heavy canvas.

Automobile brush
For washing exterior walls; stiff-bristled fiber brush fits extension handle connected to garden hose.

Extension handles
Poles with threaded end for extending reach of tool: broom, squeegee, mop or wax applicator, for example.

Rubber gloves
Protect hands from chemical liquids: natural-rubber or latex type for mild cleaning agents; neoprene-rubber type for harsh, acidic or alkaline cleaning agents such as acids or solvents.

Swivel-headed flat mop
Threaded socket of head for extension handle pivots 360; head can hold attachment such as lamb's wool pad *(top)* or scrubbing pad *(bottom)*.

Window brush
For applying cleaning solutions and gentle scrubbing; bristles of natural boar.

Strip washer
Water-retaining tool for applying cleaning solutions and gentle scrubbing; washable fleece of blended fibers fits on plastic, T-shaped handle.

Scrubbing pad
Scrubbing tool fitted with pad color-coded by abrasion level: white (mildest), blue, green, brown, black (harshest).

"Dry"-cleaning pad
For gentle rubbing of delicate or non-washable surfaces; bag of soft-knit cloth filled with fillings of chemically-treated natural rubber.

Putty knives
For gentle scraping: flexible, plastic or nylon type *(left)* for delicate surfaces; metal type *(right)* for other surfaces.

Wax applicator
For applying floor waxes, polishes and sealers; wooden head holds replaceable lamb's wool pad.

Steel wool
For gentle abrasion; pads or rolls of finely-shredded steel available in range of grades.

Spray container
For misting cleaning solutions; plastic container fitted with trigger-action sprayer.

Squeegees
Heavy-duty type with metal frame and rubber blade 1/8 to 1/2 inch thick *(top)* best for clearing liquids off floors; type with brass, stainless steel, or aluminum frame and rubber blade 1/16 to 1/8 inch thick *(bottom)* best for drying windows.

Dry-chemical sponge
For gentle rubbing of delicate or non-washable surfaces; of chemically-treated, open-cell, natural gum rubber.

String mop
Water-retaining tool for applying cleaning solutions and gentle scrubbing; use type of blended-fiber string.

Toothbrush
For scrubbing surfaces hard to reach.

Sponge
For applying cleaning solutions and gentle scrubbing; of natural sea sponge, reconstituted plant fiber or polyurethane foam.

Cloths
For applying or wiping off cleaning solutions and gentle rubbing; of soft, white, 100%-cotton fibers hemmed at edges.

Scrub brush
For gentle to hard scrubbing; bristles range from soft to stiff: type of natural-plant fibers best for use with acids or solvents; type of synthetic or tampico fibers best for light to moderate scrubbing.

Tile grout brush
For scrubbing grout between ceramic tiles; single row of stiff, synthetic fibers.

Sponge mop
For applying cleaning solutions and gentle scrubbing; replaceable sponge fits head with wringer attachment connected to extension handle.

Follow common-sense rules for home cleaning and stain removal. Set up properly for the job, assembling the tools and supplies needed. Move heavy furniture or appliances carefully to avoid injury *(page 124)*. Protect surfaces from contact with a cleaning agent by covering them with dropcloths or plastic sheeting. Resist the temptation to overreach; set up a ladder or scaffolding to work comfortably and safely at heights *(page 122)*. Outdoors, plug a power tool only into an outlet protected by a ground-fault circuit interrupter (GFCI). Read the safety information in the Emergency Guide *(page 8)*.

Develop a strategy for cleaning and stain removal in your home that is appropriate to its specific features and your lifestyle. Establish daily, weekly, monthly, seasonal and yearly routines, scheduling tasks of manageable groupings in a sensible sequence at a reasonable pace; indoors, you may wish to vary your approach between cleaning room by room and cleaning like-items together. Keep cleaning and maintenance instructions supplied by the manufacturer for the items of your home, simplifying the job of cleaning and stain removal—and reducing the risk of inadvertent damage.

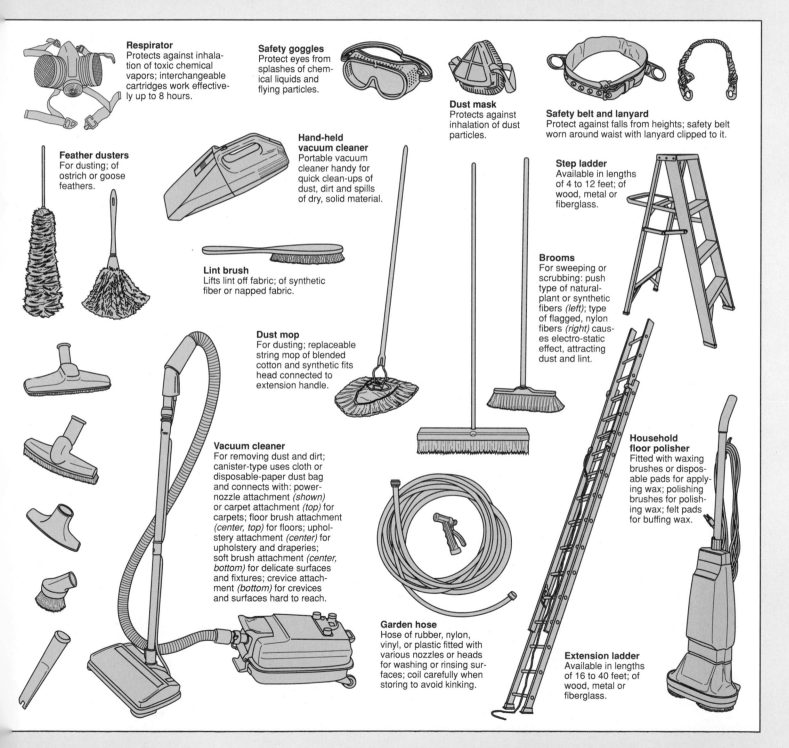

Respirator
Protects against inhalation of toxic chemical vapors; interchangeable cartridges work effectively up to 8 hours.

Safety goggles
Protect eyes from splashes of chemical liquids and flying particles.

Dust mask
Protects against inhalation of dust particles.

Safety belt and lanyard
Protect against falls from heights; safety belt worn around waist with lanyard clipped to it.

Feather dusters
For dusting; of ostrich or goose feathers.

Hand-held vacuum cleaner
Portable vacuum cleaner handy for quick clean-ups of dust, dirt and spills of dry, solid material.

Step ladder
Available in lengths of 4 to 12 feet; of wood, metal or fiberglass.

Lint brush
Lifts lint off fabric; of synthetic fiber or napped fabric.

Brooms
For sweeping or scrubbing: push type of natural-plant or synthetic fibers *(left)*; type of flagged, nylon fibers *(right)* causes electro-static effect, attracting dust and lint.

Dust mop
For dusting; replaceable string mop of blended cotton and synthetic fits head connected to extension handle.

Vacuum cleaner
For removing dust and dirt; canister-type uses cloth or disposable-paper dust bag and connects with: power-nozzle attachment *(shown)* or carpet attachment *(top)* for carpets; floor brush attachment *(center, top)* for floors; upholstery attachment *(center)* for upholstery and draperies; soft brush attachment *(center, bottom)* for delicate surfaces and fixtures; crevice attachment *(bottom)* for crevices and surfaces hard to reach.

Household floor polisher
Fitted with waxing brushes or disposable pads for applying wax; polishing brushes for polishing wax; felt pads for buffing wax.

Garden hose
Hose of rubber, nylon, vinyl, or plastic fitted with various nozzles or heads for washing or rinsing surfaces; coil carefully when storing to avoid kinking.

Extension ladder
Available in lengths of 16 to 40 feet; of wood, metal or fiberglass.

WORKING WITH RENTAL TOOLS

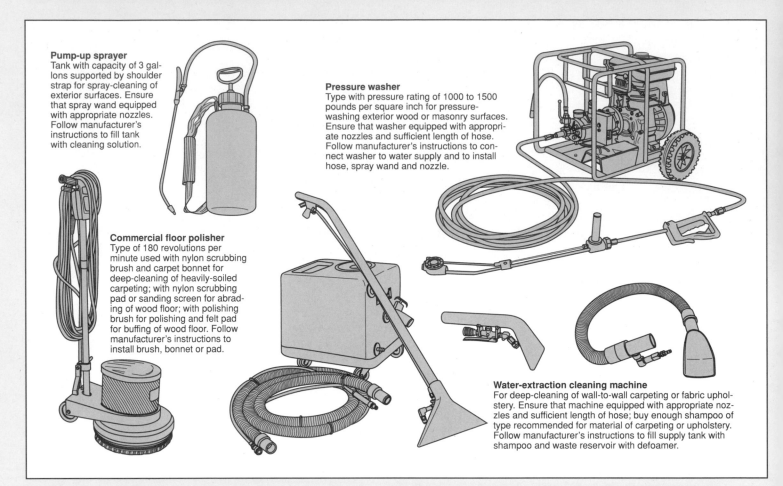

Pump-up sprayer
Tank with capacity of 3 gallons supported by shoulder strap for spray-cleaning of exterior surfaces. Ensure that spray wand equipped with appropriate nozzles. Follow manufacturer's instructions to fill tank with cleaning solution.

Pressure washer
Type with pressure rating of 1000 to 1500 pounds per square inch for pressure-washing exterior wood or masonry surfaces. Ensure that washer equipped with appropriate nozzles and sufficient length of hose. Follow manufacturer's instructions to connect washer to water supply and to install hose, spray wand and nozzle.

Commercial floor polisher
Type of 180 revolutions per minute used with nylon scrubbing brush and carpet bonnet for deep-cleaning of heavily-soiled carpeting; with nylon scrubbing pad or sanding screen for abrading of wood floor; with polishing brush for polishing and felt pad for buffing of wood floor. Follow manufacturer's instructions to install brush, bonnet or pad.

Water-extraction cleaning machine
For deep-cleaning of wall-to-wall carpeting or fabric upholstery. Ensure that machine equipped with appropriate nozzles and sufficient length of hose; buy enough shampoo of type recommended for material of carpeting or upholstery. Follow manufacturer's instructions to fill supply tank with shampoo and waste reservoir with defoamer.

"GREEN"-CLEANING

Cleaning tips for a healthy environment. Each time you work with a cleaning agent, you are adding a substance into the air, onto a surface or down the drain. Few cleaning agents qualify as dangerous to the natural environment in the amounts typically used by a household, but many commercial cleaning agents do contain substances that accumulate in the natural environment when we apply or dispose of them—especially if they are used carelessly or excessively. Follow the guidelines below to develop a "green"-cleaning strategy for your household that helps to protect the health of the natural environment:

• Reduce your need for strong cleaning agents that may contain substances harmful to the environment—and save yourself time and energy in the long run—by frequently spot-cleaning and light-cleaning using only water; or, if necessary, use a solution of a little dishwashing liquid and water.

• Avoid using too much of a cleaning agent. To remove heavy grime, for example, apply a mild cleaning agent and allow it to soak thoroughly, change to a technique or a tool that is abrasive, or simply repeat an application of a cleaning agent—these approaches usually work just as effectively as opting for the strongest cleaning agent possible.

• Most bacteria typically found in the home are harmless—and will quickly resettle on a surface even if it is cleaned with a strong "disinfectant" type of cleaning agent. Use common sense and judgment whenever you are cleaning; a cleaning agent used improperly or needlessly may be more harmful than the bacteria it is intended to thwart.

• Whenever possible, avoid using cleaning agents packaged in aerosol containers that may introduce toxins into the air or which may be inhaled; use cleaning agents packaged in pump-action spray containers instead.

• Safely dispose of leftover cleaning agents *(page 121)* to avoid putting undue strain on sewage treatment plants, septic systems and groundwater supplies.

• Avoid the use of paper towels; use cloths of 100% cotton made out of old bed linen or purchased at a hardware or clothing store.

• Keep on hand a supply of mild, biodegradable, household products that serve as effective cleaners for many surfaces and stains: washing soda, baking soda, borax, pure soap and soap flakes, white vinegar and clear ammonia.

CHOOSING CLEANING AGENTS

CLEANING AGENT	USE	CHARACTERISTICS
Abrasive cleaner	Removing stains from durable surfaces	Powder or liquid form sold under many brand names. Apply powder undissolved or mixed with water into paste; apply liquid undiluted. Available at supermarket.
All-purpose cleaner	Light to heavy cleaning of most interior and exterior surfaces	Powder or liquid (also spray) form sold under many brand names. Apply powder mixed with water; apply liquid undiluted or mixed with water; apply spray undiluted. Available at supermarket.
Ammonia	Heavy cleaning of glass surfaces	Liquid form. Type containing ammonium hydroxide in 2-3% solution recommended. Apply undiluted or mixed with water. Available at supermarket.
Ammonium sulfamate (herbicide)	Removing organic stains from exterior wood and masonry surfaces	Powder form. Apply mixed with water. Available at garden supply center.
Citrus-based solvent	Removing stains from durable surfaces	Liquid form. Type containing D-limonene in 86-90% solution recommended. Apply undiluted or mixed with water. Available at janitorial or chemical supply center.
Degreaser	Removing oily and greasy stains from durable surfaces	Liquid form sold under many brand names for specific cleaning problems and surfaces. Apply undiluted or mixed with water. Available at building or janitorial supply center.
Dishwashing liquid	Light cleaning of most interior and exterior surfaces	Liquid form sold under many brand names. Apply undiluted or mixed with water. Available at supermarket.
Dry-cleaning fluid	Removing stains from non-washable and delicate washable surfaces	Liquid form sold under many brand and chemical names. Type containing chlorinated hydrocarbon such as 1-1-1 trichloroethane and perchloroethane most common. Apply undiluted. Available at janitorial supply center.
Household laundry bleach (chlorine bleach)	Removing mildew from most durable interior and exterior surfaces	Liquid form sold under many brand names. Type containing sodium hypochlorite in 5-6% solution recommended. Apply mixed with water. Available at supermarket.
Hydrogen peroxide	Removing stains from delicate surfaces	Liquid form. Type containing peroxide of hydrogen in 3% solution recommended. Apply undiluted or mixed with water. Available at drugstore.
Laundry detergent	Removing stains from most surfaces; enzyme type for delicate surfaces	Powder form sold under many brand names; enzyme type identified on label. Apply undissolved or mixed with water. Available at supermarket.
Lemon juice	Removing stains from delicate surfaces	Liquid form. Citric acid in 3-5% solution is active ingredient. Apply undiluted. Available at supermarket.
Mineral spirits	Removing stains from wood surfaces	Liquid form. Apply undiluted. Available at building supply center.
Oxalic acid	Removing rust stains from exterior wood and masonry surfaces	Powder form. Pure type recommended. Apply mixed with water. Available at janitorial or chemical supply center.
Oxygen bleach	Removing mildew from exterior wood and masonry surfaces	Powder form sold under many chemical names. Type containing sodium perborate or sodium borate recommended. Apply mixed with water. Available at janitorial or chemical supply center.
Phosphoric acid	Removing rust stains and efflorescence from masonry surfaces	Liquid form. Type in 75-85% solution recommended. Apply mixed with water. Available at janitorial or chemical supply center.
Rubbing alcohol (isopropyl alcohol)	Removing stains from durable surfaces	Liquid form. Type containing isopropyl alcohol recommended. Apply undiluted. Available at drugstore.
Sodium bicarbonate (baking soda)	Removing stains from delicate surfaces; neutralizing acids	Powder form. Apply undissolved or mixed with water. Available at supermarket.
Sodium metasilicate (truck wash)	Removing organic stains from exterior wood and masonry surfaces	Powder form. Pure type recommended. Apply mixed with water. Available at automotive, janitorial or chemical supply center.
White vinegar	Light cleaning of glass surfaces; removing stains from durable surfaces	Liquid form. Type containing acetic acid in 4-8% solution recommended. Apply undiluted or mixed with water. Available at supermarket.

Using cleaning agents. A typical cleaning agent works on the soil of a surface by breaking down and dissolving it or by altering its pH or acidity, weakening its "hold" on the surface. By one or the other of these processes, the cleaning agents listed in the chart above will handle most cleaning problems with most household surfaces. Use the chart to help you identify the cleaning agent you may need for a job; if you need to buy a cleaning agent, use the chart to familiarize yourself with its characteristics and to determine where to buy it. For a special stain or surface not mentioned in the chart, consult the Troubleshooting Guide of the appropriate chapter in this book for further cleaning directions. Before buying or using a cleaning agent, check the manufacturer's instructions on the label to ensure that it can be used for your cleaning problem and type of surface; commercial cleaning agents contain a variety of ingredients specially to attack specific problems. Always follow any instructions on the label for mixing and applying the cleaning agent; avoid mixing different cleaning agents together unless specifically instructed by the manufacturer. Wear the appropriate safety gear for the cleaning job; when finished, safely dispose of leftover cleaning agents (page 121).

MEASURING CLEANING AGENTS

VOLUME	1 gallon	1 quart	1 pint	1 cup	1 fluid ounce	1 tablespoon
U.S. CONVERSION	128 fluid ounces 16 cups 8 pints 4 quarts	32 fluid ounces 4 cups 2 pints	16 fluid ounces 2 cups	8 fluid ounces 16 tablespoons	1/8 cup 2 tablespoons 6 teaspoons	1/2 fluid ounce 3 teaspoons
METRIC CONVERSION	3.8 liters	.95 liters 950 milliliters	.47 liters 470 milliliters	240 milliliters	30 milliliters	15 milliliters

Mixing cleaning solutions correctly. Before starting a cleaning job, make sure that you have enough of the needed cleaning agent on hand. Never use more than the recommended amount of a cleaning agent to mix a cleaning solution. Keep on hand a range of graduated measuring cups and measuring spoons for use in mixing cleaning solutions, referring to the chart above for help in making any necessary measurement conversions. For example, if you estimate that you need 2 gallons of cleaning solution for a job and you are directed to mix 1 cup of a recommended cleaning agent per gallon of water, you will need to buy a container holding at least 16 fluid ounces or 470 milliliters of the cleaning agent. Or, if you are directed to test the cleaning solution on the surface, you can mix a small test batch of the cleaning solution in the same proportions—in this example, mixing 1 tablespoon of the cleaning agent per cup of water. In another example, if you are directed to use 1/8 cup of a cleaning agent and you have no measuring cup, you can measure 2 tablespoons of the cleaning agent to achieve the exact same result.

CLEANING TOOLS

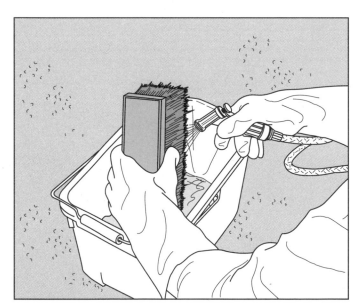

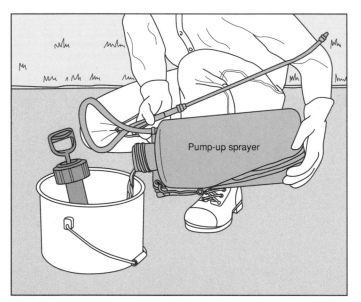

Washing tools. After each cleaning job, take the time to carefully clean and store your tools properly, keeping them ready and in good condition for the next cleaning job as well as minimizing safety hazards. To clean a tool such as a brush, pad or cloth, first soak it in any solvent recommended by the manufacturer of any commercial cleaning agent you used. Wearing rubber gloves, wash a tool such as a broom thoroughly using a solution of dishwashing liquid and water, then rinse it under running water *(above)* and wring or shake it out until it is almost dry; for a pad or cloth, wash and rinse it in the clothes washer. When your tools are dry, put them away.

Washing containers. After a cleaning job, empty and clean each container—such as a bucket or the tank of a pump-up sprayer. With a pump-up sprayer, first fill the tank and soak it with any solvent recommended by the manufacturer of any commercial cleaning product you used. Wearing rubber gloves, wash the tank thoroughly using a solution of dishwashing liquid and water, filling it and swishing it around, then emptying it *(above)*; pump solution through the hose and out of the spray nozzle to clean them. Repeat the procedure with water to rinse the tank, then let it dry. Dispose of waste solvent and water as you would any cleaning agent *(page 121)*.

SAFELY DISPOSING OF CLEANING AGENTS

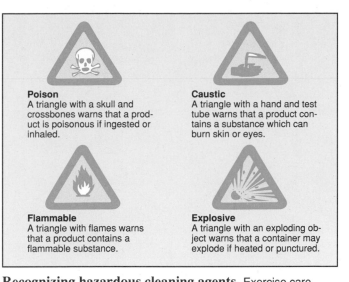

Poison
A triangle with a skull and crossbones warns that a product is poisonous if ingested or inhaled.

Caustic
A triangle with a hand and test tube warns that a product contains a substance which can burn skin or eyes.

Flammable
A triangle with flames warns that a product contains a flammable substance.

Explosive
A triangle with an exploding object warns that a container may explode if heated or punctured.

Recognizing hazardous cleaning agents. Exercise care in handling a leftover cleaning agent; it may be flammable, poisonous, caustic or explosive. Familiarize yourself with warning symbols that may appear on the label of a product *(above)* and take the time to minimize danger to you, your family and your neighborhood by discarding or storing a dangerous product safely. Keep children and pets away from the work area. Wear the proper safety gear: rubber gloves and long sleeves; safety goggles to protect your eyes from splashes; a respirator for a product that emits toxic vapors. Wash yourself, your clothes and your tools *(page 120)* thoroughly.

Neutralizing cleaning agents. Before discarding a strong acid or alkaline solution, follow any instructions on its product label to neutralize it, if possible; otherwise, discard it safely *(step below, left)*. To neutralize a solution, wear rubber gloves and safety goggles. For a bucket of an acid solution such as phosphoric acid or ammonium sulfamate, add the contents of a 1-pound box of sodium bicarbonate (baking soda) to it while stirring it with a stick *(above)*. For a bucket of an alkaline solution such as ammonia or sodium metasilicate, add 1 quart of white vinegar to it. Discard a neutralized solution as you would any other liquid.

Safely discarding cleaning agents. Discard a cleaning agent following any instructions on its product label. **Caution:** Never pour a hazardous product down the drain or throw it out with your other home refuse. If possible, return the product to its original container and cap it tightly. Otherwise, wear rubber gloves and safety goggles to funnel the product into a glass or plastic container *(above)*. Label the container and store it in a cool, dry spot until you can discard it safely. If your community has no designated Household Hazardous Waste Clean-up Day, consult your local department of environmental protection or public health for proper discarding procedures.

Safely storing cleaning agents. Store a cleaning agent following any instructions on its product label. If possible, store the product in its original container, tightly capped; do not remove the label. If you use another container, label it clearly. **Caution:** Never store a poisonous product in a container that might lead a child to mistake the contents for food or drink; never store a caustic product in a container that might be corroded by it. Store cleaning agents well out of the reach of children. If possible, use a lockable cabinet with sturdy shelves *(above)*. Ensure the storage site is located in a cool, dry area, away from sunlight and heat or ignition sources.

WORKING SAFELY WITH LADDERS OR SCAFFOLDS

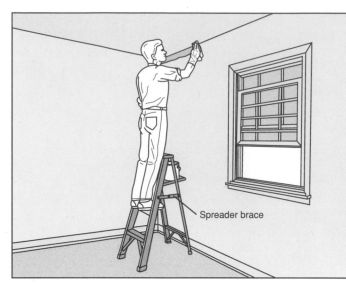

Siderail

Spreader brace

Using a stepladder. To work at a height up to 10 feet off the ground, use a stepladder; ensure that it is at least 2 feet longer than the height at which you need to stand. Do not use the step-ladder if a foot is worn, a step is loose or a spreader brace does not open fully. Set up the stepladder on a firm, level surface, opening its legs completely and locking its spreader braces. Indoors, set up the stepladder well away from stairs and overhead obstructions *(above, left)*; if necessary, place a rubber mat under the feet to keep them from slipping. Outdoors, if the ground is soft or uneven,

place boards under the feet *(above, right)*; if necessary, dig up the soil with a spade to level them. Pull down the bucket tray, placing tools and materials on it before climbing the stepladder. Face the stepladder to climb it, using both hands to grasp the steps rather than the siderails. Lean into the stepladder, keeping your hips be-tween the siderails; do not stand higher than the third step from the top. Never overreach or straddle the space between the stepladder and another surface; climb down and reposition the stepladder.

Fly section

Using an extension ladder. To work on the roof or at a height greater than 10 feet off the ground, use an extension ladder; to get onto the roof, ensure that the ladder can extend 3 feet above the edge of it. Place the unextended ladder on the ground perpendicular to the wall, its fly section on the bottom and its feet out from the wall or roof edge 1/4 of the height to which it will be raised. With a helper bracing the bottom of the ladder, raise the top of it above your head and walk under it toward the bottom of it, moving your hands along its rails and pushing it upright. With your helper holding the ladder upright, brace the bottom of it with your foot and pull on the rope to raise the fly section *(left)* to the height desired; slowly release the rope until the fly section locks. Carefully rest the ladder against the wall or roof edge. If the ground is soft or uneven, place a board under the feet, dig-ging up the soil with a spade to level it, if necessary. Drive a wooden stake 3 feet into the ground between the ladder and the wall, then tie each rail to it. Face the ladder to climb it, using both hands to grasp the rungs. If the ladder rests against a gutter, lay a 2-by-4 inside it to keep it from crush-ing under the ladder weight. Get on and off the roof safely *(page 123)*.

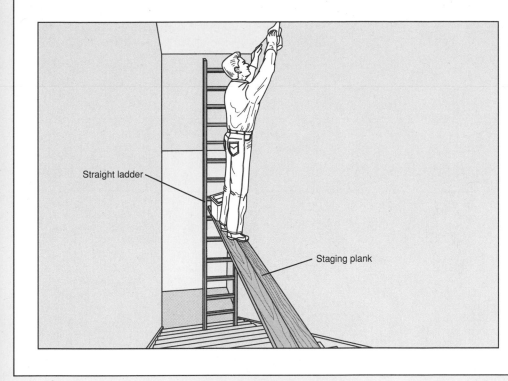

Using a scaffold. To work at heights along an exterior wall, rent scaffolding equipment at a tool rental center and follow the manufacturer's instructions to set it up. To work at heights over stairs, set up a temporary scaffold *(left)* using a sturdy, straight ladder and staging planks—available at a building supply center. Set up the ladder near the bottom of the stairs, its feet flat on a tread and butted against a riser; lean the top of it against an upper floor wall or the staircase balustrade, its rails flat and secure. Set up a pair of staging planks as a level working surface: one end of them flat on a tread and butted against a riser; the other end of them resting on and extending at least 1 foot beyond a rung of the ladder. If the distance spanned by the staging planks between the tread and the rung of the ladder is more than 6 feet, lay a second pair of staging planks on top of them for added strength and rigidity.

Straight ladder

Staging plank

WORKING SAFELY ON THE ROOF

Getting on and off the roof. Never work on the roof in wet, cold or windy weather. **Caution:** Do not work on a roof that slopes more than 6 inches per foot; have a professional do the job. Set up an extension ladder *(page 122)*. Wearing a tool belt to carry tools, have a helper steady the ladder, then climb it until your feet are on the rung at or just below the eave. Holding onto the top of the rails, keep your left foot on the rung and step onto the roof with your right foot *(above, left)*. Grasp the right rail with your left hand, then remove your right hand from the top of it and step onto the roof with your left foot. When both feet are on the roof, let go of the ladder. Avoid walking along the roof edges. If the roof slopes less

than 4 inches per foot, walk up it diagonally to the desired point. If the roof slopes between 4 and 6 inches per foot, walk straight up to the ridge and along it, then down to the desired point. Return to the ladder the same way. To get off the roof, have a helper steady the ladder. Stand to the left of the ladder and face it, then grip the top of the rail closest to you with your right hand. Swing your left foot onto the center of the rung at or just below the eave and grasp the top of the other rail with your left hand *(above, center)*, pivoting on your right foot. Grasping the rails, swing your right foot onto the center of the rung below your left foot *(above, right)*, then climb down.

MOVING HEAVY OBJECTS

Using permanent rollers. For a major appliance other than a gas type, install permanent rollers under it if you move it often for cleaning; buy appliance rollers at a home center. Wearing work gloves and sturdy shoes with non-slip soles, work with a helper to install the rollers. Unplug the appliance and tape or tie down any unsecured part of it such as a door. Carefully pivot and slide the appliance out of its position to an open area. Install the rollers one by one under opposite sides of the appliance. With your helper carefully tilting up one side of the appliance, retract its feet and position a roller under it, centered with the feet. Slowly lower the appliance to rest it securely on the roller. Use the same procedure to position a roller under the opposite side of the appliance *(left)*. Then, roll the appliance back into position and plug it back in.

Appliance roller

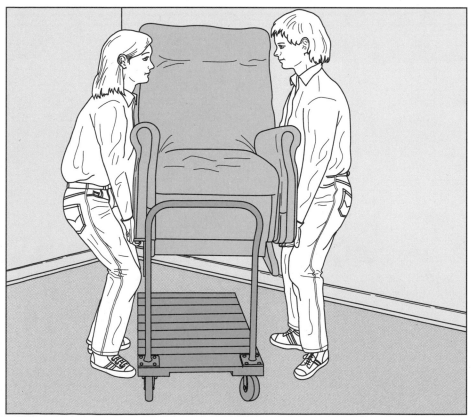

Using a dolly. Rent a flat dolly equipped with wheel locks at a tool rental center. Wearing work gloves and sturdy shoes with non-slip soles, work with a helper to lift a heavy object onto the dolly. Position the dolly with its wheels locked near the object. With your helper on the opposite side of the object, stand facing it with your feet planted firmly, then bend your knees until you can grip it securely at knee height; be sure to grip a non-moving part of it. Keeping your back straight and your elbows bent slightly, straighten your knees while hoisting the object straight up. Walk slowly with the object, resting as necessary, to position it over the dolly *(left)*. Standing with your feet planted firmly and keeping your back straight, bend at your knees to lower the object into place on the dolly. Unlock the wheels to move the dolly, then follow the same procedure to lift the object off it.

Lifting a heavy object alone. Lift a heavy object alone using the squat-and-lift method, holding it close to your torso and minimizing the bending and compression of your spine. Wearing work gloves and sturdy shoes with non-slip soles, stand facing the object with your feet planted firmly on each side of it. Bend your knees and lower yourself until you can grip the object securely at knee height *(left)*; be sure to grip a non-moving part of it. Keeping your back straight and your elbows bent slightly, straighten your knees while hoisting the object straight up. Walk slowly with the object to your destination, resting as necessary. Standing with your feet planted firmly and keeping your back straight, bend at your knees to lower the object into place.

LIFTING A STAIN WITH A POULTICE

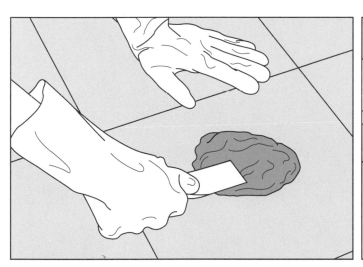

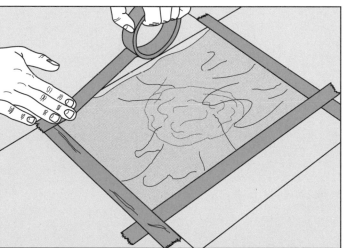

Using a poultice. For a stubborn, sticky or oily stain on a porous surface, use a poultice. Wearing rubber gloves, prepare a poultice of a liquid ingredient and a dry ingredient: cornstarch or talcum powder for a light-colored surface; fuller's earth otherwise. For the liquid ingredient, use: household laundry bleach for a surface of marble, granite or fiberglass; mineral spirits for a surface of plaster or drywall or a wallcovering; a citrus-based solvent for a surface of brick, stone, ceramic tile, porcelain or enamel. Mix the poultice in a clean container into a thick, uniform, putty-like paste, adding a small amount of the dry ingredient and pouring in the liquid ingredient a little at a time. Test the poultice on an inconspicuous spot of the surface, letting it dry before brushing it off; if the test spot is damaged, try a poultice of a milder liquid ingredient. Otherwise, use a plastic spatula to apply a thick, even coat of the poultice on the surface *(above, left)*. Cover the poultice with plastic sheeting and seal the edges of it with masking tape *(above, right)*, then let it dry—this may take 24 hours. When the poultice is dry, remove the plastic and gently sweep it off the surface using a soft-bristled fiber brush. Clean traces of the poultice off the surface using a clean, white, lint-free cloth dampened with water, then wipe it dry with another cloth. If necessary, repeat the procedure.

INDEX

Page references in *italics* indicate an illustration of the subject mentioned. Page references in **bold** indicate a Troubleshooting Guide for the subject mentioned.

A

Acoustic tiles, *39*
Air conditioners, *108-109*
Aluminum siding, *25*
  See also Exterior walls
Appliances, **92,** *93-109*
  Air conditioners, *108-109*
  Baseboard heaters, *109*
  Clothes dryers, *102*
  Clothes washers, *101*
  Dishwashers, *100*
  Electronic equipment, *104*
  Furnace filters, *107-108*
  Heat pumps, *109*
  Humidifiers, *105-107*
  Refrigerators, *99-100*
  Small appliances, *103*
  See also Ranges
Ashes, 78, *79-80*
Asphalt. *See* Driveways

B

Baseboard heaters, *109*
Bathrooms, **84,** *87-91*
  Bathtubs, *88*
  Ceramic tiles, *87, 90, 91*
  Shower doors, *89*
  Sinks, *88*
  Stain removal, *90-91*
  Toilets, *89-90*
Bathtubs, *88*
Blinds, 110, 112-113
Bricks, *41*
  Fireplaces/wood stoves, *82-83*
  See also Exterior walls
Burn marks, **56,** *60*
Butcher blocks, *87*

C

Cabinets, *86*
Carpets, **56,** *56-65*
  Area rugs, *58, 61-62, 64-65*
  Burn marks, *60*
  Chewing gum, *61*
  Deep-cleaning, *62-64*
  Spills, *57*

Stain removal, *59-60*
  "Steam" cleaning, *63-64*
  Vacuuming, *58, 61*
Ceilings, **36,** 38-39
  Acoustic tiles, *39*
  Drywall/plaster, *38*
  Fans, *115*
  Stain removal, *42-43*
  Stucco, *39*
Ceramic tiles, **44,** *46, 49, 54*
  Bathrooms/kitchens, **84,** *87, 90, 91*
Chandeliers, *115*
Chemicals:
  Emergency procedures, 9-12
  Safety precautions, 8
  See also Cleaning agents
Chewing gum. *See* Gummy substances
Cleaning agents, 119, 120
  Disposal, *121*
  Environmental concerns, 118, *121*
Clothes dryers, *102*
Clothes washers, *101*
Computer monitors, *104*
Concrete. *See* Driveways; Efflorescence
Countertops, *86,* 90
Creosote, **78,** *82*

D

Dishwashers, *100*
Doors, **28,** *35*
Draperies, **110,** *112*
Driveways, **16,** *17-21*
  Etching, *20*
  Sealing, *21*
  Spray-cleaning, *20*
  Stain removal, *18-19*
"Dry"- cleaning, *40, 43*
Dryers, *102*
Drywall, *38, 40*

E

Efflorescence, 16, 22, 26
Electrical emergencies, *11-12*
Electronic equipment, *104*
Emergency procedures, 8, **9,** *9-13*
Environmental concerns, 118, *121*
Etching of concrete, 20
Exterior walls, **22,** *23-27*
  Efflorescence, *26*
  Stain removal, **24,** *26-27*
  Washing, *25*

F

Fireplaces, **78,** 79-82
  Accessories, *81*
  Ashes, *79-80*
  Brick/stone surfaces, *82-83*
  Glass doors, *81*
  Screens, *81*
  Stain removal, *83*
First aid, *10, 12-13*
Fixtures, **110,** *111-115*
  Ceiling fans, *115*
  Light, *114-115*
  Window, **110,** *112-113*
Floors, **44, 55**
  Marble, *48*
  Spills, *45*
  Stain removal, 54-*55*
  Tiles
    ceramic, *46, 49, 54*
    resilient, *46, 47-48, 54*
  Wood, *50-54*
Furnace filters, *107-108*
Furniture, **66,** 67-77
  Laminates, *73*
  Plastics, *73*
  Wicker, *71*
  Wood, *73-76*
  See also Upholstery

G

Gas appliances:
  Ranges, *94, 95-98*
  Shutting off, *93*
Glass:
  Furniture, 72
  Shower doors, 89
  Fireplace doors, 81
  See also Windows
Gummy substances, *16, 27, 55, 61, 90*
  See also Stains

H-K

Heat pumps, *109*
Humidifiers, *105-107*
Kitchens, **84,** *86-87*
  Butcher blocks, *87*
  Ceramic tiles, *87, 90, 91*
  Sinks, *86*
  Stain removal, *90-91*

L

Ladders, *122-123*
Laminates, *73, 86*
Lamps, *114*
Leather upholstery, **66,** *71, 76*
Light fixtures, *114-115*

M

Marble, *48, 83*
Mattresses, *72*
Microwave ovens, *103*
Mildew, *35, 42,* 49, 54, 59, 68, *90*
Mirrors, **72**

O-P

Ovens, *96-97*
    Microwave, *103*
    See also Ranges
Paths. *See* Walks
Patios, **16,** *17-21*
    Etching, *20*
    Sealing, *21*
    Spray-cleaning, *20*
    Stain removal, *18-19*
Plaster, *38, 40*
Polishing, *47-48*
    See also Waxing
Poultices, *43, 83, 125*
Pressure washing, *25*

R

Ranges:
    Electric, *94, 96-97, 98*
    Gas, *94, 95-98*
    Hoods, *98*
Refrigerators, **92,** *99-100*
Resilient tiles, **44,** *46, 47-48,* 54
Rugs. *See* Carpets
Rust stains, 18, 24, 59, *80, 91*

S

Safety precautions, 8
    Disposal of cleaning agents, *121*
    Environmental concerns, 118, *121*
    Ladders, *122-123*
    Lifting, *124-125*
    Roofs, *123*
Screens, *32, 81*

Service panels, *11, 93*
Shower doors, *89*
Sinks, *86, 88*
Soap scum, *91*
Spills:
    Carpets, *57*
    Chemical, *10-11*
    Driveways/walks/patios, *18*
    Floors, *45*
    Upholstery, *67*
Spray-cleaning, *20*
Stain- guard, *65,* **66**
Stains:
    Bathrooms/kitchens, *90-91*
    Carpets, *59-60*
    Driveways/walks/patios, *18-19*
    Exterior walls, 24, *26-27*
    Fireplaces/wood stoves, *83*
    Floors, 54-*55*
    Upholstery, 68, *76-77*
    Vinyl/leather, *76*
    Walls/ceilings, *42-43*
    Windows, *34-35*
    Wood furniture, *75-76*
Stair runners, *58*
"Steam" cleaning:
    Carpets, *63-64*
    Upholstery, *69-70*
Stone surfaces, **22,** *82-83*
    See also Marble
Stoves. *See* Ranges
Stucco, *39*

T

Television screens, *104*
Tiles:
    Resilient, *46, 47-48,* 54
    See also Ceramic tiles
Toilets, *89-90*
Tools, *116-118*
    Ladders, *122-123*
    Washing, *120*
    See also Cleaning agents
Troubleshooting Guides:
    Appliances, *92*
    Bathrooms and kitchen, 84
    Carpets, 56
    Driveway, walks and patios, 16
    Emergency guide, 9
    Exterior walls, 22
    Fireplaces and wood stoves, 78
    Fixtures, 110

Floors, 44
Furniture, 66
Walls and ceilings, 36
Windows and doors, 28

U-V

Upholstery, *67-71, 76-77*
    Leather, **66,** *71, 76*
    Spills, *67*
    Stain removal, 68, *76-77*
    "Steam" cleaning, *69-70*
    Vinyl, **66,** *70, 76*

W

Walks, **16,** *17-21*
    Etching, *20*
    Sealing, *21*
    Spray-cleaning, *20*
    Stain removal, *18-19*
Wallcoverings, *40, 42, 43*
Walls, **36,** *37-43*
    Brick, *41*
    Drywall/plaster, *40*
    Stain removal, *42-43*
    Stucco, *39*
    Wallcoverings, *40*
    Wood panelling, *41*
    See also Exterior walls
Washers. *See* Clothes washers; Dish washers
Water-extraction cleaning. *See* "Steam" cleaning
Water marks:
    Hard water, *91*
    Walls, *42*
Waxing:
    Wood floors, *52-53*
    Wood furniture, *75*
Wicker furniture, *71*
Windows, **28,** *29,* 35
    Screens, *32*
    Stain removal, *34-35*
Wood:
    Floors, *50-54*
    Furniture, *73-76*
    Blemishes, *75-76*
    Panelling, *41*
Wood stoves, **78,** *79-81*
    Ashes, *79-80*
    Brick/stone surfaces, *82-83*
    Exteriors, *80*
    Stain removal, *82-83*

ACKNOWLEDGMENTS

The editors wish to thank the following:
Amicale Appliance Service, Montreal, Que.; Sharon Arkinson, Public Relations Manager, VELUX-CANADA Inc., Kirkland, Que.; Association of Specialists in Cleaning and Restoration International, Annapolis Junction, MD; André Babineau, Owner, Ameublement Comme Neuf Appliances enr., Montreal, Que.; Hector Benitez, Director, Active Maintenance Service, Montreal, Que.; Harold Bedoukian, Ararat Rug Co. Ltd., Montreal, Que.; Bionaire, Montreal, Que.; Building Service Contractors Association International, Fairfax, VA; Marshall Byle, President, Ontario Chimney Sweeps Association, Tiverton, Ont.; Canadian Window and Door Manufacturers Association, Ottawa, Ont.; Chem-Dry ® of Montreal, Joe Minichiello, Owner, Montreal, Que.; Choisy Laboratories, Louiseville, Que.; Carpet and Rug Institute, Washington, D.C.; Castex Industries Inc., Holland, MI; Brian B. Coffey, Development Manager, Lever Brothers Limited, Toronto, Ont.; Paul de Wit, Honeywell Ltd., Montreal, Que.; Frank S. Fitzgerald, CAE, Fitzgerald Corporation, Chicago, IL; John Ghio, Director of Technical Services, W.M. Barr and Co., Klean-Strip Division, Memphis, TN; Louis Gleicher, New York Marble Works Inc., New York, NY; Claude Grisé, President, Les Fenêtres Vimat-Rosemont Windows, Montreal, Que.; Tobi Haynes, Aslett-Browning Inc., Pocatello, ID; Gerry Halton, Robert Hunt Corporation, Montreal, Que.; Ron Hebdon, Regional Coordinator, Servpro, San Diego, CA; William Hildebrand, Technical Director, Superior Oil Co. Inc., Indianapolis, IN; Abe Kelly, P.Eng., Canadian Wood Energy Institute, Board of Directors, Wood Heating Alliance (U.S.A.), Member; Marshall Kern, Biologist, Technical Service and Development, Dow Chemical Canada Inc., Sarnia, Ont.; Oleh Z. Kowalchuk, Manager of Training and Technical Support, Ronald D. Gunn, Product Manager, Laundry, Larry Gammon, Product Manager, Ranges, John Dieroff, Product Manager, Refrigerators, CAMCO Inc., Mississauga, Ont.; Steve Lappin, President, Total Leather Care, Oceanside, NY; Robin Law, Plant Manager/Chemist, Lyon Chemical Co. Ltd., Marietta, GA; Metropolitan Home Services and Cleaning of Canada, Ltd., Montreal, Que.; Ed Mutter, National Sales Manager, TUWAY AMERICAN GROUP, Rockford, OH; Marcel Néron, Director, Cheminée Poêle à Bois Néron inc., Montreal, Que.; North American Cleaning Equipment, Toronto, Ont.; Phil Padron, Chemist, K O Manufacturing, Springfield, MO; Revac Distribution, Montreal, Que.; William M. Rodgers, General Manager, Set Consumer Products, Cleveland, OH; Roger Salamon, Vice-President, Midland Chicago Corporation, Alsip, IL; Pascal Silvano, Les entreprises Raymond Gaudet Inc., Que.; Dean Skiles, Owner, Aladdin Housecleaning and Maid Service, Louisville, KY; Robert A. Smith, Vice-President, Sales, Pressure Systems Supply, Siloam Springs, AR; William (Bill) Spears, Consultant, IKS, Montreal, Que.; William A. Staples, Director, Consumer Sales, Emerson Builder Products Division, Emerson Electric Co., St. Louis, MO; Thomas G. Stewart, Lever Brothers Limited, Toronto, Ont.; John E. Tadych, President and Rob Korman, Chemical Assistant, American Building Restoration Chemicals Inc., Milwaukee, WI, (800) 346-7532; TECHNI-SEAL, Montreal, Que.; Estelle Tredway, National Moving & Storage Association, Alexandria, VA; Vision Carpet Cleaning, Montreal, Que.; Washington Toxics Coalition, Seattle, WA; Ed Weill, Director, Product Development and Quality Assurance, American Stone-Mix, Inc., Towson, MD; Jill and Ray Woolfrey, St. Donat, Que.

The following persons also assisted in the preparation of this book:

Elizabeth Cameron, Marc Cassini, Naomi Fukuyama, Shirley Grynspan, Donald Harman, Graphor Consultation, Nancy Kingsbury, Jenny Meltzer, Heather Mills, Shirley Sylvain, Dianne Thomas and Bryan Zuraw